Ron van d

About Island Press

Since 1984, the nonprofit Island Press has been stimulating, shaping, and communicating the ideas that are essential for solving environmental problems worldwide. With more than 800 titles in print and some 40 new releases each year, we are the nation's leading publisher on environmental issues. We identify innovative thinkers and emerging trends in the environmental field. We work with world-renowned experts and authors to develop cross-disciplinary solutions to environmental challenges.

Island Press designs and implements coordinated book publication campaigns in order to communicate our critical messages in print, in person, and online using the latest technologies, programs, and the media. Our goal: to reach targeted audiences—scientists, policymakers, environmental advocates, the media, and concerned citizens—who can and will take action to protect the plants and animals that enrich our world, the ecosystems we need to survive, the water we drink, and the air we breathe.

Island Press gratefully acknowledges the support of its work by the Agua Fund, Inc., Annenberg Foundation, The Christensen Fund, The Nathan Cummings Foundation, The Geraldine R. Dodge Foundation, Doris Duke Charitable Foundation, The Educational Foundation of America, Betsy and Jesse Fink Foundation, The William and Flora Hewlett Foundation, The Kendeda Fund, The Andrew W. Mellon Foundation, The Curtis and Edith Munson Foundation, Oak Foundation, The Overbrook Foundation, the David and Lucile Packard Foundation, The Summit Fund of Washington, Trust for Architectural Easements, Wallace Global Fund, The Winslow Foundation, and other generous donors.

The opinions expressed in this book are those of the author(s) and do not necessarily reflect the views of our donors.

GREEN BUILDING TRENDS: EUROPE

GREEN BUILDING

TRENDS: *EUROPE*

JERRY YUDELSON

ISLANDPRESS
WASHINGTON | COVELO | LONDON

Library of Congress Cataloging-in-Publication Data

Yudelson, Jerry.
    Green building trends : Europe / Jerry Yudelson.
        p. cm.
    Includes bibliographical references and index.
    ISBN-13: 978-1-59726-476-1 (cloth : alk. paper)
    ISBN-10: 1-59726-476-8 (cloth : alk. paper)
    ISBN-13: 978-1-59726-477-8 (pbk. : alk. paper)
    ISBN-10: 1-59726-477-6 (pbk. : alk. paper) 1. Sustainable
buildings—Europe—Design and construction. 2. Buildings—Energy
conservation—Europe. I. Title.
    TH880.Y636 2009
    720'.47094—dc22

                                                2008047818

Printed on recycled, acid-free paper ⊛

Design by Joan Wolbier

Manufactured in the United States of America
        10 9 8 7 6 5 4 3 2 1

*For Madhu, a great friend and
faithful companion whose bright
candle burned out much too quickly,
and for Jessica, without whose
steadfast and spirited support
this book wouldn't have
come to completion.*

CONTENTS

PREFACE

Throughout the early part of this decade, as interest in green buildings began to grow dramatically in the United States, I heard occasionally that the Europeans are far ahead of Americans in green building technology and approaches. I wondered whether that was true; other than some interesting project examples from Sir Norman Foster's projects in Germany and the United Kingdom, it was hard to glean much information from American building and architecture magazines. To be sure, plenty of projects have been completed in the United States by well-known European architects, such as the Seattle City Library by Rem Koolhaas of the Netherlands' OMA firm, but these were not designed particularly with green principles in mind.

In 2002, on a trip to Oslo to talk at the Sustainable Building conference, I looked for examples of green architecture in Norway, but I really didn't find any exemplary projects. In fact, an American firm, NBBJ, had designed one of the greenest buildings in Oslo, the Telenor (state telephone company) headquarters. What I did find out was that the Norwegians placed far more emphasis on town planning than on building design, even in a cold northern country (about 60° north latitude). The goal, I was told, was that no one would live more than 300 meters from three essential services: a transit stop, a grocery store, and an elementary school. As for buildings, the most interesting thing I learned was that many were designed without internal load-bearing walls, so that uses could be reconfigured endlessly over many decades, as buildings might shift from residential to various commercial uses or vice versa. A similar pattern of use is becoming more common in the United States as mixed-use projects seek to accommodate, for example, hotel, office, and residential uses.

Through my work with the U.S. Green Building Council, beginning in 1999, I became aware that there was an established green building rating system in the United Kingdom, promulgated by the Building Research Establishment (BRE), called the BRE Environmental Assessment Method (BREEAM), which had quite a bit of commercial uptake.[1] BREEAM uses a system of independent, authorized building assessors to review documentation and assign ratings to buildings. Through early 2008, about 1,200 commercial buildings and 100,000 homes had received BREEAM ratings, a good record for a country with one fifth the population of the United States (about equal to the number of commercial buildings certified by the U.S. Green Building Council's Leadership in Energy and Environmental Design [LEED] system as of the spring of 2008).

Still, I wondered what Europeans knew about green building design that we didn't (and should). Were their buildings greener because they cared more about people (therefore designing buildings with more daylighting and natural ventilation), because energy prices were much higher (driving interest in low-energy design), because codes and customs demanded a different design approach, or because architects and engineers there thought it was the right thing to do?

A dinner meeting in 2003 with the British engineer Guy Battle, of London's Battle McCarthy firm, also piqued my interest in European approaches. Battle had been retained to participate in the early-stage design charrette for a project in Portland, Oregon that eventually became the world's largest LEED Platinum-certified building. Battle's approach brought bioclimatic design considerations to a very large (412,000–square-foot) complex health care building; it included consideration not just of building-integrated photovoltaics but also of building-integrated wind power systems, in this case on top of a 200-foot-tall building. Battle also advocated for natural ventilation approaches, using thermal chimneys that relied on the buoyancy of heated air to cause it to rise out of a building. All of these approaches aimed toward zero-net-energy buildings that would generate enough power on site for all their needs.

In 2007, an article in the *New York Times* magazine by architecture critic Nicolai Ouroussoff, "Why Are They Greener Than We Are?,"[2] further excited my interest in European approaches and led directly to this book. In that article, Ouroussoff wrote of a number of European examples of green architecture that made it appear that all of European design was much more advanced than in the United States and Canada.

In September 2007, I was invited to speak at an architectural conference in Frankfurt, Germany sponsored by Somfy, a French manufacturer of dynamic façades, where I learned more about European approaches to designing energy-efficient façades. I followed up that trip with three more each to the United Kingdom and Germany and with side visits to the Netherlands and Luxembourg in the spring of 2008. At each visit, I learned more about European approaches to green design and became more convinced that Americans could benefit from learning more about what was being done in Europe. My last visit to the United Kingdom was in June 2008, where I addressed a conference of shopping center developers in London and visited a new green building sponsored by the country's largest building product distributor. My visit gave further insights and impetus to this work.

From talking with dozens of European architects, engineers, planners, and developers, I came away convinced that architects, engineers, builders, and developers in North America could learn some valuable lessons. This book is a compilation of these lessons. I think that the project examples, technologies, and approaches presented in this book are fairly representative of European approaches, but they are by no means exhaustive.

One further note: I've tried to showcase leading-edge examples and more up-and-coming architects, so I've avoided some buildings by many architects well known in the United States. This is not to slight their many achievements but to produce a more contemporary dialog about what defines green architecture in economically advanced countries.

What's the upshot? What should we learn from European approaches? First, we've been much too timid in our approaches to green building design. We should be aiming at buildings that reduce energy use by 90 percent compared with current codes while maintaining comfort, health, and productivity for building occupants and reducing environmental impacts of building design, construction, and operations essentially to zero. Second, starting with zero net impact as the goal radically changes building design and construction, product, and technology selection, and that's the real lesson to learn from our European colleagues.

—Jerry Yudelson
Tucson, Arizona
January 2009

ACKNOWLEDGMENTS

I want to acknowledge all the architects, engineers, planners, and developers who met with me and provided information for this book. I'm especially thankful to David Cook for writing the foreword. David is an Englishman and a partner in Stuttgart's Behnisch Architekten, one of Europe's leading design firms, which is also doing significant work in the United States.

Thanks also to Christoph Ingenhoven of Ingenhoven Architekten, Düsseldorf, for the hospitality he showed me and in having members of his staff guide me through some of his more significant projects in Germany and Luxembourg. Thanks also to Robert Hösle of the Behnisch firm for a guided tour of their project Therme, Bad Aibling in Bavaria. Thanks to Rab Bennetts for arranging a similar guided tour of New Street Square in London and to the many architects and engineers in the United Kingdom, Germany, Holland, Switzerland, and Austria who shared their precious time, along with expertise and insights. The professionals in the United States and Europe who consented to be interviewed for this book deserve special thanks.

A special thanks to Thomas Saunders of the United Kingdom's Building Research Establishment (BRE) firm for keeping me up to date on the BRE Environmental Assessment Method (BREEAM) program and to Heather Topel and Daniel Bridge of London's EDAW planning firm for guiding me through the intricacies of the United Kingdom's Eco-Towns experiment, outlined in Chapter 7. Thanks also to Anna Braune, former executive director of the Deutsche Gesellschaft für Nachhaltiges Bauen (German Sustainable Building Council), for information on the group's green building certificate program. Thanks to architect Katrin Klingenberg, of the Passive House Institute–U.S., for reviewing the PassivHaus material in Chapter 1 and to architect Anja Caldwell and Professor Ulf Meyer for reviewing the information on German green buildings, as well as the entire manuscript.

Many thanks also to Gretel Hakanson, my editorial associate. This is our sixth green building book together in the past 3 years, and her contribution grows with each project. Thanks also to my wife, Jessica, for putting up with all this globetrotting and for deferring her "honey do" list for many weekends while I was traveling and writing.

Thanks to my editor at Island Press, Heather Boyer, who reined in some of my overexpansive prose, provided key input on the book's structure and composition, and helped guide a rough manuscript into the book that you now hold. Thanks to Heidi Ziegler-Voll of Creative Tornado for providing illustrations for this book and to Susanna Sirefman of New York City for providing a critical overview of the rough draft.

I also want to thank Brian Libby, a Portland, Oregon–based architectural writer, for providing the research and write-up of Sir Norman Foster's projects in the United Kingdom and Germany, and Arunima Chatterjee, at the time an architectural graduate student at the University of Arizona, for providing research services. Thanks also to Paul Ehrlich for his strong insights into the technology opportunities found in European green buildings and to the Mechanical Contractors Education and Research Foundation for sponsoring a research project on this topic.

I owe a final thanks to the many people who participated in interviews, provided expert guidance, arranged project visits, and provided photos and renderings for this book, and to those who served as reviewers and critics. The opinions in this book are mine alone, but without their help I wouldn't have known how to start and, more importantly, how to finish this book.

These people include, in the United Kingdom, Craig White, David Lloyd Jones, Ken Shuttleworth, Sean Affleck, Bill Bordass, Bill Watts, Adam Ritchie, Andy Ford, Guy Battle, David Richards, David Strong, Alan Short, Katy Janda, Larry Malcic, Michael Beaven, Mikkel Kragh, Matt Cartwright, Patrick Bellew, Jerry Percy, David Kirkland, and Michael Taylor; in the Netherlands, Tjerk Reijenga, Arno Ruigrok, Arco Rehorst, and Glenn Aaronson; in Germany, Helmut Meyer, Ben Dieckmann, Georg Vahlhaus, Heide Schuster, Mathias Haeussler, Johannes Kreissig, Sybille Fanelsa, Beata Reinartz, Peter Mosesle, Martin Haas, Eva Schmincke, Tajo Friedemann, Christian Wetzel, Thomas Spiegelhalter, Winfried Heusler, Dieter Grau, Gerhard Hauber, Hartwig Kunzel, Klaus Sedlbauer, and the office of Thomas Herzog; in Austria, Georg Reinberg and Filipa Fernandes; in Switzerland, Hansjuerg Etter; in France, Katia Vlahovic and Carlos Esteves; and in Portugal, Elsa Monteiro and Álvaro Portela. Finally, in the United States and Canada, I would like to thank the reviewers and those we interviewed about European green building approaches, including John Echlin, Bob Berkebile, Bob Shemwell, James Andrews, Kevin Burke, Tim McGinn, and Bruce Fowle.

FOREWORD

Architecture and the Human Condition[1]

B ehnisch Architekten and Transsolar have established and maintained a long-term working relationship, completing numerous projects in both Central Europe and North America. The common foundation of this collaboration is the belief that stimulating, high-quality built environments can be realized with far less consumption of natural resources. Curiosity, commodity, and delight drive a design process characterized by both the discovery of new topics and technologies and the desire to improve on what has already been achieved.

For the last 15 years, ever-increasing pressure has come to bear on developments in terms of building technology and architecture, particularly in Europe. The focus has been on the need to handle natural resources in a more economical and responsible manner.

As architects, we recognize that any undertaking as substantial as the construction and subsequent operation of buildings consumes considerable natural resources. How can architects and environmental engineers create buildings that are better integrated in the world, and how we can place less strain on our environment through the process of building? These goals seem contradictory in their very essence. We believe that we are charged with balancing the respectful tempering of the natural environment, based on local cultural and climatic conditions, with the basic necessity of providing shelter. This is often easier said than done, as common procedures and readily available technologies on one side of the Atlantic are not necessarily applicable or are less accepted on the other.

However, as an example, we were able to bring many of the lessons learned on previous projects to one of the largest Leadership in Energy and Environmental Design (LEED) Platinum-certified buildings in the United States, the Genzyme corporate headquarters in Cambridge, Massachusetts, a project completed in 2004. Here a truly integrated design approach and continued dialog with both developer and tenant allowed us to pursue strategies not easily adopted in the commercial U.S. market. Many of the individual design moves are simple, but they have a major impact on the operation of the building: creation of a shallow plan building out of a predefined volume by introduction of a central atrium; light redirectional systems at the façades and the head of the atrium (an idea imported directly from Germany); use of the central atrium as a return air duct; challenging of conventional reliance on raised floors and dropped ceilings, resulting in reduced floor-to-floor heights; tapping of waste heat from a neighboring power plant as a heating and cooling source; and exposure of thermal mass, allowing a natural dampening of internal temperature swings. All these strategies have been practiced on numerous projects in Germany. The Norddeutsche Landesbank in Hannover is a fine example of how a similar range of simple yet effective strategies can be combined carefully to produce a large-scale, environmentally responsible building.

Buildings can be spoken of in terms of sustainability only if they suit their purpose and are efficient to operate. Otherwise, they consume resources unnecessarily, are a burden to the owners, and risk premature replacement. The design process entails consideration of the life-cycle cost of a building, in terms of both economics and environmental impact; for buildings with a design life of 60 years, the cost of ownership and operation far exceeds the cost of construction. Therefore, the approach to the construction of any new facility should be to maximize the efficiency of the building fabric in order to conserve resources in future operation. In this context, the existing building stock must be seen as an important resource, and new buildings must be flexible in order to respond to ever-changing patterns of life.

For us, sustainability in architecture is really about acknowledging the diversity of patterns of use and promoting qualities that stimulate the senses, leading to enjoyment of occupying the building. In each project, we seek to adopt strategies that recognize the building's occupants and their response to their immediate environment as an integral part of these systems. Throughout, we seek to ensure that the cycles of nature are properly recognized and considered a dynamic quality rather than seen as a nuisance.

Interestingly, it could be argued that you could build an energy-efficient building that could easily be a hostile architectural environment that hardly anybody would use but would still be considered a sustainable building, at least in terms of today's common understanding. But in truth it would not be sustainable at all, for if nobody uses it, it is not efficient as a building and therefore is useless and a waste of resources, both financial and environmental.

Where can we, as designers and builders, best make a difference? Where can we effectively save energy and materials? Without a doubt, it is the users of a building who can influence ecological value through their behavior and energy demands. However, in our efforts to provide idealized conditions for buildings in the second half of the 20th century, the rhythms of nature were increasingly ignored. The construction of buildings has led to growth in the implementation of technical equipment and with it—perhaps most notably in the case of office buildings—numerous examples of stagnant, often inhospitable spaces with obvious consequences for occupant satisfaction, staffing efficiency, and attendance levels.

In short, many buildings that stand in our cities today promote anything but intensive use; instead, they are a continuing drain on resources. The inefficient application of technology not only consumes energy but also produces heat as a byproduct, contributing to greater dependence on cooling systems in the summer. This vicious cycle is difficult to break.

We believe that it is essential to return to basic ecological principles in the development of buildings. In recognizing the cycles of nature as a quality to be emulated, we continue to question seemingly simple truths, such as our current definition of comfort. This is a design and construction issue that challenges certain preconceptions about the city, questioning both lifestyles and how people perceive their built environment.

We believe that it is our responsibility to integrate technical and aesthetic aspects in the search for sustainable architecture. We are convinced that it is necessary to espouse a holistic view, one driven by environmental quality rather than formal architectural considerations. But it is simplistic for the design focus to be centered on energy consumption while overlooking physical parameters; it is also insufficient to judge a "sustainable" architecture based on energy consumption per square meter, for neither approach adequately addresses qualities and the individuality of the human condition.

Many of our own projects are developed according to simple principles, nonetheless resulting in sophisticated environmental concepts that respond to the manifold needs of the individual, recognizing fluctuations in seasonal conditions and affording a degree of individual control. We do not claim that any of the concepts we apply are revolutionary, but they certainly go a long way to creating user-friendly environments that promote well-being and personal enjoyment.

Unfortunately, acting responsibly in the design and construction of individual projects is not going to make much of a difference. In a world of an expanding population and exploding consumption levels, current strategies cannot sustain prosperity by restricting industry and curtailing growth. More radical moves are essential in the planning of our cities; we must avoid repeating the mistakes of the past. For as Herbert Girardet offers in his book *Surviving the Century*,

> If everybody all over the world were to adopt London consumption patterns, we would need three planets rather than the one we actually have available to live on. So, for the rest of the world to copy London lifestyles—requiring over 6 hectares per person, rather than the 1.8 hectares of productive land actually available per head of the world's population—would be an unrealistic proposition. As the world industrializes and urbanizes, a growing mismatch emerges between human demand patterns and the capacity of the planet to supply. So, we need to find ways to reorganize our urban, economic and technical systems.[2]

Ecology and *sustainability* are two terms central to the current debate on the process of building and its potential impact on the natural environment and resources; both need amplification.

The term *ecology* stems from the Greek words for "house" and "discipline" and refers to the "household of nature." We often use the term *ecology* incorrectly as being something inherently healthy (implying that a balanced ecological system is in itself good, with humankind as the central element), so that systems are considered well balanced if they create a living environment for humankind. Such a view is anthropocentric and presumptuous.

Sustainability has come to mean all things to all people. Increasingly misused in architecture, the term is in danger of becoming a mere label. For us sustainability is less a political than a humanistic issue. In our short occupation of the earth, we have acutely threatened its future and our habitat. Now we appear to be rapidly gaining a common understanding of the urgency of these matters. Perhaps we have finally reached a tipping point where we cannot remain in denial. However, people don't change their habits easily unless there are good reasons for doing so, and we obviously cannot rely on morals alone.

Perhaps the real reason people don't change is that they don't see any immediate benefit. Climate change is undoubtedly upon us, but its worst effects will not be felt next week or next year, so in the short term most people continue to live in a manner that is clearly unsustainable. Rewards are needed, not threats. We must therefore ensure the correct incentives. But who is to take the lead here? If governments continue to subsidize the oil industry at the expense of developing technologies based on renewable energy, then the uptake will naturally be slowed.

As architects and engineers, we are undoubtedly experiencing a change in attitude toward building as many clients expect us to design, develop, and deliver environmentally responsible buildings. Led by various not-for-profit organizations, business has recognized the value of a healthy indoor and outdoor environment. In 1993 the U.S. Green Building Council was founded, and soon thereafter it initiated the LEED rating system, a tool that looks beyond the purely quantitative aspects of the environmental impact of buildings. It is a system that will continue to evolve, but it is the most comprehensive evaluation system today.

It is fascinating to attempt to draw parallels between our works, past and present, on both sides of the Atlantic. Although the cultures are quite different, the problems encountered during planning and construction are quite similar. Current commissions such as Harvard's first Science Complex clearly illustrate the value of an extended client dialog that has enabled us to introduce sophisticated responses to the onerous requirements of a modern laboratory complex. Naturally, there were certain preconceptions to be overcome, but this is true in any project.

Generally, we believe that the key differences between working on either side of the Atlantic may be briefly described by the following (at least these might be common American perceptions of why there are differences in design and why European green design is considered to be more advanced):

- One could argue that historically Europeans have attached greater value to the quality of their working environment. This attitude manifests itself in buildings that are expected to last longer, achieved through higher implicit standards of design and construction. In Central Europe, we are fortunate to have many specialist suppliers and contractors operating right on our doorstep. We continue to work with many to develop new products and systems and attempt to introduce them on our projects.

- Higher standards are undoubtedly influenced, indeed promoted, through appropriate codes and standards that, for example, demand access to daylight. This automatically results in shallow–floor plan buildings where natural ventilation and daylighting strategies can be adopted easily. We hope that the introduction of the European Union's Energy Performance Certificates will also help promote efficiency levels in the construction and property industries.

- In general, energy prices have been much higher in Europe, making the conservation of energy in design and operation a simple economic issue. As natural resources continue to dwindle, it is only natural that Europe carefully attempts to control its reliance on foreign partners. Therefore, we have seen an appreciable push for renewable energy, particularly in Germany, where there is a definite reluctance to revert to the nuclear option. The lifting of restrictions and the promotion of locally generated energy that can be sold back to the grid have certainly helped this push. This is surprisingly not the case in many other countries, even in Europe.

- At the risk of generalizing, our experience has shown that comfort standards on both sides of the Atlantic are different. The mild Central European climate can often be tackled without the extensive use of mechanical systems. Indeed, many of our buildings are developed without them. In Central Europe, it appears that there is a greater acceptance of natural phenomena and that people here are prepared to tolerate a greater range of indoor temperatures without complaint. This certainly makes the design process a little easier.

The United States is a vast country with many different climate zones, and therefore many of the strategies used in Central Europe are not easily transferred. We don't consider this a problem; it's an opportunity to exploit in the pursuit of a contextual form of architecture, which has little to do with style and more to do with performance.

—David Cook, *principal*
Behnisch Architekten
Stuttgart, Germany

INTRODUCTION

European Green Buildings in Context

Although North American green building practices and technology have come a long way in the past 15 years, it's realistic to say that Western European architects, engineers, and builders are ahead of us in the widespread use of passive design techniques, integrating solar power into building design and producing low-energy buildings.

As an example of good European design, consider the Doxford Solar Office building, completed in 1998 by David Lloyd Jones and Studio E architects (see Chapter 2 for more on his work) and shown in Figure I.1. This is a low-energy office building with the entire south-facing façade composed of building-integrated photovoltaics (BIPVs), generating 73 kilowatts (peak) of power, a design innovation I've hardly ever seen in the United States or Canada. The south façade is a completely integral system built in conjunction with a major German manufacturer, Schüco, profiled in Chapter 6. Expected annual net energy use of the 4,600–square-meter (49,500–square-foot) building is 115 kilowatt-hours per square meter (10.6 kilowatt-hours per square foot).

The Doxford Solar Office is located at a business park near Sunderland, in the United Kingdom. It was the first speculatively constructed office building to incorporate BIPVs, and the resulting solar façade was the largest constructed in Europe at that time.[1]

FIGURE I.1. Designed by Studio E Architects, the Doxford Solar Office is an early example of a low-energy building with a building integrated photovoltaic system. *(©Dennis Gilbert/VIEW)*

This example of a highly integrated sustainable office building from more than 10 years ago, developed for strictly commercial uses, brings up some interesting questions that this book was written to answer. For example, what do the Europeans know (and do) that we don't, and why? What are some fundamental differences in the way Europeans and Americans or Canadians approach sustainable design? When comparing the driving forces for sustainability in Europe and the United States, it's also instructive to consider the experiences and perspectives of leading practitioners, some of whom have practiced in both places.

John Echlin is an American architect and former design principal of an architecture firm in Portland, Oregon who worked in Switzerland for two firms over a period of 7 years in the 1990s.[2]

> What drives buildings in the U.S. are free-market conditions and private development. There's no doubt that in Europe what drives things are essentially culture and public benefit. In the U.S., we typically build buildings to last 20 years and don't really think much beyond that. But in Europe the cultural norm is really to build permanently. Because of that, all building strategies relate to finding the most permanent solution. It tends to drive efficiency in operations and promote design approaches that make multiple uses out of single elements.

Larry Malcic is director of design in London for the large international architecture firm HOK.[3]

> In London there has been a kind of constant theme of sustainability. Energy-responsible design is partially driven by the much higher energy prices in Europe, but also it's a kind of cultural attitude. Particularly starting with our work in the Netherlands and Germany, there's a real attitude that culturally says we have a custodial responsibility for where we live, for our buildings, our towns, and our cities.
>
> On an island like the U.K., there's a pretty clear consciousness that there isn't someplace else to move on to. That contrasts significantly with the American approach of you build it, you use it, and then you move on because there's always someplace to move on to. Here, the landscapes are manmade; the parks are manmade. So there's a recognition that we have to deal carefully with what are, in fact, finite resources. I think that is a fundamental cultural difference.

Does the extensive European use of sustainable building approaches result from specific climatic, cultural, political, and economic factors that might not be found in the United States, making comparisons between the two continents difficult and lessons learned harder to extract? Let's take a look at both sides of the Atlantic.

DRIVING FORCES IN EUROPE

Climate

Many of the innovative European technologies come out of Germany and the United Kingdom, with a significant contribution from smaller countries and regions such as Switzerland, Austria, the Netherlands, and Scandinavia. These countries tend to have cold winters and mild summers, with lower humidity than is found in much of the United States. In that respect, architects and engineers are designing mostly for a different climatic situation, one in which heating energy use is far more significant than cooling energy use. For example, European latitudes range from 47° in Zürich, to 50° in London and Frankfurt, to 59° in Oslo and Stockholm. (The northern border of the United States is defined mostly by latitude 48°, so most of Central and Western Europe is farther north than any major U.S. city; e.g., Boston lies at 42°.[4]) The counter to this notion of colder climates in Europe is the prevalence in North America of the fully sealed, all-glass high-rise office building, which needs air conditioning year-round for comfort in almost any climate.

The climate in the United Kingdom is quite mild, certainly by Central European standards, with no location more than 60 miles from the ocean. In that respect, London's climate is quite similar to that of the coastal zone of the western United States, from San Francisco northward, except that those latitudes range from 38° in San Francisco to 48° in Seattle.

Culture

The lack of daylighting in most large-floorplate, open plan offices in the United States would surprise and dismay most European engineers. Daylighting of all workspaces is pretty much a cultural norm in Europe, as a fundamental sign of respect for workers' mental and physical health. As a result, European office buildings tend to be less efficient from a real estate investment viewpoint (i.e., with a lower ratio of net to gross leasable area, given that all high-rise buildings need about the same amount of core space for elevators, lobbies, fire escapes, and restrooms).

For example, German building regulations for worker health and safety (similar to those of the Occupational Safety and Health Administration in the United States) require that a permanent workstation have direct access to fresh air and natural light; therefore, the maximum room depth is limited to about 5 meters (16 feet) from a window, unless higher ceilings are provided (for daylighting), in which case one might be 7 or 8 meters from a window.[5] This requirement makes European buildings longer and narrower than most typical American office buildings. Part of the reason is that the great building boom in the United States and Canada after World War II coincided with the advent of modern air conditioning, removing previous constraints on the use of glass and the need for operable windows in office buildings.

Europeans don't seem to be as sensitive as Americans to temperature excursions in the workspace. They would find somewhat comical Americans' insistence on wearing the same clothing in the office year-round and expecting the same 72°F to 75°F (22°C to 24°C) temperatures, with little variation. This expectation of year-round constant indoor air temperature is a great hindrance in adopting natural ventilation and using radiant space conditioning systems, which can't deliver the instant response of overhead-ducted, forced-air heating, ventilation, and air-conditioning systems. In the United States, we're beginning to see some changes on this front, especially since 2004, when the American Society of Heating, Refrigerating and Air-Conditioning Engineers published its first adaptive comfort research and standards. However, one deterrent to the use of alternative comfort systems is that most office leases in the United States still specify narrow temperature ranges, giving designers far less latitude for using radiant heating and cooling.

Deciding when to open the windows to let natural ventilation into the building can be a major stumbling block to wider adoption of such systems. I visited the national telephone company's new office complex building in Oslo, Norway in 2002 and found out that the group's manager made this decision. I couldn't imagine an American manager even wanting the responsibility for making that decision. Of course, American engineers are dismayed by the prospect of having to take user preferences for natural ventilation into account because it makes achieving constant interior temperatures far more difficult, especially in hotter, more humid climates.

Politics

The European Union adopted its Energy Performance of Buildings Directive (EPBD) in 2002. Individual countries are responsible for full implementation by 2010, and many were well on the way by 2008. The goal is to reduce energy use in buildings to help meet the Kyoto Protocol targets for reductions in greenhouse gas (GHG) emissions. As one example, the German government plans to reduce GHG emissions 40 percent below 1990 levels by 2020. We'll see later in the book how some of the individual countries are implementing the EPBD. Going beyond just labeling buildings to actually implementing GHG reductions takes a comprehensive national approach that most European governments are still struggling to implement. (By contrast, at a 2008 G8 summit, former president George W. Bush pledged only that the United States would take until 2050 to reduce GHG emissions to 1990 levels.)

The most aggressive responder so far to the EPBD has been the United Kingdom, which has pledged that all new public (or social) housing, a much larger component of housing construction than in the United States, would be carbon-neutral by 2016, all new private housing by 2018, and all new commercial buildings by 2019.

In 2008, the United Kingdom implemented the directive's Energy Performance Certificates (EPCs) for all new commercial construction, which will publish the projected energy use of new buildings and give them a grade from A to G, with A being the best, essentially a zero-net-carbon building, and G being the worst. Most new buildings in the United Kingdom are expected to get grades of D and E, which would represent the average energy use of the current building stock. I expect that the simple task of grading the buildings will lead to a dramatically increased demand from commercial building owners, developers, and managers for low-energy building engineering services in the United Kingdom.[6] In turn, this should spur innovation and the adoption of new design approaches and new energy efficiency technologies. At this time, we have no such government mandate in the United States and Canada. One of the big issues in the United Kingdom is the cost of EPCs, which could cost a lot more than expected and take a lot longer to be issued.[7]

Other countries in Northern and Western Europe are expected to follow suit in the next 3 years, because the EPBD applies to all members of the European Union, so that much of the continent should become a hotbed for building technology innovation and low-energy design, including for retrofits. (Some European countries are not European Union members, including Switzerland and Norway.)

Economics

Energy prices historically have been much higher in Europe than in the United States, about twice as high according to some of the people we interviewed, because European governments have taxed fuels more aggressively than those in the United States. As an example, in April 2008 I drove a rental car in Germany and paid about $9.00 per gallon (€1.49 per liter) for diesel to fill my tank.

The psychology of saving energy is more deeply ingrained in Europe than in the United States because of a long history of higher fuel prices and fewer indigenous oil and gas resources. Of course, all countries were shocked at the fourfold increase in crude oil prices that began in 2004 and continued into the summer of 2008, and energy conservation became even more of a practical economic imperative. Even with the retreat in prices later in 2008, the message was clear: Pay attention to energy costs, now and in the future. Nonetheless, Europeans generally consider the more casual approach to controlling energy use in buildings in North America both wasteful and impractical.

I examined electricity prices from the city electric utility in Düsseldorf, Germany, and they appeared to be about the equivalent of 17 cents per kilowatt-hour, certainly higher than in many locations in the United States. Higher electricity prices make investments in energy-efficient technologies more attractive. Some of this cost comes from "Ökosteur," ecological taxes, adopted in the late 1990s.

Economics drives most change in the advanced economies. Higher energy prices in the United States are going to drive us more toward European approaches to building design and comfort engineering that place greater emphasis on achieving radically improved energy efficiency without adding initial costs to the building.

European consumers are 50 percent more likely than Americans to buy green products, according to a 2007 study.[8] Europeans are 25 percent more likely to recycle and 30 percent more likely to influence their friends and family about the environment. However, they are more price sensitive than Americans; for example, Europeans are 25 percent less likely to pay 20 percent more for eco-friendly products. Europeans also believe more strongly that companies need to be sensitive to their environmental impact. Buildings cost more than in the United States because of the focus on quality and durability. Also, European building owners are more willing to pay for art and to integrate new buildings more wholly into the urban fabric.

DRIVING FORCES IN THE UNITED STATES AND CANADA

Are the United States and Canada subject to the same or similar forces as Europe that will drive innovation in green buildings and more energy-efficient climate control systems?

Climate

The United States has a far greater diversity of climate zones than most of Northern and Western Europe, where the greatest amount of green design and green engineering innovation is taking place. Therefore, we are unlikely to be able to use specific European approaches throughout the United States. However, challenges to the conventional rules of building design are likely to increase because of the higher cost of energy and a greater demand for low-energy buildings. In addition, as we will see in Chapter 1, many European approaches such as the PassivHaus are adaptable to the United States in principle but may need some modification in practice.

That this argument may not hold much water is indicated by a recently completed student union building at Tulane University in New Orleans. Located in a hot, humid climate that argues for full-on air conditioning, the 148,000–square-foot building nevertheless uses a variety of European strategies designed into the project by Germany's Transsolar climate engineers (see

Chapter 6). These include shade, radiantly cooled surfaces, and air movement, with daylighting and natural ventilation year-round, especially in the spring and fall.[9]

Global warming may cause two things to happen soon. First, we'll all have to design for warmer climates. Second, we'll have to "future-proof" our buildings for this possibility, providing space for adding more cooling equipment in the future. Therefore, figuring out how to meet the goals of comfort, energy efficiency, and economy are going to be challenging for both Europeans and North Americans.

Culture

As the North American culture continues to become more diverse, there is an opportunity to change the expectations of building occupants toward accepting greater temperature swings in the workplace. Many studies of energy efficiency in buildings are beginning to focus on the role of education, training, communication, and motivation to change ingrained comfort habits in the workplace.

In the short run, the best way to do this is with occupant education, changes in building leases' temperature requirements, and building systems that work autonomously or anonymously (e.g., a green light as a signal to open windows in the fall and spring "shoulder" seasons, a red light as a signal to keep them closed).

Designers and contractors must engage with building occupants before imposing new climatic regimes on the building to get their assent and to educate them about their operating responsibilities. For buildings that are going to be occupied by a single company, educational institution, or government agency, the easiest way is to engage occupants during the design process. However, even when this is done, the results are not always encouraging. It does seem that 20 percent of building occupants will always be unhappy with the environment.

Politics

The shock of high oil, gas, and coal prices is likely to drive political change toward mandating higher levels of building energy efficiency and providing incentives for making this change. In July 2008, for example, California adopted a standard for new buildings that increases energy efficiency requirements by 15 percent over the state's already stringent energy codes.[10] I think it likely that the new president and the new Congress in 2009 are going to grapple seriously with domestic energy prices and building practices. They will quickly discover that buildings are easy to regulate because building energy conservation measures are in a unique position of having positive life-cycle costs.[11]

Some states are not waiting for federal action. In 2006, California enacted far-reaching legislation to control GHG emissions. By August 2008, some thirty-one states already had Leadership in Energy and Environmental Design (LEED) initiatives in place, many of them requiring LEED Silver or better performance in their own buildings, including California, Arizona, and Indiana.[12]

As of late August 2008, more than 850 U.S. mayors from cities representing 80 million citizens had signed on to the U.S. Conference of Mayors' Climate Protection Agreement, committing their cities to reducing greenhouse gas emissions 7 percent below 1990 levels by 2012.[13] They will need to cut building energy use dramatically to have a chance of meeting these goals.

Economics

Economic factors are driving architects, building owners, engineers, and contractors to seek high-performance building solutions with zero net energy use, an approach that will inevitably popularize European design approaches that are already achieving energy use per square foot 50 percent or more below U.S. norms for green buildings.[14]

However, there is an issue with design fees. One architect with both German and American design experience expressed it this way: Design teams in the United States are paid half the money (in fees) in half the time (months) to design twice the square footage one really needs, at half the cost (of a European building) with twice the annual energy use, a quadruple loss for the environment. Her conclusion: You get what you pay for.[15]

An increasing number of U.S. and Canadian projects are demonstrating high levels of energy savings on conventional budgets.[16] This will increase demand from owners and developers for architects, engineers, and contractors to achieve the same results, again driving design and construction toward European radiant cooling and natural ventilation approaches and toward integrated design methods.[17]

The life-cycle costs and benefits of high-performance buildings are shifting as energy prices rise and the costs of achieving superior results continue to fall. Innovative financing methods are arising to fill the gap, ranging from the established energy service companies to more innovative municipal and nonprofit financing programs, such as that found in the Clinton Climate Initiative.[18]

In 2008, researchers reached a definitive verdict: LEED-certified and Energy Star–rated buildings get higher rents, greater occupancy, and higher resale values than their competitors.[19] This knowledge will drive the rapid adoption of such buildings throughout the U.S. and Canadian commercial sectors, again forcing building teams to become much more familiar with European approaches.

The basic conclusion I draw from this analysis of trends is that North Americans are going to see dramatic changes in building envelopes, ventilation, space conditioning, climate control, and similar systems over the next 5 years. Many of these technologies, systems, and products will derive from current practices in Western and Northern Europe, especially those found in Germany and the United Kingdom.

A 2006 study of green offices in the United Kingdom built in the 1990s offers a laundry list of green measures that have been incorporated in U.K. projects about a decade earlier than in the United States.[20]

- On-site renewable energy, especially solar and geothermal
- Solar shading devices
- Atrium space integrated with the climate management system
- Triple glazing (typically one outer layer and a double-skin inner layer)
- Operable windows
- Use of water instead of air for cooling
- Radiant cooling systems, including chilled beams and chilled ceilings
- Façade venting for natural ventilation
- Shallow (or narrow) floor plan, offering daylighting to all workspaces
- Mixed-mode ventilation, using thermal chimneys whenever possible
- BIPVs
- Rain capture and water recycling

IMPRESSIONS FROM DESIGNERS

Bruce Kuwabara is a Toronto-based Canadian architect. His firm, KPMB Architects, designed the Canadian embassy in Berlin, perhaps a unique cross-cultural experience for a North American green architect. His testimony is unequivocal:[21]

> Frankly, the difference [in producing a building in Germany and one in Canada] is so great that one wonders whether we inhabit the same world. No one talks about designing a sustainable building in Berlin because it is so ingrained in the culture. Water management and recycling are fundamental to every project, not just as demonstrations but also as law.
>
> It was also clear to us how exterior building enclosures have been the subject of tremendous technical and, indeed, aesthetic development in Europe. Certain glass types in large sizes are only available in Europe. We know that things are changing here. We see European manufacturers of curtain walls, for example, penetrating the North American market on high-profile public projects.

Architect John Echlin has a foot in both worlds.[22]

> Façade design and double-skin façades are certainly important in Europe, and I think there's a lot of experimentation being done here in the U.S. based on those [innovations]. I think the whole notion of passive solar and active systems, the active façade, is coming directly from Europe. With essentially all of these things [that we associate with European design], we're on a learning curve, whereas they've been doing them for 20 years.

Bruce Fowle is head of New York's FX Fowle Architects, with a long history of collaboration with European designers such as Renzo Piano and a strong body of domestic work in sustainable design. He says,[23]

> European society places greater value on its architecture and is more willing to do it right, no matter what the cost, than in America. The architect enjoys a celebrity status there and has greater influence on what things look like and cost.
>
> The principles of sustainability in many parts of Europe are much more seamlessly integrated into the way of life and into architecture, such that they are holistically considered a part of good design practice and not singled out as a separate metric, something that Americans should strive to achieve.

Bob Shemwell is a partner and well-known green architect with Overland Partners in Texas. His associate principal James Andrews was educated in the United Kingdom and worked there from 1990 to 2002.[24] Andrews says,

> [As architectural students], we studied engineering and buildings like the Houses of Parliament that have early central heating and mechanical air systems. With that as a background on your doorstep, the whole collaboration with engineers becomes part of the course of architecture. When you look at some of the eminent architects today like Foster, Grimshaw, and Rogers, you see how they begin very early on approaching new mechanical, plumbing, electrical strategies for the buildings. Doing that has a huge impact on their form and in the

way that they create space. The mechanical systems and the harvesting of natural light, those are two real drivers in Europe that haven't been as important in the everyday commercial architecture in the U.S. until the development of LEED.

Shemwell has worked with European architects and has completed projects in other countries, so his experience is broad based. He says,

> I think the Europeans have been more serious in the past about their fundamental understanding of the materials and systems. That being said, what I've tended to notice with the Europeans is that you have either firms that are fantastic or firms that are not very good. There's not a lot of middle ground. America has been very good about having a very solid middle ground with fewer architects at both the top and bottom of the spectrum. It's not unlike our culture in general. Europe tends to be that way sociologically and financially as well.[25]

Shemwell's comment suggests that when we look at the leading practitioners of sustainable design in Europe, we shouldn't get too much of an inferiority complex because they may represent the handful of firms that win most of the major design competitions. The real benefit in North American practice is the rapid spread of what we learn about sustainable design throughout a large number of firms. Good examples of this include underfloor air distribution systems and green roofs. Asked what is the most important thing American architects need to learn from Europe, Shemwell says,

> I think the systems-based building approach is where their best architects are extremely good. They start their building design thinking about systems. They really think about the marriage between the natural daylight, natural ventilation, mechanical ventilation, and artificial light.
>
> Going forward, one of the big things that we're going to be looking for is for architects to develop expressions that reinforce cultural values, regional identity, local materials, the tone and tenor of the climate, sky, land, and landscape. If you're not really partnering with what nature is providing in a specific place and learning from that in a very careful way, then I don't think you're actually practicing sustainable design.

Dr. Katy Janda is an American academic conducting research at Oxford University. She is particularly focused on understanding how different countries are planning for low-carbon futures.[26] Here's what she has to say about the differences between "there" and "here":

> One of the big differences between the U.S. and the U.K. is that I think there's more emphasis on green in the U.S. and less on energy efficiency. In the U.K. there's more emphasis on energy efficiency and less on green. I think that the whole green building idea seems to have a little bit less force behind it here than it does in the U.S.
>
> In the U.K., the primary push for making change in the building stock is the CO_2 reduction target. The government set a reduction target of 60 percent (compared with 1990) by 2050. That really galvanizes a response, whereas our federal government has not made any such commitment. In fact, in response to more recent evidence, the newly formed U.K. Department of Energy and Climate Change has pushed those reduction targets back even farther, to 80 percent.[27] From an American perspective, that's difficult to imagine. Obviously, the primary push for sustainable building and sustainability in the U.K., in my experience, tends to be more focused on carbon reductions and also adaptability to climate change.

Adaptability refers to creating buildings that are not just more energy efficient but can withstand blackouts and are less dependent on electricity, for instance, and less grid dependent. That's a different type of building from the standard green building in the U.S. I wouldn't say that kind of dialog is dominant, but it's present.

The notion of long-term adaptability ties in with the evolution of much current American thinking about green buildings being autonomous with respect to energy and water needs, using primarily on-site systems. Finally, Janda talks about the roles of regulation and market forces in Europe. That's one of the fundamental current differences that are likely to converge over the next 5 years as we face up to the carbon reduction challenge.

Government incentives [for energy-efficient buildings] are a little less obvious in the U.K. and that's predominantly because regulations are so much more prominent. In Europe in general, and especially in the U.K., people expect the government to regulate. The whole attitude, "we want a tax credit or a hand out. Give us a piece of the pork," which we have in the U.S., is not present in the U.K. For instance, the U.K. has actually declared that all new public housing is going to be zero carbon by 2016. The government just declared that, and now the market is saying, "Wait, how do we do that? What does it actually mean?" That [declaration] would never happen in the U.S. The market forces aren't as influential in the U.K. as they are in the U.S. People don't expect the market to deliver the magic here.

Kevin Burke is an architect and a partner with William McDonough + Partners in Charlottesville, Virginia. He is leading the firm's design of a new office park, Park 20|20, in Beukenhorst Zuid, Hoofddorp, in the Netherlands. William McDonough + Partners is collaborating with Dutch architecture firm KOW. His European experience is based on several projects there over the past decade.[28]

We are collaborating with a diverse group of Dutch engineers on the Park 20|20 project, including the environmental engineering firm Search. Search is a broadly based environmental firm that has become very focused on the implementation of Cradle-to-Cradle strategies in buildings.[29] They're providing a broad range of services on the project, including helping us identify Dutch manufacturers interested in Cradle-to-Cradle, in order to get their products certified and implemented within the building.

Search is helping with the engineering of the various sustainable design technologies in the project, including the geothermal system, wastewater treatment system, and renewable energy systems. They're also tracking the various sustainability measures using one of the Dutch sustainability guidelines, Greencalc, which is roughly akin to our LEED system, although with more of an energy focus.

The bar for high-performance green buildings is set very high in the Netherlands. The Dutch have been pursuing optimized energy performance in their buildings for a lot longer than we have. Standard practices and levels of performance would be considered advanced engineering in the U.S.

Dutch architects have the benefit of a wide range of building systems that have been developed to help support sustainable design objectives. For instance, high-performance building envelopes, including double skins, are much more prevalent because of the focus on optimizing the thermal performance of the exterior skin. In addition, operable shading devices are much more prevalent, allowing the building to provide optimized shading while being responsive to exterior light levels.

What can we in the United States and Canada make of all this? My bottom line for American architects, engineers, planners, and builders is simple: Get with the sustainability program as currently practiced in Europe or risk becoming obsolete and uncompetitive. A design convergence is happening in the developed countries, based on a common concern about climate change and future-proofing buildings for an era of expensive energy and carbon-neutral considerations. Each successful example of low-carbon buildings with strong aesthetics will give rise to dozens of imitators, and the firm that doesn't figure out how to use the technologies and design approaches outlined in this book is going to fall behind competitors who do, both in project awards and in the ability to attract and keep the talent that every design and construction firm needs to stay competitive.

CHAPTER 1

The PassivHaus Concept and European Residential Design

In my research for this book, I found many interesting innovations, both cultural and technical, in the European approach to green buildings. Perhaps the most interesting and potentially most meaningful in terms of its impact on energy use and climate change is the approach taken in Central Europe to building design: the Passive House (PassivHaus in German).

For a moment, suppose you were assigned to design an energy-efficient home for a client in the United States or Canada. That appears easy enough. After all, you just add more insulation, upgrade the windows, maybe use some innovative technology such as structural insulated panels or insulated concrete forms, install a more efficient heating and hot water system, upgrade the Seasonal Energy Efficiency Ratio of the air conditioner, and maybe even add a solar water heater, and you're done. For the most part, you would save about 50 percent of the energy use of a conventional home. But now suppose your client wanted to save 90 percent, without sacrificing indoor air quality or reducing the number of windows. That would be a very difficult task, particularly without adding many solar panels for heating and hot water. Well, it turns out that the PassivHaus standard addresses exactly that 90 percent savings assignment.

European governments take far more seriously the problem of global warming than the U.S. government. But while the United States has taken some steps to lower commercial building energy use, Germans and Austrians have tackled the housing sector. Like the United States and Canada, they're still struggling with the more important issue of what to do with the existing housing stock. This is a more critical problem because the turnover of housing stock is much lower in Europe, because of slower population growth, less workforce mobility, and a large number of historically significant buildings, which makes renovating them to be more energy efficient more challenging. The Germans and Austrians are not alone. Each of the twenty-seven countries in the European Union must adopt national standards to achieve carbon dioxide reduction goals. However, according to one expert, only four countries currently have both government and private sector programs to achieve this goal, even though the European Union's 2002 energy directive for building performance is supposed to be fully implemented by 2010.[1]

In April 2008, I attended the annual PassivHaus conference in 2008 in Nürnberg, a delightful medieval city in Bavaria of some 180,000 people, known to most Americans (if at all) only as the place where Nazi war crimes trials took place after World War II, memorialized in the well-known movie *Judgment at Nuremberg*.

The conference is the brainchild of Professor Wolfgang Feist, an academic impresario of residential and commercial green building who has managed over 12 years not only to popularize the PassivHaus concept but also to have it accepted by the German authorities as the national standard. Attracting more than 1,000 serious researchers, businesspeople, students, and foreign visitors, the Passivhaustagung is a great place to begin considering what we can learn from the green building movement in Europe.

WHAT'S A PASSIVHAUS?

The basic concept behind the PassivHaus is quite simple. In a continental climate dominated by energy use for heating during a longer cold season, one should build a house like a thermos bottle that recovers most of the heat in the outgoing air to warm the incoming air. That's it. It is quite simple in concept but very hard to implement in the field because it requires rigorous attention to construction detail, basically sealing up all potential outside leak points.

Look at Figure 1.1. The opposite of the thermos bottle is the coffee cup, which cools off quickly and needs reheating to stay warm, as might be the case in a typical American home.

The PassivHaus standard is quite exacting because it's aimed at achieving an incredibly low heating energy use of 15 kilowatt-hours (of primary energy) per square meter per year. Consider that the average new home in the United States is about 2,400 square feet, or about 220 square meters. To meet the standard, you shouldn't use more than 3,300 kilowatt-hours per year, considering both gas and electricity for heating. Now, look at your own electricity and gas bills. In the United States, in which natural gas is the dominant fuel for heating, cooking, and hot water outside the Northeast, the average annual use of natural gas in single-family homes is 800 therms, or 23,000 kilowatt-hours, seven times the PassivHaus standard, not counting electricity use, which averages nearly 12,000 kilowatt-hours.[2] (In California, with its mild climate, the numbers are closer to 6,000 kilowatt-hours for electricity and 460 therms [13,000 kilowatt-hours] for gas.)

Passive houses are superinsulated, walls, roof, and below, using the best windows in the world. It's hard to beat a German window manufacturer for quality. Consider what a well-insulated window will do for you. The German design standard for windows in passive homes is that when it's 20°F outside and 72°F inside the home, the surface temperature of the window in the room won't be below 67°F (a 3°C difference), so your body won't sense a cold surface when you're in the room. You can do this only with triple-glazed windows that have no thermal bridges, or "heat freeways," between inside and outside. Feel a standard U.S. builder-grade aluminum frame window on a cold winter night, and you'll instantly feel a surface that's as cold as a refrigerator, so the room is losing heat even while the double-

FIGURE 1.1 The PassivHaus system acts like a thermos bottle that holds heat in the building without further energy needs.

glazed window with "low-e" coating is keeping out some of the cold. The cold surface you feel is a thermal bridge that is steadily transporting nice, expensive heat from inside the house to the outside.

What gives the PassivHaus its importance is a strong commitment by the German central government to reduce the entire country's carbon dioxide emissions significantly by the year 2020. There's no way to do this without the PassivHaus being adopted on a massive scale. Consider that all of Germany lies at the latitude of Canada and that heating energy use can represent more than 80 percent of all energy use for heating, cooling, and hot water in the home. You can see why the Germans (and the Swiss and Austrians also, by the way) focus on improving residential design and energy performance.

What's the goal of the PassivHaus movement in Europe? To reduce energy use in residential homes and apartments (considering only heating energy use) by 95 percent of today's average home, which uses about 300 kilowatt-hours per square meter per year. To meet these energy targets Professor Feist and his colleagues are determined to revolutionize the way homes are built and operated.

Passive Homes, the German and Austrian Way

Most of the world's estimated ten thousand passive houses are in Germany and Austria, where winter design temperatures are about 9°F to 16°F.[3] These homes are built to standards that require approximately R-50 walls (equal to about 15 inches of fiberglass batts or 8 inches of sprayed polyurethane foam[4]) and triple-glazed U-0.14 (R-7) windows, with maximum air leakage rates of 0.6 air changes per hour. As a result, these homes have the most efficient building envelopes in the world.

In a typical PassivHaus in Central Europe there is a heating coil in the ventilation duct. Most of these heating coils circulate hot water produced by a gas-fired water heater or a heat pump water heater. So they're not truly passive, but they certainly are low-energy.

What you should get is a home that is very comfortable, with quite low energy bills. Because Central European PassivHaus designers deliver heat mainly through ventilation ducts, heat recovery ventilators act as the key residential heating appliance. In some very cold climates of the United States, such as Minnesota and Wisconsin, there will still be a need for supplemental heat beyond that delivered through the ventilation system.

PassivHaus technical specifications are strictly established in Germany and Austria, and they are generally well understood by builders. The annual energy consumption for space heating must be no more than 15 kilowatt-hours per square meter. (Note that this level of energy use would equate to an annual energy use for heating of 2,800 kilowatt-hours—about 100 therms—in a 2,000–square-foot house, pretty low by American standards in cold climates.)

For an entire residence, the PassivHaus standard specifies that the maximum annual energy budget for all purposes (including space heat, domestic hot water, lighting, appliances, and all other electrical loads) must be no more than 120 kilowatt-hours per square meter (11 kilowatt-hours per square foot, or about 760 therms per year for a 2,000–square-foot house in the United States). Although this is a small energy budget, it is not zero energy by any means. If you want a net-zero-energy house, you'll have to supply the balance with solar thermal and photovoltaic panels for both heating and hot water. In a mild climate without a significant air-conditioning need, these systems would be quite affordable in most parts of the United States and Canada, taking into account energy prices along with current local, federal, and utility subsidies.[5]

The Innovator, Wolfgang Feist

Unlike many academics, Professor Feist emphasizes the practical nature of the PassivHaus standard and its usefulness in North America.[6] He says 15 kilowatt-hours per square meter (1.4 kilowatt-hours per square foot) is not arbitrary but a good benchmark.

> The definition of a PassivHaus doesn't need any [particular] number. As long as you build a house in a way that you can use the heat-recovery ventilation system—a system that you need anyway for indoor air requirements—to provide the heat and cooling, it can be considered a PassivHaus. Since you need a house to be tight, you need a supply of fresh air. If you need that anyhow, the idea is to do everything else—the heating and cooling and dehumidification—with the ventilation system. To do that, the peak load for heating and cooling has to be quite low, including appliances.

Delivering heating by methods other than through the ventilation system has adverse impacts, according to Feist. For example, direct electrical heating is inexpensive to install, but the primary energy use (for electric power production) is extremely high, so he thinks that's not a good idea, in most cases. Woodstoves are okay with him, but a good one is quite expensive, so you should use just one stove. If you do that, and you still want to have good thermal comfort all around the building, you will need quite good insulation. Because biomass is limited, if you burn biomass (e.g., in the form of wood pellets) in your house, the house should be well insulated—in the range of what is required for a PassivHaus. Keeping the heat source in the ventilation system (in the form of a hot water coil) is not necessary, but in Feist's opinion it's the cheapest way.

Feist believes that in many of the milder climates of the United States, low-energy houses can indeed include standard exhaust-only or supply-only ventilation systems and not use heat recovery ventilators.

> If you can meet the requirements for a very low amount of additional energy, in summer and in winter, without a heat-recovery ventilator, why not? In San Francisco, for example, you don't need a heat-recovery ventilator; just build the house with operable windows. [In colder places], I think it is important to install a heat-recovery ventilator before any other system in the house, such as a forced-air heating system.

The PassivHaus standard has very exacting requirements for window performance, specifications that would be hard to meet with standard double-pane, low-e windows that are the current U.S. definition of an energy-efficient window, with or without thermal breaks.

> The window specification depends on the climate. In Central Europe, we need an R-7 [U-0.14] window. You would not need the same window in Florida or California. The reason for the U-value that we now require in Europe is *the comfort of the occupants*. It is a functional definition. During the winter, the coldest surface temperature in the room will be the window. If you don't have a radiator in your room, the difference between the surface temperature of the window and the average surface temperature of the room should not be more than 3°C (5°F); that's for comfort reasons. [For this, you need very efficient windows.]

This is not as complex as it sounds. In essence, Feist believes that a home design should be kept simple, by improving insulation and windows and by installing a heat recovery ventilator. In

North American climates, the biggest problem may be changing mindsets about how to get started. For example, Feist says, "Most builders I have talked with in North America still think that increasing insulation is an expensive thing. I'm surprised, because insulation is the cheapest thing you can do." The main issue is doing away with the notion that energy efficiency upgrades must "pay back" in terms of current energy prices. He says, "I think it is important to do away with this idea of the payback calculation. We should do advertising to say that a payback calculation is not important for determining energy efficiency, because a house will be there for more than five years—it will be there for maybe 70 years."

Explained this way, do you think now that you could use the PassivHaus standard to design a 90 percent energy-efficient home just about anywhere in North America?

The Role of Government Regulation

The larger issue in adopting a standard such as PassivHaus may be in our own approach to regulation and energy codes. Germans have a long history of government regulation, including the building sector. The first laws regulating quality in buildings came about at the same time (1882) as the lawless Arizona Territory saw the gunfight at the O.K. Corral, where Wyatt Earp, Doc Holliday, and other Earp brothers gunned down the notorious Clanton gang in the aptly named town of Tombstone. In much of the United States, we're still fighting battles over the role of government regulation that the Europeans settled long ago, in favor of the government.

Germans tend to regulate everything, including buildings, in a way that most Americans do not understand and probably would not tolerate. For example, it's socially unacceptable to jaywalk in Germany. After visiting a fantastic green building near the Frankfurt Airport, I wanted to cross a completely empty street against the light. My German guide wouldn't hear of it. Why? It would set a bad example for the children, she said, and they might dash out into the street and get run over. (Good reason, except that there were no children anywhere near this busy commercial area; Germans just like "Alles in Ordnung.") What this means is that if the German government puts something in the building code, such as the PassivHaus standard, it's likely to be taken up and followed by one and all.

Building Physics

Building physics underlies the PassivHaus standard. The Germans are quite taken with the notion and language of building physics, a topic and field of study mostly unknown in North America and certainly not part of the common language and thinking of most homebuilders, architects, or engineers. Simply stated, building physics looks at heating, cooling, and moisture management in buildings from a scientific viewpoint. Simple physics principles most of us learned in high school can be used to design better buildings; for example, heat flows from warm to cold, moisture flows from wet to dry, moisture condenses on a cold surface, and heated air rises.

While in Munich, the home of *Bier und Bratwurst*, I visited the world-famous Fraunhofer Institute for Building Physics, a research station employing about three hundred people who are looking for new ways of heating, cooling, and dehumidifying buildings, using scientific research methods. I saw hundreds of mold and algae cultures being tested to see under what environmental conditions they thrive (and therefore how to prevent them from growing, by eliminating those conditions). I also went inside a three-story research building with twelve different types of building façades being tested for environmental performance. The researchers at Fraunhofer are developing new types of external and internal paints that will inhibit mold growth, even in severe wet winter weather. The institute's work will continue to form the backbone of many building regulations in future years in Germany.

WHAT CAN WE LEARN FROM THE PASSIVHAUS APPROACH?

There is no way to stop global warming over the next 40 years without significantly reducing household carbon dioxide emissions to well below 1990 levels. In the housing sector, the PassivHaus concept shows that it is possible to maintain a high-quality standard of thermal comfort with only 10 percent of the current average energy use—*if* we learn to build our homes better.[7]

The U.S. Department of Energy has been laboring for the past 20 years, with a dedicated group of researchers, to accomplish the same results with their Building America program. But I don't think it has had the impact and acceptance among practical builders that the PassivHaus standard has had in Central Europe. Part of the reason is that the United States has greater diversity in climate zones than Germany. If you live in Miami, you've got a tropical climate (wet–humid), and if you live in St. Louis or Dallas, you have cold winters and hot, humid summers (mixed–humid). If you live in Phoenix, you have desert (hot–dry), and if you live in Los Angeles, you have a Mediterranean climate. So in the United States, we need more diverse approaches that take all these different climate zones into account and then translate those differences into simple standards that every builder can use. (In fact, the federal government's Building America program has done this to some degree.) We also have to return to better skill in homebuilding, something that may have been lacking in the rush to overbuild in the first half of the present decade, but a skill of which German homebuilders are rightly very proud.

You've probably got the idea already that solutions to the problems of energy use, global warming, and carbon dioxide production will vary depending on the culture of each country. But we don't have a lot of time to make the changes in practices (and expectations among buyers) that will result in much more energy-efficient homes. My research for another book (on green homes in the United States) led me to believe that most builders have the skills and know-how to build much better, even 50 percent better than current codes (based on the 2004 International Residential Code), but that they lack motivation to do so and don't see a consumer demand for energy-efficient housing.[8] To counter that perspective, I would point out that only 5 years ago, most Americans were clearly opting for gas-guzzling SUVs, not hybrids. Five years from now, we're going to see a clear preference for cars that move away from the dominant conventionally powered, conventionally fueled automobile, perhaps in favor of the plug-in electric hybrid vehicle, as the technology of choice.

The Solar Decathlon House

The superiority of the PassivHaus concept was demonstrated in an unusual way in the summer of 2007. A team of German architecture and engineering students from the Technical University of Darmstadt, initiated by Barbara Gehrung and under the leadership of Professor Manfred Hegger, a colleague of Feist, competed with nineteen other schools in the biennial Solar

Decathlon, held on the Capitol Mall in Washington, D.C. during a hot, humid 10-day period in August. The 2007 Solar Decathlon challenged twenty college teams from around the globe to design, build, and operate the most livable, energy-efficient, and completely solar-powered house. Solar Decathlon entrants must meet all the home energy needs of a typical family using only the power of the sun. The winner of the competition is the team that best blends aesthetics and modern conveniences with maximum energy production and optimal efficiency.[9]

The objective was to design and build a 700–square-foot home that approximated realistic energy demands from a typical American household, but one that was almost or completely sustainable. The homes were judged on engineering, economic, and social criteria, including marketability. The German entry took top prize, beating out such formidable competitors as Penn State, Georgia Tech, Maryland, Carnegie Mellon, Colorado, and Massachusetts Institute of Technology.[10] Moreover, the German students' home was the only entry that generated more power than it used over the trial period. Nearly 150,000 people visited the homes in the Solar Decathlon.

FIGURE 1.2 A key to any low-energy home is windows with an R-5 to R-10 rating. German windows are made like German cars, with superior engineering. (www.energate.com)

One especially nice feature was the triple-glazed windows (quadruple on the north side) from a modest 90-year-old German company, located in Speyer, a 2,000-year-old Roman town in the state of Baden-Württemberg. The company, Häussler Fenster (Häussler Windows), produces some very attractive, highly energy-efficient windows, shown in Figure 1.2. The current head of the firm is Ludwig Häussler, the third-generation owner and an expert in wood technology. As is typical with much building technology in Germany, the windows are as finely engineered and built as their cars. (That's a lesson we could easily learn, one that many high-end U.S. window manufacturers could adopt quickly. The bigger issue is getting U.S. homebuilders to buy and install good windows instead of just trying to meet basic energy code requirements.) Germany has been increasing requirements for windows since 1977, through its Wärme Schutzverordnung (heat protection ordinance).

The German students' entry (Figure 1.3) had a number of innovative features, including photovoltaics on the shutters that kept direct sunlight from entering the building and a solar water heater for the home's hot water needs. It was also an attractive building, with a nice deck for sitting outside and a hidden bed that lies under the floor during the day (almost a Japanese futon-style solution).

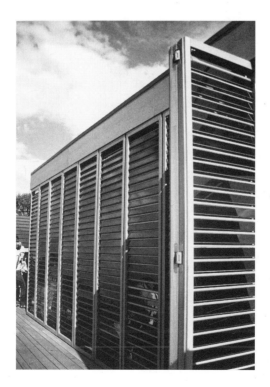

FIGURE 1.3 The German student entry won the 2007 Solar Decathlon, producing more energy than it consumed using building-integrated photovoltaic systems. (Kaye Evans-Lutterodt/ Solar Decathlon)

The Werner Sobek House

On a number of occasions in my European visits, I came across a project so unique and interesting that I felt it had to be shared in this book. Such is the case with Werner Sobek's house. One of Germany's top consulting structural engineers, Sobek is also a professor at the University of Stuttgart, and the first president of the German Green Building Council, the Deutsche Gesellschaft für Nachhaltiges Bauen.[11] In June 2000, he and his wife built the first emission-free home in Germany on a hillside overlooking Stuttgart. The four-level home on Römerstrasse, named R-128, is 250 square meters in area (about 2,700 square feet) (Figure 1.4).

What's unusual about this home? First, it's all glass and designed for disassembly: Everything is bolted together from modular components. Second, it's on a difficult sloping site, requiring careful planning and engineering, Sobek's specialty. Third, it's designed for zero emissions for heating on an annual basis.[12]

The goals were to offer the user maximum transparency, daylight, openness, and year-round comfort, the latter hard to achieve in most homes, let alone in an all-glass house. The climatic concept has cool water circulating through ceiling panels in summer to take heat out of the house; the heat energy is stored below the house and recovered for space heating in winter. This is one of the few examples I've seen of trans-seasonal thermal energy storage, a concept that could be exploited in more areas with dramatic annual temperature swings, such as the northern United States and most of Canada. In circulating water to draw heat away from the house in summer (thus cooling it) and return it back in winter, the home also draws minimal electrical energy to pump small amounts of water. With radiant heating and cooling panels covering 40 percent of the ceiling area, the home is easily made comfortable in all seasons.

Temperature and lighting levels are controlled by sensors and touch screens. Lighting can be voice activated or remote controlled. All sanitary fixtures are sensor controlled, so they are very hygienic and water conserving.

The building façade consists of triple-glazed panels with transparent foil between the outer and central panes. An inert gas fills the space between the panels. The glass alone has an R-value of about 13 (compared with most double-pane, low-e glass that has an R-value of 3 to 4), making it the equivalent of a wall with 4 inches of fiberglass insulation. Because

FIGURE 1.4 Werner Sobek's all-glass house in Stuttgart uses trans-seasonal thermal storage to provide heating in winter, along with solar photovoltaic and thermal panels.
(Roland Halbe fotografie)

of this superinsulating glass, there is no overheating in summer or overcooling in winter. According to Sobek, on a cold winter day the inside pane of the glass can feel warm, even while ice crystals are forming on the outer pane.[13]

Heat is recovered from all exhaust air, which is designed to exit through the bathrooms, doing double-duty as ventilation air. In winter, incoming fresh air is preheated through the heat recovery module to about 20°C, even at low outside temperatures. During the warm months, the ground-coupled heat exchanger cools the supply air by 6° to 7° Kelvin without any net energy input.

The flat roof contains forty-eight solar panels with a peak power output of 6.7 kilowatts, quite large for any home, even mounted horizontally. The annual output for this system in Stuttgart's latitude is estimated at about 8,000 kilowatt-hours, more than enough for heating and cooling in this climate.

Overall, the R-128 house is a great example of creative engineering to meet the goals of a passive house without sacrificing comfort, aesthetics, or light. And, to coin a phrase, "people who live in glass houses shouldn't use energy."

Passive Buildings in Switzerland

In Switzerland, the prevailing energy design standard is called Minergie (minimum energy), administered by the Swiss Minergie Association. One of the key goals for the standard is to keep the cost premium within 10 percent of a standard house while reducing annual energy consumption for heating, hot water, and ventilation, measured in terms of heating oil, to about 1 gallon (4 liters) per square meter of floor space. For a 150–square-meter home (1,650 square feet), this would imply a heating oil use of about 150 gallons per year. By comparison, some older Swiss homes might use as much as five times that amount. Americans and Canadians who heat with oil might want to compare these goals with their own energy use to get an idea of how restrictive the Swiss standard really is.

Minergie also certifies commercial buildings, apartments, townhouses, and many other types of structures. By 2007, more than 8,200 buildings had received Minergie certification, totaling more than 8.3 million square meters (nearly 90 million square feet) of floor area.[14]

To meet the Minergie standard, a new single-family house or apartment block must keep annual *primary* energy consumption for space heating, hot water, and ventilation below 42 kilowatt-hours per square meter (this is roughly equivalent to the PassivHaus standard, which is based on end use or site energy use). An annual threshold of 80 kilowatt-hours per square meter is applied to refurbished buildings (for which it's harder to retrofit the entire building envelope). Primary energy consumption includes a weighting factor for the total value of fossil fuels consumed, either directly as heating oil or indirectly as electricity. The weighting factor to convert energy use at the home to primary energy is a multiplier of 2.0, reflecting Switzerland's abundance of hydroelectric energy. For countries with less hydropower in the electricity mix, the weighting factor could be 3.0.

As of 2009, these energy targets will drop still further to 38 and 60 kilowatt-hours per square meter, respectively. Well-insulated buildings are capable of meeting these thresholds even with fossil fuel (e.g., oil- or gas-fired) heating systems. Yet experts recommend the use of heat pumps or wood-fired heating systems as a more effective means of saving energy by reducing the primary energy use for power production.[15]

Minergie certification for a single-family house provides five options for space heating: a ground-source heat pump, a wood-fired heating system in conjunction with solar collectors for hot water production, an automatic wood pellet–burning heating system, connection to a district heating system running on waste heat, and an air-to-water heat pump for space heating and domestic hot water supply.

Just like the PassivHaus, the Minergie standard requires a compact, well-insulated, and airtight building envelope in all situations. To comply with it, the envelope has to have a 15- to 20-centimeter (6- to 8-inch) thick insulation layer and, minimally, double-glazed windows. Similar to the PassivHaus approach, the Minergie standard also requires an automatic ventilation system with heat recovery. This saves energy by minimizing the net heat losses through ventilation.

Austrian Energy-Efficient Homes and Buildings

To understand the approaches taken in another cold Central European country, Austria, consider the work of a long-time green architect, Vienna's Georg Reinberg. He has been building energy-efficient buildings and homes, mostly with passive solar design principles, for nearly three decades. Reinberg's book on the subject, *Ecological Architecture: Design, Planning, Realization*, appeared in the fall of 2008, showcasing a lifetime of projects and design principles. Reinberg maintains that the PassivHaus concept needs to be expanded beyond just concern over heating and ventilation to include the embodied energy of building materials, hot water consumption, electricity consumption for appliances, and cooling energy.[16]

Take a look at the B!otop company's office building and studio, a 5,000–square-foot office building located on an existing pond, shown in Figure 1.5. It has solid wood construction (cross-laminated panels) with a solid sunlit memory wall inside. The glazed south zone serves as an opening, providing communication and a connection with water, weather, and sun. The adjacent

FIGURE 1.5 Georg Reinberg's B!otop office in Austria uses a full range of integrated design strategies to create a low-energy building.
(Rupert Steiner)

zone is illuminated diffusely; direct light comes from the north and through the inside shaded windows, creating optimal conditions for office workers.

The south façade is generously glazed and forms a connection between the inner space and the outside. The glass wall is interrupted by a blue–violet vertical collector wall covering the stairs. A footbridge over the water makes it possible to walk around the pond.

The energy design is based on highly insulated outside walls, with high-quality glazing to reduce heat losses. Supply air is fed into the building through ground channels and exhausted through a regenerating air heater. Fresh air is blown into the offices through the winter garden and is exhausted from bathrooms directly to outside, as in Sobek's design. The interior is open to the winter sun; solar gains are stored in an inner memory wall or used by ventilation equipment (heat exchanger) for warming up the fresh air.

A solar water collector provides hot water for the building. The remainder of heating needs are met by a biomass heating plant that uses wood scraps produced in the market garden. Protection against summer overheating is guaranteed by high insulation, outside shading, cooling of the input air in the ground channels, and automatic night flush ventilation. Additional cooling can be provided by concrete core activation (water running in tubes in the concrete mass).

For this office building, the large new pond is used both for swimming and for demonstrating different planting concepts. Rainwater is fed from the roofs to planted seepage areas, connected to the whole concept of green areas around the site. This building illustrates classic environmentally appropriate, low-energy architecture at its finest.

For this book, we interviewed architect Reinberg to find out more about his philosophy of sustainable design.[17]

> In the beginning, the demand was just for homes, but now more and more clients are building offices and public buildings because they also want to profit from the positive image. They also want to become independent of energy price increases, because energy is much more expensive in Austria than it is in the U.S.
>
> In Europe, beginning with the coming year [2009], every house will have to have an energy passport (*Energieausweis*). When a new home is built, the builder will have to give the owner an energy certificate. The requirements will vary by district. The document will include the home's heating demand and aspects of ecology, such as the source of electricity, warm water, and so forth.

Reinberg exhibits the typical Austrian concern for the source of energy in buildings, the primary energy demand, typically from hydropower, coal, or imported oil.

> What we are working on now is lowering the primary energy demand for all purposes. We're taking into account electricity, warm water, and heating, and we're trying to bring down the energy demand for all three of them. To do that, first, one must keep the heat inside the house in the winter. Therefore, we pay close attention to the details and use a lot of insulation, very thick walls. Normally we insulate the walls with 20 centimeters [8 inches] and the roof with 30 centimeters [12 inches] of insulation. As a standard, we use triple glazing in the windows with an inert gas fill, so we have a very good U-value. We are very careful with the details, and we build the houses airtight, so they don't lose warm air.

Most green architects and engineers share this viewpoint: First reduce energy use with conservation measures, and only then add renewable energy such as solar.

> After the house is designed to lose very little energy, then we add [solar] warm water collectors. Very often, we build warm water collectors that also serve for heating, but those collection installations have to be relatively big. For example, in Salzburg we did a sixty-four–unit housing project. The collection roof is 410 square meters [4,412 square feet], and the storage tank has a 100,000-liter [26,667-gallon] capacity. We need the storage for cloudy days. We normally use photovoltaics as shading devices. We use them for shading house façades from the sun, and then the photovoltaics also reduce electricity consumption. Photovoltaics also supplement the energy used in the collectors and ventilation system for the controlled air exchange.

Because heating is the primary concern, in terms of energy use, standards in Austria and Germany have become more rigorous. Reinberg says, "Since we have a very good standard for insulation, now we're engaging more with solar thermal collectors and photovoltaic collectors. We also use the earth's energy. We take it out indirectly with heat pumps or directly with circulating water from the ground for heat in winter and for cooling in summer." Austria also has a "feed-in tariff" for photovoltaics, a subsidy that pays about five times the amount of what you pay for taking electricity out of the grid. In this way, a homeowner can pay off a photovoltaic system in about 15 years.

Reinberg is optimistic that in the future, "we will have houses that are producing more energy than they are consuming, and we will have no more energy problems." As one final example of his design approach, he points to a kindergarten now under construction:

> The school has very good insulation. Additionally, it has photovoltaics and solar hot water collectors. The electricity generated from the photovoltaics runs a heat pump, which uses groundwater from a deep well. The groundwater is used for heating in the winter and cooling in the summer. It's balanced over the year; we don't heat up or cool the groundwater in a way that disturbs nature, but we can do all of the heating and cooling through the groundwater. This building is not consuming any additional external energy. Such things are possible now.

Low-Energy Social Housing in the Netherlands

The Dutch have long worked together cohesively because most of the country lies below sea level, and one person or one town can't keep out the sea. In April 2008, I visited respected green architect Tjerk Reijenga in The Hague. He has been designing low-energy homes and green office buildings for the past 15 years.

Reijenga took me to a nice housing development he designed on the outskirts of The Hague, De Groene Kreek ("The Green Creek"), in Zoetermeer, a group of sixty-six townhouses designed to be carbon neutral (Figure 1.6). What I like especially about the design is the fact that in the development, built around a small lake, there are no internal paved roads. At the edge of the development is a light-rail station, so there is little need to drive to work. Recycling containers are highly visible and well marked. Each townhouse has space for its own garden, and each rooftop is oriented for future retrofits of solar hot water and photovoltaics. The project was

designed in cooperation with the future residents, so they could make decisions about the layout of their homes and the space around the houses.

The Dutch system for evaluating homes includes more than energy. It's called Greencalc Plus (which provides an eco-indicator as a single number for environmental benefit) and includes consideration of water use, material choices, and transportation accessibility.[18] According to Reijenga, it is now a privatized system similar to the United Kingdom's BREEAM rating system, which is explained in more detail in Chapter 4. The Dutch also look at sustainability through the lens of a process called DCBA, in which

> D = Meet legal requirements (the normal situation).
> C = Energy-efficient design, using best practice measures and products (i.e., correct the problems of the normal situation).
> B = Bioclimatic design with use of optimized materials (minimize environmental damage).
> A = Zero-energy design, with only renewable materials, flexible, and deconstructible (completely autonomous of fossil fuels and nonrenewable resources).[19]

The Dutch aspire to very high standards in their housing and commercial buildings. The DCBA system is one way to keep moving the bar higher, focusing on continuous improvement and a growing autonomy for communities and the country as a whole.

What can we learn from these European approaches to energy-efficient homes? First of all, it's possible to design attractive, more energy-efficient homes using simple technology. Second, clear standards for home energy use are needed so that everyone knows the target at which to aim. Third, there's no escaping the need for government regulation of energy demand. Fourth,

FIGURE 1.6 Designed by BEAR Architects, De Groene Kreek near Den Haag provides access to transit and contains no internal roads.

PassivHaus probably is not a good term to use for the more active American attitude; perhaps *high-performance* would work a lot better here. Fifth, there is no current market demand for such homes; we need a lot of demonstration projects, allowing people to see that these homes are not only energy efficient, but also attractive, quiet, and comfortable. Finally, a lot of education is needed because the detailed construction techniques are not in most builders' toolkits right now.[20] I'll explore more about the PassivHaus approach in later chapters, when we look at how similar housing standards are being implemented elsewhere in Europe.

One more thing: The European approach is focused heavily on energy use, with attendant benefits of increased comfort and indoor air quality. From the standpoint of the more popular green home standards in the United States, those of the U.S. Green Building Council and the National Association of Homebuilders, that approach is much too narrow. The North American approach considers also land use impacts, links to transportation and vital services, water use, and material use. In my opinion, we need to do both: have "climate-neutral" housing and make sure that the life-cycle impacts of our total approach to homebuilding and home operations are neutral at worst. It is true that in Europe most of those other things are good design practices to begin with. Land, materials, and resources are limited and already managed with stewardship in mind, and most places already have excellent public transportation. Toxins in materials are controlled by much more stringent codes. So there is no need to give points for things that are already a given. The debate over what green building standards should entail will continue, of course, but there's no doubt that any green building should exhibit low levels of energy demand.

CHAPTER 2

European Design Innovators

Y ou're going to read now about some of the significant design innovators in European green design, architects who began this movement nearly two decades ago, when energy and environmental concerns in architecture were far less significant than they are today. When I began the research for this book, I had just a vague idea of where I would find not just the famous but also lesser-known designers and planners doing the most valuable sustainable design work. It took a year's worth of networking and on-site investigation, attending trade shows and conferences, and relying on those I interviewed to recommend others of similar mind and practice. Presented here is just a sample of what many people consider to be the leading designers, innovators, and practitioners of European sustainable design.

Early on I decided to focus mainly on the United Kingdom and Germany because that appeared to be the origin of the greatest concentration of innovative design work.[1] Perhaps the most seminal figure in European green design, one whose work is widely recognized around the world, is Lord Norman Foster of the United Kingdom.

FOSTER + PARTNERS, U.K.

The Foster + Partners firm has provided guidance to a generation of architects about how to introduce sustainable design principles and low-energy solutions into first-class architecture. A number of noteworthy projects in the firm's long history are profiled in Chapters 4 and 5. Going back nearly 20 years, Foster's projects have attempted to meld architectural innovation with a full integration of low-energy design, using daylighting, natural ventilation, and both winter and sky gardens, into what could have been more conventional glass boxes. Some of his noteworthy projects, profiled in Chapter 4, include Europe's first sustainable skyscraper, in Frankfurt, the naturally ventilated Reichstag building in Berlin, and the cigar-shaped, energy-efficient Gherkin office in London.

DAVID LLOYD JONES AND STUDIO E, U.K.

David Lloyd Jones has been designing environmental buildings for more than two decades. In 1998, he published one of the earliest books on environmental design in the modern era, *Architecture and the Environment*.[2] In the preface to that work, Lloyd Jones writes,

[By bioclimatic design] I mean an approach to design which is inspired by nature and which applies a sustained logic to every aspect of the project, focused on optimizing and using the environment. The logic covers conditions of setting (location), economy, construction, building management and individual health and well being, in addition to building physics.

For an example of his work, see the Doxford Solar Office building profiled in the Introduction and the Beaufort Court project profiled in Chapter 4.

FIGURE 2.1 Thomas Herzog's design philosophy of building orientation and massing, along with intelligent use of solar energy, is shown in the SOKA-BAU office park. *(Horst Goebe)*

THOMAS HERZOG AND PARTNERS, GERMANY

In Germany, the work and achievements of Thomas Herzog have been recognized for almost 30 years. Herzog has been very interested in incorporating renewable energy, particularly in the form of solar power, into his designs. Herzog's work represents a solid, almost engineering approach to architecture that has a great following in Germany. One of his more recent projects, SOKA-BAU in Wiesbaden, is shown in Figure 2.1.

Based in Munich, Herzog is a university professor, practicing architect, and technological innovator. He is author and editor of numerous books on architecture, construction, and technology in several languages. Of Thomas Herzog's position in the field, one commentator writes,[3]

The real significance of Herzog's work lies in his embrace of the green agenda, not just in his designs but also as a teacher and as an active campaigner in exhibitions, publications and other collaborations with fellow architects. His architecture could be seen, perhaps paradoxically, as both returning to modern architecture's proto-green roots while also transcending the modern paradigm to help bring about the more ecologically oriented one that must surely replace it.

WHITE DESIGN, U.K.

Founded in 1998 by Craig White and Linda Farrow, White Design has developed an explicit approach to sustainable design that deserves a wider following. Specifically, the firm's approach contains the following elements.

- Engages with the client to jointly develop the design and to help them understand how to manage the energy use of the building after occupancy

- Follows low-energy design principles and incorporates double glazing, rainwater harvesting, biomass boilers, natural daylighting and ventilation, and thermal mass into buildings wherever possible
- Uses a life-cycle approach that considers the occupation and eventual disposal of buildings as well as the design process and construction phase
- Follows good practice such as recycling existing on-site buildings or materials wherever possible, promoting a local (50-mile radius of site) supply chain, and supporting innovative recycling projects involving the local community. (For example, for Ann's Grove School, a local industry was established as a result of an initiative during the design stage exploring insulation materials made from recycled fabrics. The school also uses a software tool that allows them to compare technologies for reducing carbon emissions against capital cost and payback implications.)

As for trends likely to influence design in the United Kingdom over the next 5 years, White Design says,[4]

The debate about whether a zero-carbon house is possible is complex and on going; it is likely to influence design debate significantly over the next decade. We believe it is already possible to achieve a zero-carbon community, which is where we intend to focus our design and consultancy activities.

We will be exploring how future targets for low-carbon communities engage with the complex issue of behavior change and encouraging people to lead more sustainable lifestyles.

We also believe that materials such as ModCell, prefabricated straw bale panels, and housing concepts like Balehaus will become mainstream in the U.K. housing market.

FIGURE 2.2 ModCell's use of prefabricated straw panels is a unique twist on the straw bale building technique. *(White Design)*

In the Ann's Grove Primary School, in Sheffield, White Design insulated the walls and roof of the main school building with recycled denim and the school hall with recycled newspaper. Shown in Figure 2.2, ModCell is an innovative straw bale panel that is produced near the site for each project, using standard equipment, allowing the construction of a PassivHaus level of wall insulation right out of the box.

BENNETTS ASSOCIATES ARCHITECTS, U.K.

Rab Bennetts founded the eponymous Bennetts Associates Architects and is one of the leading proponents of green buildings in the United Kingdom. Bennetts is well known for several landmark projects, including the Brighton Library. He started the firm in 1987 and now employs about seventy people at two offices in London and Edinburgh.

Bennetts shared his philosophy of sustainable design with me through a presentation he made in 2008 to the Liberal Democrats and Councilors, the third largest political bloc in the U.K. Parliament.[5] His basic point is that good design alone can substantially reduce carbon dioxide emissions from buildings, without economic hardship, a proposition to which most U.K. green architects would readily assent. For long-term sustainability, Bennetts asserts five basic principles for all buildings:

- Efficiency
- Simplicity
- Robustness
- Adaptability
- Low CO_2 emissions

To arrive at the ultimate goal of low carbon emissions, he cites six design steps:

1. A good brief with a clear requirement for low-energy design, along with the selection of the proper consultants
2. Passive design (what we would call passive solar design, including orientation, massing, daylighting, solar shading, nighttime flushing, and natural ventilation)
3. Active energy-efficient engineering (e.g., displacement ventilation, chilled beams, energy-efficient lighting, peak-shaving electrical control systems)
4. Commissioning and building management (relaxing comfort criteria in design, managing the energy use of electronic equipment, conducting post-occupancy evaluations, making sure everything actually works as intended, and then operating the building to get the results predicted, steps overlooked by most architects and engineers)
5. Appropriate choice of fuels, which in the United Kingdom means biomass boilers and ground-source heating and cooling via heat pumps as well as solar and wind power systems in addition to electricity and gas from the national grid
6. Design for local conditions, with no "one-approach-fits-all" design solution (if there were one, it wouldn't really be design), design for objectives such as low carbon emissions, and, of course, design for good architecture

Bennetts's approach right now is very simple: "CO_2 drives everything." We can expect to see more European architects adopting this motto as the enormity of the global warming challenge becomes more apparent over time. I visited Bennetts Associates' New Street Square project, a four-building office complex in London completed in June 2008, which includes a number of energy-saving and environmental features such as high-performance glazing and green roofs, along with an innovative green wall on a two-story conference center (figures 4.4 and 10.2). This is a good example of contemporary sustainable design in the United Kingdom.

HOPKINS ARCHITECTS, U.K.

Sir Michael and Lady Patty Hopkins started Hopkins Architects in London in 1976. The firm first came to my attention with its role as the design architects for a Leadership in Energy and Environmental Design (LEED) Platinum research laboratory at Northern Arizona University in Flagstaff, the first highest-ranked LEED building completed in Arizona. Michael Taylor, one of the directors, who's been at the firm since the early 1990s, says that their approach is to start every project with the most extreme wish list of things they'd like to include, then narrow it down to the items that are the best value for the client. In the case of the northern Arizona project, the client's wish list for sustainable design measures added enough cost that a large amount of space was removed from the building program to accommodate it. Taylor says that managing costs is the hardest part of sustainable design.

The firm is bringing its low-energy design approach to the United States in projects including a chemistry building at Princeton University and Kroon Hall at Yale University, through collaborations with American architects. At Princeton, they're experimenting with new low-energy façade designs, working with the Italian firm Permasteelisa.[6] That firm's "Blue Technology" concept treats the façade (building envelope) and the building's environmental systems as an integral whole, looking for synergistic solutions that allow transparency through the façade without compromising occupant comfort or energy consumption, and at a cost comparable to more conventional solutions.

Hopkins Architects' approach is to embed sustainability so fully into the process that the architecture is always the best they can do, without reference to whether it's fully green. Taylor believes that basic architecture works the best for long-term sustainability, in paying close attention to the form, scale, and orientation of buildings.

He says that changing occupant behavior is the key to getting effective, low-energy results. For example, if people are willing to have inside temperatures range from 19°C (66°F) to 25°C (77°F) instead of insisting on a more restrictive 22°C to 24°C (72°F to 75°F) year-round, the energy use of the building will be a lot lower, especially during the peak cooling periods.

Hopkins projects of note include the 1999 Jubilee campus for the University of Nottingham, the 1994 Inland Revenue Centre at Nottingham (the first building ever certified as Excellent under the BREEAM, it won the Green Building of 1996 Award), and the British Parliament's new offices, Portcullis House, in 2000. In 2008, the Hopkins firm received *Building* magazine's "Sustainable Architect of the Year" award.[7]

Like many British architects, Michael Hopkins regards engineers as equal partners in developing a design appropriate to place. He says, "Engineers are the first people one thinks of when one starts to build up a design team. The best ones are our philosophers. I have this recurring feeling that the best architecture grows out of the engineering, so you want the engineers in there to contribute to ideas right from the very beginning."[8]

MAKE ARCHITECTS, U.K.

Ken Shuttleworth is a successful architect who left Foster + Partners in 2004 to found Make Architects. I met with Ken and his partner, Sean Affleck, in London in May 2008. Their motto is "Death to the glass box" because of the high energy use of all-glass façades. As a firm that designs buildings ranging in scale from residential towers and office developments to urban master plans, Make is leading the effort to make these buildings more energy efficient by cutting the amount of surface area devoted to glass (which is the least energy efficient wall section) and replacing it with a very artistic approach to the building envelope.

FIGURE 2.3 Make Architects' approach of providing adequate lighting in an unusual and tight envelope is shown well by this building (right) at the University of Nottingham.
(Zander Olsen, Make Architects)

Sean Affleck's presentation at London's 2008 Ecobuild conference showed me how the sustainable line of thinking can lead to some wildly innovative design approaches, that sustainable architecture can be exuberant rather than stuffy. His approach is to get rid of the all-glass curtain wall and aim to have at least half the façade consist of insulated panels, many with artistically cut shapes. Right there, he says, we can cut 20 percent of energy use. The glazing doesn't have to be uniform, either. In a residential building, for example, one can increase the amount of glass for views from a living room while reducing it for privacy in a bedroom.

The firm is willing to experiment with newer green technology. In a twenty-eight–story residential tower in Leeds, they proposed a 40-kilowatt wind turbine at a cost of about $100,000, with an estimated 5- to 8-year payback period. Affleck's personality reflects the firm's approach: exuberant. Another project using an innovative approach to glazing and materials at the University of Nottingham is shown in Figure 2.3.

Make's philosophy of sustainable design is expressed eloquently in the following:

> With the built environment making a major contribution to the world's carbon dioxide emissions, we believe that architects have an urgent duty to design buildings to work harder and perform better. We are passionately committed to designing buildings that minimize environmental impact and optimize energy efficiency.

ARUP ASSOCIATES, U.K.

The Arup Associates architecture firm is part of the larger Arup group of engineers and planners. Arup Associates has completed major sustainability projects in the United Kingdom, continental Europe, and Asia.

As told to me by Michael Beaven, an architect and director of Arup Associates, the firm's approach to sustainable development centers around six core principles:[9]

- Integration: Effectively integrate environmental, social, and economic considerations (the "triple bottom line").
- Stakeholder involvement: Support all stakeholders.
- Precautionary behavior: Measures to protect environmental and social integrity should not be postponed because of scientific uncertainty about actual impacts.
- Generational equity: Promote fairness and equal access to opportunities, as implied in the original definition of *sustainable development*.
- Continual improvement: It's imperative to take action now, while recognizing that future products, technologies, and systems will be better.
- Ecological integrity: Protect biological diversity and maintain essential ecological processes.

I also met with David Richards, a director of Arup Associates engineers and planners in London. Richards expressed his design approach in terms of six sustainable goals that they use to start each project:[10]

- Carbon neutrality
- Water neutrality
- Use of sustainable materials
- Flexible design to adapt to future climate change
- A positive contribution to the local community
- Sustainable operations, including monitoring

In Richards's view, every project needs a sustainable strategy, starting with these six objectives and then proceeding to specified outcomes that can be measured. Using these desired outcomes, the team will develop specific design themes and create a sustainable design plan. Having spent 7 years in New York City at Arup's office, he thinks that engineers in the United States have

50 percent less time to think on projects, because of the typical fee structure, and instead prefer to wait until an architect has mostly finished the schematic design to step in and start fixing things.

For Citi, the firm completed a major data center in Frankfurt, Germany in April 2008 and expects to receive a LEED Platinum rating with 58 points out of a possible 69. The 10,000–square-meter (107,000–square-foot) data center is located inside a 20,000–square-meter building. The building has an extensive green roof and an intensive green wall watered by recovered drainage, and it uses wastewater, water economy, and ozone purification (instead of chemicals) for the cooling tower, which in turn provides free evaporative cooling.

By focusing heavily on façade engineering for all projects, Arup Associates hopes to downsize or eliminate the conventional heating, ventilation, and air conditioning (HVAC) systems in most projects and bring down their total cost from 25 percent of the building to about 5 percent while spending more on the façade. The attitude of the firm is that one can always add HVAC later if the first design doesn't provide enough cooling. The Citi project exemplifies this ideal. Power consumption is 40 percent of that of a conventional data center, all power to the site is from renewable sources, and 90 percent of the wastewater is reused.

SHORT AND ASSOCIATES, U.K.

Cambridge professor Alan Short is one of the significant innovators in British sustainable design. Short is a unique architect, committed to a research agenda for all his projects, many of which cleverly use sound engineering principles in pushing the envelope of low-energy buildings. I'll profile three of his projects later, including a new building at the University College London, completed in 2005 to house the School of Slavonic and East European Studies. In the 1990s, the firm completed an early green building with natural ventilation, the Queens Building at De Montfort University in Leicester, which won the United Kingdom's "green building of the year" award in 1995.[11] Completed in 2000, the University of Coventry is an excellent example of natural ventilation and daylighting.

INGENHOVEN ARCHITEKTEN, GERMANY

Christoph Ingenhoven started his firm in 1985 at the tender age of 25. Such a thing is almost unheard of in Germany; no one goes out on his own so early in a career. Beginning in the early 1990s, Ingenhoven began to create a significant body of work focusing on low-energy design for large buildings, replete with natural light and natural ventilation. The firm's headquarters is at Plange Mühle, a refurbished former flourmill in Dusseldorf's Media Harbor, where it employs around 100 architects, interior designers, drafters, and model makers.

Ingenhoven Architects is a leader in sustainable building and ecological design; its work is guided by the principles set out in standards such as LEED, Minergie in Switzerland, and BREEAM in the United Kingdom. The RWE headquarters in Essen, completed in 1996, is one of Europe's early ecologically oriented high-rise buildings that, with its double-façade technology, allows each floor to be naturally ventilated. The Lufthansa

Aviation Center, completed in 2006, uses only one third of the energy of a conventional office building. The new Main Train Station (Hauptbahnhof) in Stuttgart, to be built from 2009 to 2018, was awarded Holcim's Global "Gold" Award in 2006 for its sustainable design approach.[12] A zero-energy station, it will use no heating, cooling, or mechanical ventilation and will be lit during the day mainly with daylighting. In a later section, Ingenhoven's latest work and a classic green building are profiled.

BEHNISCH ARCHITEKTEN, GERMANY

Originally working with his father, Stefan Behnisch has operated the firm of Behnisch Architekten independently since the early 1990s. Behnisch is perhaps the best-known German architecture firm working in North America, based largely on the Genzyme Headquarters building in Cambridge, Massachusetts, the first large (350,000–square-foot) LEED Platinum building in the United States. Begun in 2000 and finished in 2003, this building exemplifies many of the sustainable design principles found in Behnisch's European work. The firm's philosophy is also described in the foreword by David Cook, one of the partners.

Behnisch Architekten's offices in Stuttgart occupy two buildings accessed through an alley off a main street not far from the city's Hauptbahnhof. The firm has a polyglot staff from many countries in Europe, North America, and Asia, fluent in both German and English. Behnisch is hard at work on a new large-scale bioscience campus in Allston, Massachusetts for Harvard University that will be completed around 2012.

Behnisch Architekten and engineering firm Transsolar continue to jointly exhibit their work in a traveling show touring North America from 2007 to 2009. What I found remarkable about this exhibit is that it not only represents the joint work but also reaffirms the philosophy and shared thinking of both the architect and the engineer in a way that I've seldom seen in the United States.

ATELIER DREISEITL, GERMANY

Atelier Dreiseitl is one of the leading landscape architects of Germany, working also in the United States and Singapore. I first became acquainted with the work of Herbert Dreiseitl in 2002 through a presentation at the U.S. Green Building Council's Greenbuild conference. Dreiseitl is a German landscape architect with two unusual obsessions: He is devoted to the natural form water wants to take as it flows through the landscape, and he uses his original training as an art therapist to make his landscape creations into healing places for both people and the planet. Atelier Dreiseitl has created some of the more interesting internal and external landscape designs in Europe. Their work has become known in the United States through collaborations for the 40,000–square-foot green roof on Chicago City Hall and the Tanner Springs Park, a 40,000–square-foot constructed wetland park in Portland, Oregon.

Sunk 5 feet below street level, Tanner Springs Park cleanses rainwater and provides a passive recreational experience in the middle of a bustling urban district. I lived near this park in 2006 and used to walk along the boardwalk over the water, admiring what Dreiseitl had done, especially the paean to the former Tanner Springs buried 40 feet below. The park features a 200-foot-long (60-meter) Art Wall composed of 368 railroad rails, rising up from the wetland in a vertical undulating pattern, with ninety-nine pieces of fused glass hand-painted by Dreiseitl. He calls this an "authentic and artistic ecology."[13]

Dreiseitl's articulates his philosophy about the use of water inside and outside buildings in this way:

> Water is far from being just a designer's resource or a material: it begs to have its vital possibilities rediscovered. This starts at the beginning of the planning process for water projects, and involves linking up and integrating elemental themes. Knowledge of water's particular qualities as a material [is] needed, and often experiments [are needed] to give an idea of the ensuing result.[14]

Working with water is also a great teacher. Dreiseitl says, "Water is full of dynamism, and it needs a sense of movement in the thinking and ideas of the people dealing with it." In his view, there is a special inner flexibility "needed to work with water successfully." For Dreiseitl, landscape design is more than plants, sidewalks, planters, and ponds; one also needs to capture the soul of a place and then express it in design using the full dimension of one's own inner landscape.

Dreiseitl's firm also provided the landscape architecture for SolarCity Linz, a new city to serve a projected population of 25,000 along the Danube River in Austria, described in Chapter 7. The principles: First control rainwater, then limit access to protected nature areas, beginning with wetlands, and then create attractive diversions in the form of passive and active recreation areas, including a bathing lake and new sports center, along with designated walkways through and adjacent to the nature areas.[15] Early indications (after completion in 2005) are that local wildlife has adapted well to the new wetlands, even in areas adjacent to buildings.

This chapter has presented just a sample of the sustainable design thinking, exemplified in realized projects of the past 15 years, coming out of Europe that we can use in the United States and Canada. As we go through the book, you'll see many project examples that show much that we can admire and emulate.

CHAPTER 3

European Green Buildings Today: What Do They Know That We Don't?

Because of the strong focus on energy savings in the colder countries of Northern and Western Europe, it's easy to overlook some of the sustainable design efforts under way in the Mediterranean countries, such as Italy, southern France, and Spain. For example, Spain has had a Consejo Construcción Verde España (Spain Green Building Council) since 1998.[1] Many other European countries are forming national green building councils.[2] Additionally, there have been Leadership in Energy and Environmental Design (LEED)-certified buildings in the United Kingdom, Germany, Italy, and Spain, using the U.S. standard. For example, the Herman Miller facility in Chippenham, U.K. was certified LEED Gold at the end of 2007.[3] The Alvento Business Park in Madrid, Spain received an LEED Silver rating in 2006. Two facilities operated by the U.S. Navy in Italy received LEED Certified and Silver ratings in the past few years. As mentioned in Chapter 2, the data center in Frankfurt designed by Arup Associates for Citi, completed in 2008, expects to receive a LEED Platinum rating.

One of the key driving forces of European energy-efficient design is the European Union's 2002 Energy Performance of Buildings Directive (EPBD).[4] Each of the twenty-seven member states of the European Union is responsible for individual implementation of the EPBD through national laws.[5] The main focus of European sustainable building design at this time is on reducing energy use directly and carbon emissions indirectly. The EPBD has five main themes:

- *Certificates*: When buildings are constructed, sold, or rented out, an energy performance certificate must be made available to the owner or by the owner to the prospective buyer or tenant, as the case might be.
- *Inspection*: All larger boilers and air-conditioning units must be inspected to ensure proper operation.
- *Experts*: Qualified experts must carry out inspections and provide the analysis for the certificates.
- *Calculations*: Energy use estimates must be made with adequate software whose calculation methods are transparent and widely accepted.
- *Minimum energy performance requirements*: For new buildings with a total useful floor area greater than 1,000 square meters (10,000 square feet), each country shall require that every project consider the technical, environmental, and economic feasibility of alternative systems such as decentralized energy supply systems based on renewable energy, combined

heat and power systems, district heating or cooling (if available), and heat pumps under certain conditions. In addition, owners of existing buildings greater than 1,000 square meters that undertake major renovations shall be required to upgrade their energy performance to meet new minimum requirements.

You can see that this is a comprehensive program that we should emulate in the United States and Canada. Without clear standards for new buildings and major upgrade requirements for existing buildings, we'll never be able to reduce the carbon emissions from residential and commercial buildings, which contribute 40 percent of the total in both Europe and North America.

What's driving the EPBD is the heightened European concern over the role of building energy and materials use in global carbon dioxide production, constraints on energy supplies, and the potential for catastrophic changes in the global climate as a result of increased carbon dioxide concentrations in the atmosphere. European national governments have been far more willing to accept the conclusions of climate science than American or Canadian governments and have been willing to take that science and develop practical public policies for reversing the growth of carbon emissions, including subsidies, laws, and regulations to implement these policies.

As for future development of the EPBD in Europe, Bill Bordass of the United Kingdom's Usable Buildings Trust provides his assessment of the situation:[6]

> The directive is currently under review in Brussels. Written submissions were invited earlier this year [2008] and are being collated in preparation for a process that will lead to revisions in 2010. To avoid any confusion, the European Commission plans not just to make amendments but to publish a new version of the directive. I suspect that this will require Display Energy Certificates (DECs) on a wider range of commercial buildings and possibly all.[7] DECs may also need to be based on actual energy use. The new requirements would probably come fully into force 2 to 3 years after 2010.

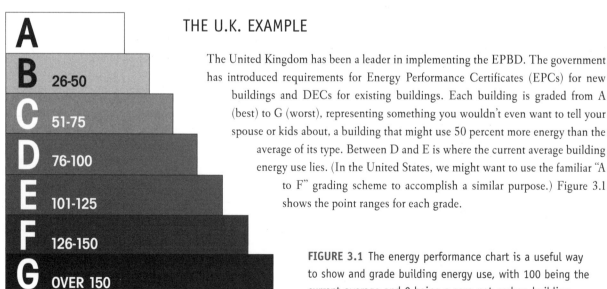

THE U.K. EXAMPLE

The United Kingdom has been a leader in implementing the EPBD. The government has introduced requirements for Energy Performance Certificates (EPCs) for new buildings and DECs for existing buildings. Each building is graded from A (best) to G (worst), representing something you wouldn't even want to tell your spouse or kids about, a building that might use 50 percent more energy than the average of its type. Between D and E is where the current average building energy use lies. (In the United States, we might want to use the familiar "A to F" grading scheme to accomplish a similar purpose.) Figure 3.1 shows the point ranges for each grade.

FIGURE 3.1 The energy performance chart is a useful way to show and grade building energy use, with 100 being the current average and 0 being a zero-net-carbon building.

The current timetable of regulation in the United Kingdom follows. Most of these dates deal with the EPCs. The primary difficulty in the United Kingdom today appears to be training enough qualified assessors to make the required analyses.[8]

April 2008 EPCs required on construction for all dwellings.

EPCs required for the construction, sale, or rent of buildings, other than dwellings, with a floor area greater than 10,000 square meters (107,000 square feet).

July 2008 EPCs required for the construction, sale, or rent of buildings, other than dwellings, with a floor area greater than 2,500 square meters (27,000 square feet).

October 2008 EPCs required on the sale or rent of all remaining dwellings.

EPCs required on the construction, sale, or rent of all remaining buildings, other than dwellings.

Display energy certificates required for all public buildings larger than 1,000 square meters (10,700 square feet).

January 4, 2009 First inspection of all existing air-conditioning systems larger than 250 kilowatts must be completed.

January 4, 2011 First inspection of all remaining air-conditioning systems larger than 12 kilowatts must be completed.

What does a building owner get from an EPC except compliance with the law and an expensive invoice from the consultant performing the analysis? According to one industry source,

> An EPC will provide an energy rating for a building that is based on the performance potential of the building itself (the fabric) and its services (such as heating, ventilation and lighting). The certificate provides an energy rating of the building from A to G, where A is very efficient and G is the least efficient. The energy performance of the building is shown as a carbon-dioxide (CO_2)–based index. The EPC is accompanied by a report that provides recommendations on using the building more effectively, cost-effective improvements to the building and other more expensive improvements which could enhance the building's energy performance.[9]

The DECs will work much the same way, except that they will use the actual energy performance data of existing buildings. The difficulty is to establish an effective way to compare buildings fairly and generate a grade based not just on square footage but also on the number of occupants, daily and yearly occupancy schedule, presence or absence of a data center, and similar considerations. Right now, news stories from the United Kingdom indicate that a shortage of qualified assessors and disputes over methods are likely to force the government to delay the implementation timetables somewhat, but the die has been cast.

The BREEAM Green Building Rating System

The United Kingdom's Building Research Establishment (BRE) is the leading authority on sustainable design in that country. Privatized in recent years, it developed the BRE Environmental Assessment Method (BREEAM), which has certified more than 1,200 commercial buildings (about the same as the U.S. Green Building Council's LEED system through early 2008) in a

TABLE 3.1 **2008 BUILDING RESEARCH ESTABLISHMENT ENVIRONMENTAL ASSESSMENT METHOD RATING CATEGORIES AND WEIGHTINGS.**

RATING CATEGORY	WEIGHTING
1. Building management	12
2. Health and well-being	15
3. Energy	19
4. Transport	8
5. Water	6
6. Materials and waste	12.5
7. Waste	7.5
8. Land use and ecology	10
9. Pollution	10
TOTAL	**100**

country one fifth the size of the United States and more than 100,000 housing units.[10] More than 800,000 buildings (including homes) are currently registered and pursuing a rating.[11]

BREEAM rates buildings according to the nine major categories shown in Table 3.1, with a single score at the end, similar to the LEED system. At 27 percent of the total, energy and transport are given weightings similar to those of the LEED for New Construction system (version 2.2).

The scores translate into the following rating categories:

1. Pass
2. Good
3. Very Good
4. Excellent

More than 600 buildings have been rated Excellent by BREEAM. BREEAM can be used to rate all types of buildings, with special systems including

- Schools
- Courts
- Offices
- Health care facilities
- Industrial buildings
- Ecohomes (now superseded by the Code for Sustainable Homes; see Chapter 4)
- Prisons
- Multifamily residences
- Retail space

To be launched in 2009, there will be also a "BREEAM in Use" standard similar to the U.S. Green Building Council's LEED rating system for existing buildings.[12]

Table 3.2 shows the progress of the BREEAM rating system in recent years, along with the total number of buildings rated in each category. In addition to these totals, BREEAM had certified 109,450 homes as of December 2008.

One critique of BREEAM, similar to that leveled against the U.S. Green Building Council's LEED system, is that

> There is no measurement of how the building performs once occupied. It is believed there has been little or no measurement of carbon emissions from the 628 buildings to have been designated "Excellent" so far. Total emissions are strongly influenced by tenant behavior, from the type of fit-out, the number of people in the building and the hours the building is in use each day, to the amount of electrical equipment installed and the occupier's understanding of how to run the heating and cooling efficiently.[13]

This has been a general issue with all green building rating systems and will undoubtedly be addressed by both BREEAM and LEED in the next few years. In 2008, BREEAM introduced a new and higher rating of Outstanding to denote the few projects now exceeding the Excellent rating level. (Personally, I'm waiting for an even higher level of complete sustainability, perhaps for restorative buildings, which I expect will be called Splendid or the British favorite, Brilliant.) Also, in 2008 BREEAM made major changes to the system, including introducing new environmental weightings, mandatory credits, and a two-stage certification process, design stage and post-construction. Benchmarks were set for carbon dioxide emissions to align BREEAM with the new EPCs. Finally, BREEAM introduced a "Core and Shell" rating system, similar to what has been in the LEED system since 2004.

BREEAM is exporting its system, with buildings currently certified in Luxembourg, Hungary, and the United States. BREEAM assessments are under way in countries as diverse as Dubai, France, Italy, Mauritius, Poland, the Philippines, Qatar, Sweden, and Turkey. In 2008, the International Council of Shopping Centers adopted BREEAM as a standard for rating shopping centers throughout Europe,[14] and the Dutch Green Building Council also adopted BREEAM as its standard.[15]

What I especially like is that BREEAM will create a "bespoke" rating system for unusual building types, such as recreation, laboratories, hotels, and various higher education structures, recalling the days when English gentlemen bought only custom-tailored (or "bespoke") suits from shops located along Savile Row in London. The U.S. approach with LEED has been the reverse, to make most of the diverse building types fit into a straitjacket made originally for office buildings, although this is changing, with rating systems specifically for schools and retail buildings introduced in 2007 and 2008.

All in all, BREEAM is a worthy competitor to LEED in the United States and is likely to be the dominant rating system in many European countries and perhaps in some other countries that prefer to follow a U.K. rather than a U.S. model. It illustrates green building rating systems that actually work because they're in tune with the marketplace realities but retain a sense of higher purpose.

TABLE 3.2 TOTAL NUMBER OF BUILDING RESEARCH ESTABLISHMENT ENVIRONMENTAL ASSESSMENT METHOD RATINGS, BY CATEGORY.

BUILDING TYPE	TOTAL (SINCE INCEPTION)	2008 (PARTIAL)	2007	2006
Schools	58	35	19	2
Customized ("bespoke")	244	68	77	37
Offices	1,196	371	179	132
Industrial	410	128	59	55
Ecohomes	6,000	1,647	1,284	1,223
Retail	43	35	4	1
Schools	58	35	19	2
Military	79	26	31	22
Total	**8,088**	**2,345**	**1,672**	**1,474**

Information current as of August 29, 2008, provided by the Building Research Establishment to the author.

Post-Occupancy Evaluations

One Achilles heel of all green buildings is that almost none of them are properly evaluated after a break-in period, so one does not know whether they are actually achieving the anticipated levels of performance. Bill Bordass is one of the United Kingdom's leading experts on this subject, having formed the Usable Buildings Trust with his colleagues.[16]

His commentary on the current situation with building energy measurement and ratings is not very encouraging if one expects to have a large number of buildings thoroughly evaluated anytime soon.[17]

> [On the requirement for DECs in certain buildings with more than 1,000 m² useful floor area], there are a few teething problems at the moment.
>
> European countries do not have anything like Energy Star's "Portfolio Manager," which sorts the energy efficiency of different building types into percentiles.[18] The system used in England starts with fixed benchmarks based on fairly "lightly stressed" buildings (i.e., not allowing for long occupancy hours, high occupancy densities, high use of IT or energy used by things we call "specials," for example, swimming pools, data centers, parking lot lighting, and so on). To be allowed to correct for "specials," you have to examine them separately, for example by sub-metering a server room and getting a report on its performance and scope for improvement.
>
> It is also vital that occupancy hours and levels are verified; otherwise, there will be a temptation to inflate the numbers to get better benchmark comparisons, while space utilization surveys often reveal that monitored person-hours of occupancy are typically about half managers' initial estimates. In the first year or two of certification, robust data to verify usage patterns and "specials" may well not be available, so heavily used buildings may be judged to be performing more poorly than they really deserve.
>
> This may look unfair, but the view in England and Wales was that if you want to motivate energy and carbon-saving improvements, a benchmarking system was needed to provoke people to want to undertake further investigation and improvement. However, until teething troubles with the issues outlined above have been dealt with in the public sector, I think it would be unwise to make DECs mandatory in the commercial sector. But the commercial sector is not standing still; some companies are already making preparations, either by planning to prepare Display Energy Certificates voluntarily or by undertaking voluntary peer group comparisons that can supplement the government's system.

GERMANY GOES GREEN(ER)

Germany is the largest country in the European Union, with a 2008 population of more than 82 million.[19] As a country with no domestic oil production, Germany is heavily reliant on nuclear and coal-fired electricity.[20] Germans appear to be solidly behind the movement toward more sustainable living, and German architects have been designing sustainable buildings for nearly two decades. Figure 3.2 shows the RWE utility headquarters building in Essen, Germany, in the Ruhr River Valley industrial region, designed by Ingenhoven Architekten and completed in 1996, the first high-rise, low-energy building in that country.

The idea to build a more sustainable Germany took root in the late 1970s with the advent of the Green Party, whose motto, "Neither right nor left, but forward," finally found a place in German political life in the 1980s.[21] The current coalition government led by Prime Minister Angela Merkel announced a goal of cutting greenhouse gas (GHG) emissions 36 percent below 1990 levels by 2020, probably the most radical proposal by the government of a large country.[22] A 2008 survey of climate change performance ranked Germany and Sweden tops in terms of taking action to control GHG emissions.[23]

In 2000, Germany passed a law to promote renewable energy resources, and it has multiplied the use of such sources as the sun, wind, and biomass. According to German figures, renewable energy sources generated well over 200 billion kilowatt-hours in 2006, which corresponds to the annual electricity use of some 10 million households. Overall, this generation met about 8 percent of the country's annual total energy consumption.[24]

Through large state subsidies, Germany has become the leading country in use of renewable energy. It has an installed capacity of more than 18,000 megawatts of wind energy (equivalent to the power output of eighteen large coal-fired power plants). Germany also has more than 6 million square meters (65 million square feet) of solar collection area in use. This is 40 percent of the solar panel surface area installed in the entire European Union.

In 2006, renewable energy resources allowed Germany to reduce its total expected carbon dioxide emissions by more than 10 million metric tons. Thanks to renewables such as solar and wind, the government estimates that this reduction will rise to 120 million metric tons by 2012. The German government is also providing subsidies and cheap credits through state banks to provide loans to homeowners to improve heating efficiency in homes.

FIGURE 3.2 RWE Essen from Ingenhoven Architekten is the first large low-energy building in Germany with natural ventilation, solar integration, and a host of other eco-friendly features. *(H. G. Esch, Hennef)*

The German Sustainable Building Rating System

The German Sustainable Building Council (GeSBC, or Deutsche Gesellschaft für Nachhaltiges Bauen, DGNB) was formed in 2007. By the fall of 2008 the council had held its first annual conference, Consense, in Stuttgart, and had grown to more than 400 members with a permanent secretariat, also in Stuttgart.[25] Werner Sobek, whose house is profiled in Chapter 1, serves as president. The GeSBC is working hard to go beyond just the EPBD standards and introduce a full German rating and certification system for sustainable buildings, developed together with the German Federal Building Ministry.

Anna Braune, former executive director of the GeSBC, ran a growing staff from an office in Stuttgart. Here's her August 2008 update on the status of the GeSBC and its rating system.[26]

Today [the GeSBC develops] a certification system or rating tool for new office buildings, which covers more than fifty criteria that we call the sustainability issues and are translated into sustainability criteria. We have now more than fifty criteria with quantification rules and target values for new construction office buildings. The system is a little bit different from other systems because we have a target-oriented management system. For example, an organization might have a goal to save water. When you break that down they may say, "This year we want to reduce water use by 10 percent." Then we ask, "What are the measurements to determine reduced water use?" This target-oriented thinking is one of the overarching ideas of the whole system. This year we started with the testing phase. At the end of this year we will have the evaluation. At the beginning of 2009, in January, we will hand off the first certificates (called in German the *Gütesiegel*, or "seal of quality"). Currently we have more than thirty projects, with fifteen in the certification process as finished projects. The others are in the pre-certification process since they are still ongoing.

We took the Olympic idea of bronze, silver, and gold medals. It's a way of communicating the level of building quality. Additionally, each building will have a numeric rating. In Germany, a rating of 1 is the best and 6 is the worst. With the medal, there will be a quantified number as well; this is very German. When a building is certified, it gets a German Sustainable Building Certificate (GSBC).

The German Sustainable Building Certificate takes many aspects of sustainability into account. The primary goal of sustainable building is quality, considering a comprehensive range of aspects. For example, to be sustainable a building has to be economically efficient, environmentally friendly, and easy on resources. But the building also has to be comfortable and healthy for users and optimally fit into its cultural surroundings. Sustainable buildings therefore retain their value for the long term—for investors, owners, and users equally.

One of the main differences compared to other certification systems is that [our rating system] is a target-oriented tool. We have a very systematic way of providing target values. You get ten points in each category when you fulfill the highest target value, and then it is mainly proportionately less when you have fewer than the maximum number of points. To be certified, you have to reach a minimum of certain mandatory criteria, with ten points being the maximum. That's how you get to the overall rating.

Sustainable Cities Take Root

In 2008, the city of Marburg became the first in Germany to require that every home install solar water heating, both in new construction and with any major renovation such as a reroofing.[27] Near Cologne, the city of Nippes has established eco-communities, including a car-free subdivision consisting of single-family townhouses and apartment buildings that will eventually house 400 families, with no internal streets and parking only at the outskirts.[28]

The city of Freiburg im Breisgau, located in the Black Forest of southwestern Germany, quite close to France and Switzerland, began eco-initiatives in the 1970s, with plans for bicycle trails, resulting today in 500 kilometers (300 miles) of bike trails. Local residents use their bicycles for more than a quarter of all trips. In 1973, the city center banned all cars and allows only pedestrians, a model being adopted in many other places in Europe. The district of Vauban in Freiburg has become known as the most eco-friendly residential zone in Germany; begun as an initiative in 1993, by 2006 it housed 6,000 people. (For more on this project, see Chapter 7.)[29]

Solar architect Rolf Disch constructed Schlierberg, the first all-solar development in

Freiburg. This new solar village incorporates natural resources into the overall construction concept, the choice of materials, and the water and energy systems. Inhabitants are encouraged to get creative with the aesthetic design, incidental costs and operating expenses are low, and there is an efficient system of ecological mobility by public transport, by bike, or on foot.[30]

Disch has become well known both for his work at Freiburg and for the concept of the Plusenergiehaus, a home that will produce more energy than it consumes. According to Disch, "the Plusenergiehaus has a designed energy use of 10 to 15 kWh/sqm/year, which is only 10 percent of the heating energy demands of a conventional house. The building envelope is compact, avoiding projections and recesses. The U-value of the exterior wall and the ceiling is U = 0.12 (R-50 in American units). All the envelope surfaces are absolutely windproof. The generous windows on the south side with their special triple glazing helps to make optimal use of the sun even on days with little solar radiation. On particularly hot summer days, the photovoltaic station and the south-facing balconies provide shade to the windows."

The Plusenergiehaus aims to meet the total energy needs of the house in a regenerative way and even to produce a surplus. Therefore, each house has a solar power station of its own on its roof with an output of 3.0 to 12.0 kilowatts, depending on its size.[31]

One of the more interesting projects in another part of Freiburg, the Rieselfeld district, is a group of solar townhouses designed by architect Thomas Spiegelhalter (now a professor at the University of Southern California) and built in 1997. Located on the site of a former sewage treatment plant and shown in Figure 3.3, the 14,000–square-foot project has passive and active solar systems, no air conditioning, natural ventilation, thermal mass for passive heating and cooling, rainwater harvesting systems, recycled materials, and rainwater-permeable landscaping.[32] The yearly energy use for heating and hot water has been measured at 31 kilowatt-hours per square meter, about twice the PassivHaus standard but very good compared with conventional construction.

FIGURE 3.3 Freiburg is known for its many ecological innovations, and this 1990s solar townhouse by Thomas Spiegelhalter is one of them. *(Thomas Spiegelhalter)*

Implementing the EPBD in Germany

In Germany most aspects of the EPBD were implemented through the Energy-Saving Ordinance of 2002, including a calculation method for energy performance, requirements for new building design, Energy Performance Certificates for new buildings and some major refurbishments, requirements for nearly all cases of modernization of fabric elements, and inspection of boilers. However, the earlier ordinance did not provide for EPBD requirements for certificates in cases of sale and renting of existing buildings, display of certificates in buildings for public services frequently visited by the public, or inspection of air-conditioning units.

The 2007 law included a requirement known as EnEV (Energie Einspar Verordnung), the Ordinance on Energy-Saving Thermal Insulation and Energy-Saving Appliances in Buildings. The EPC is called an Energieausweis (Energy Passport) and rates nonresidential buildings on a scale of 0 to 1,000 for their primary energy demand, where 0 is a totally autonomous building, off the grid in every respect. For residential buildings, the Energieausweis scale runs from 0 to 400.[33] Table 3.3 lists the reference values for metered energy consumption in nonresidential buildings. Because the 2007 ordinance did not change the level of requirements, the EPBD requirements will be enforced gradually through a new Energy-Saving Ordinance of 2009, which was issued in 2008. This will still meet the European Union's 2010 deadline.

Current energy conservation requirements will be strengthened initially by 30 percent in 2009 and in 2012 again by another 30 percent. A more extensive report on the status of German implementation is available but is current only through March 2008.[34] German law requires that all energy-saving regulations be economically reasonable. Because of the significant rise of energy prices, the government expects that additional costs of the regulations out to 2010 can be recovered within a few years through energy savings.

TABLE 3.3 GERMAN STANDARDS FOR REFERENCE (CONVENTIONAL) BUILDINGS (GREEN BUILDINGS SHOULD BE WELL BELOW THESE NUMBERS), KILOWATT-HOURS PER SQUARE METER PER YEAR.[A]

BUILDING TYPE	HEATING AND HOT WATER	ELECTRICITY
Office buildings, no air conditioning	135	55
Office buildings, with air conditioning	190	155
Hotels	120	95
Restaurants	320	135
Department stores, with air conditioning	85	150

Source: www.buildingsplatform.eu/cms/index.php?id=118&publication_id=3143, p. 6, accessed August 29, 2008.

[A]To translate kWh/sq. m/year to square footage, divide by 10.76. To get from kWh to Btu, multiply kWh by 3,413. So 135 kWh/sq. m/year = 12.5 kWh/sq. ft./year = 42,662 Btu/sq. ft./year = 0.43 therms/sq. ft./year.

THE FRENCH HQE SYSTEM

France is the second most populous country in the European Union, slightly larger than the United Kingdom and Italy, with a population of about 63 million.[35] The current driver of French sustainable development and green building programs is the Grenelle Environment Policy, adopted in October 2007, which created a plan for promoting sustainable development, establishing renewable energy and green building construction as national priorities.[36] In terms of specific goals, the policy calls for all new buildings to use less than 50 kilowatt-hours per square meter per year by 2012 and to be carbon neutral by 2020. Within the next 5 years, the policy is expected to reduce commercial energy consumption by 20 percent and residential energy use by 12 percent.

Since 2004, the French have had an eco-building rating system known as Haute Qualité Environnementale

(HQE), or High-Quality Environment, run by the nonprofit Association HQE.[37] Originally developed in 1992, the strictly voluntary HQE standards deal with the following features:[38]

Eco-construction
- Blend in harmoniously with the immediate environment
- Integrated choice of building materials and products, including wood
- Low noise and low pollution generated by the building site

Eco-management
- Reduction in energy use
- Reduction in water use and increase in rainwater harvesting
- Reduction in building waste generation
- Cleaning and maintenance

Indoor environment
- Thermal comfort, including humidity control
- Acoustic comfort
- Views to outdoors and daylighting
- Odors

Health
- Health conditions
- Indoor air quality
- Indoor water quality

HQE's overall goal is to generate 30 percent energy savings, particularly in the residential sector, to reduce overall national greenhouse gas emissions by 40 percent, and to produce 16 percent water savings. (France gets the majority of its electricity from nuclear energy, which creates no direct greenhouse gas emissions.)[39]

HQE began certifying individual projects only in 2005. The process costs between $22,000 and $38,000, similar to the costs of certifying a project in the United States under the LEED system.[40] As of April 2008, there were 150 HQE-certified buildings and more than 450 additional projects going through the process. HQE looks at each project individually, detailing the specific process and issues.[41]

According to one source, the HQE approach "involves setting up an Environmental Management System (EMS), which includes an examination of the site, the objectives of the operation and the needs of the future users. The building owner elaborates on the construction plans and the scheduling of the building, the implementation and the oversight of the construction, to manage the quality of the processes."[42]

The HQE buildings to date have been public (social) housing and government buildings. The first private French commercial building to be certified is a 10,000–square-meter (108,000–square-foot), eight-story office building in Auberviliers, near Paris, known as EMGP 270 and shown in Figure 3.4. The building has two levels of parking and ground-floor retail, with seven stories of offices above the retail podium. The owner is the development firm ICADE, and the architect is Brenac & Gonzalez, Paris.[43]

Completed in June 2005 at a cost of about $25 million, the building has demonstrated 30

percent energy savings against a conventional building. Overall energy use is 253 kilowatt-hours per square meter per year (23.5 kilowatt-hours per square foot per year), compared with 380 kilowatt-hours per square meter per year for a typical French office building. However, because temperature settings were limited to a narrow range of 22°C (72°F) to 24°C (75°F), energy use was 40 percent higher than predicted because the chilled beam system had to run all year long. The design temperature settings were 20°C (68°F) to 25°C (77°F), but the facility management team subverted the design to avoid complaints by building users.[44] This result demonstrates the critical role of communication between the design team, occupants, building owner, and building operators in achieving low-energy building results. (In this project, the owner did distribute a CD-ROM about the building to occupants, explaining some of the green features.)

The specific eco-building features included triple-glazed windows; a north-oriented entrance to achieve a glazed side that wouldn't need air conditioning; chilled-beam cooling for space conditioning; daylighting; T-5 fluorescent lights; office space with user-adjustable air diffusers, temperature controls, and light dimmers; motor-controlled blinds with automatic shutdown depending on solar heat gain; and a building management system with 75 sub-meters for each component of energy use.

The lighting design uses 600 windows along the building façade, framed in twelve colors, giving the building a distinct visual identification. By night, light colors in five sequences illuminate the windows. There is also an 800–square-foot light wall in the lobby.

The chilled beams represent a new approach of adaptable active beams with adjustable air velocity, cooling capacity, and supply airflow rates.[45] Because the beams can operate at variable water temperatures and supply airflow, the building enjoys free cooling much of the year through the evaporative coolers on the roof, without use of the electric chillers.

GREEN BUILDING IN SWITZERLAND

A good example of green commercial buildings in Switzerland is the Eawag Forum Chriesbach office and research facility, designed by Zürich-based planning team Bob Gysin and Partner Architects. This project began in 2002 with a vision of a sustainable research facility by Eawag (Swiss Federal Institute for Aquatic Science and Technology), a building with office space for 150 people that would use only 36 kilowatt-hours per square meter per year of site energy, including construction processes, and 65 kilowatt-hours per square meter per year of

FIGURE 3.5 Designed by BGP Architekten, Forum Chriesbach is a model low-energy building in Switzerland that provides wonderful daylighting for a Swiss research institute. *(Photography by Roger Frei, Zürich; courtesy of Bob Gysin + Partner BGP Architekten ETH SIA BSA, Zürich and Eawag Empa, Dübendorf)*

primary energy. The 8,533–square-meter (92,000–square-foot), five-story building, shown in Figure 3.5, began operation in the summer of 2006.

In the winter, Forum Chriesbach is heated directly with an air-to-earth heat exchanger and indirectly via heat recovery ventilation, which captures waste heat leaving the building and transfers it efficiently to the incoming fresh air. In the summer, the building is cooled off at night via passive cooling, using the internal atrium to create a stack effect for exhausting air from the offices. A chilled ceiling system cools meeting rooms, using groundwater. There is a 77-kilowatt (peak) photovoltaic system that produces about 60,000 kilowatt-hours of electricity per year and a solar thermal system using vacuum tube collectors that produces 24,000 kilowatt-hours of thermal energy for heating and hot water.

One of the goals of the project was to come close to the 2,000-watt society (see Chapter 9) in terms of energy consumption in office buildings of 600 watts per capita, or 5,100 kilowatt-hours per person per year.[46] Primary energy use in the building is only 31,000 kilowatt-hours per year (3,000 liters of oil, or less than 800 gallons), about that of a single-family house. Figure 3.6 compares a current Swiss energy code, including embodied energy of building materials and construction, a typical Minergie standard building, the 2,000-watt goal, and the Eawag Forum Chriesbach building's planned annual energy use. Actual energy use measurements after the first 2 years of operation reveal that this project achieves a 65 percent reduction in primary energy use against the referenced code building and a 35 percent reduction against current Minergie standards.[47] The figure of 23 kilowatt-hours per square meter per year site energy use is deceptively low, however, because there is a rather generous 55–square-meter (592–square-foot) per person space allowance in this building and because it also contains a 150-seat cafeteria and seminar and meeting rooms for 180 people.[48] Nevertheless, this building demonstrates that a well-designed office building can cut conventional energy use significantly without sacrificing user comfort. This project is well worth studying because it replicates the size and layout of many conventional smaller office buildings in North

America. This building also illustrates what will be increasingly perceived as a challenge for green buildings: As the energy use for building occupancy declines, the embodied energy of building materials and construction will become a higher percentage of the total use. At Forum Chriesbach, for example, the "gray energy" is almost one third of total energy use and is an irreducible minimum. A second point worth mentioning is that electricity use for lights and equipment is almost 75 percent of the total site energy use (and 87 percent of primary energy use) because the tight building envelope reduces heating and cooling demand almost to nothing.

GREEN BUILDING IN ITALY

In Italy, as of March 2008, building energy certificates (called CasaClima) have been issued throughout the country for new buildings (the equivalent of 700,000 apartment units) and for property transfer of existing medium and large buildings (10,000 buildings, equivalent to 110,000 apartments).[49]

The first Italian association of architects promoting green building awareness, the Associazione Nazionale Architettura Bioecologica (ANAB), was founded in 1989.[50] In addition to the EPBD mandatory certification of building energy use in Italy, ANAB has developed a volun-

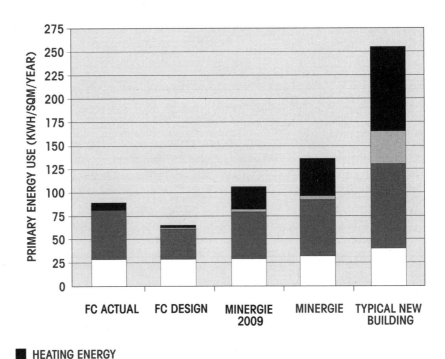

FIGURE 3.6 Forum Chriesbach (FC) cuts heating and cooling energy use almost to zero while holding overall annual primary energy use, including embodied energy, to about 20,000 Btu/sq. ft.
(Courtesy of Bob Gysin + Partner BGP Architekten ETH SIA BSA, Zürich and Eawag Empa, Dübendorf)

tary certification system based on sustainability parameters. The certification system is called SB100 (which stands for "sustainable buildings with 100 actions").[51]

The Istituto Nazionale di Bioarchitettura (INBAR) is another nonprofit association of professionals, technicians, and other experts, active since the mid-1990s in promoting awareness, information, and education for future generations of professionals on green building issues.[52] Together with the Italian federation of construction cooperatives, INBAR launched a network of construction cooperatives named La Casa Ecologica, whose aim is specifically to promote sustainable homes. Homes certified under that system receive from INBAR the *marchio* INBAR, verifying the achievement of certain energy and environmental performance levels in new home construction.

A 2006 survey of 250 Italian cities and towns showed that 55 percent had already adopted building regulations aimed at increasing the construction of houses that are green and have low energy consumption and low environmental impact. To achieve these objectives, cities offer homebuilders tax discounts, increased floor area ratios for low-emission buildings, and rebates on property taxes. About 16 percent of cities and towns surveyed chose to designate certain areas for sustainable buildings.[53]

In the Mediterranean region, the architect's approach to sustainable design is heavily influenced by the need for solar control and natural ventilation, as exemplified by the iGuzzini Headquarters Office Building, in Recanati, Italy.

Completed in 1997 by Bologna-based Mario Cuccinella Architects, the headquarters office building for iGuzzini Illuminazione SRL, a lighting manufacturer, cost €2.6 million. The building is designed to house the administrative, commercial, and management offices of the iGuzzini company and seeks to optimize the control of natural light, exploit natural ventilation, and use thermal mass for cooling.[54]

To begin the project, iGuzzini commissioned a 3,000–square-meter (32,000–square-foot) extension to its existing headquarters. The new building is designed to create a modern and comfortable work environment while minimizing energy consumption. Architectural and environmental strategies are integrated to achieve this goal. The building is organized around a central courtyard where the new extension connects to the old building. This light-filled atrium is an integral part of the building environmental control system. Glazed skylights work together with openings in the façades and cool thermal mass in the floors to create a flow of air that cools and ventilates the building.

As shown in Figure 3.7, the south-facing main façade is entirely glazed. It is protected from the summer sun by an overhanging shading roof that is designed to allow sunlight penetration in the winter. The east and west façades are opaque to avoid overheating from the early morning and late afternoon sun. The shading roof is positioned to allow winter sun to enter the building, providing both solar heat gain and daylight. Sun hits the floorplates and is absorbed into the floor to keep the building heated in winter. The final element of the design is the landscaping of both of the internal garden and the surrounding industrial site, to create a cooler microclimate.

The offices occupy four floors and are organized around a central atrium that contains a garden made from stone scales and bamboo canes. The height of the atrium—reaching the full height of the building up to the skylights—and the prevailing use of glass ensure maximum natural light.[55]

The central space acts as the fulcrum for natural ventilation, functioning as a "mechanical void" where hot air from the offices collects and is expelled through ventilation grilles next to the skylights. Together with controlled opening of the façade this contributes to cooling in midseason. The north and south façades are completely transparent.

FIGURE 3.7 At the iGuzzini office building, Mario Cuccinelli Architects crafted an elegant addition to an existing building with great attention to both daylighting and solar control in Italy's hot, sunny climate.
(© MCA, photograph by Jean de Calan)

Exposed concrete soffits and internal block walls increase the building's thermal mass so that night flush ventilation can be used to cool the structure.

Inside the building, further control of lighting is provided by venetian blinds and by a light shelf that reflects natural light toward the ceiling for better distribution deep into the offices. Outside the southern entrance, an inclined green area serves as a covered parking space. Inside the atrium, the choice of low-maintenance stone and bamboo for the winter garden enhances productivity by providing a natural scene right outside the office windows.

GREEN BUILDING IN THE NETHERLANDS

Although it is a small country, in terms of both land mass and population, the Netherlands has long been recognized for its contributions to sustainable buildings and sustainable urban design. On a visit to Amsterdam in 2008, I marveled at how well the Dutch accommodated the millions of bicycle riders in this flat country, providing them with their own paved roads and traffic signals, separate from both cars and pedestrians, a far cry from the dangerous and little-used bicycle lanes situated directly alongside traffic on many U.S. roadways.

Centric ICT Headquarters, Gouda

In 2008 the leading Dutch development firm OVG completed a 17,000–square-meter (183,000–square-foot) office building in Gouda to serve as the headquarters for Centric ICT (Figure 3.8). The project received a Dutch Greencalc score of 203 points, with a carbon reduction of about 50 percent compared with the climate (baseline) year of 1990.[56] Compared with the current Dutch building code, this equates to 25 percent less energy use and places the building in the top ten Dutch registered and measured sustainable buildings. The dynamic heart of the building is

formed by an inviting atrium with an interaction between mezzanine floors, stairwells, elevators, and conference rooms. Energy-saving measures include an underground heat-and-cold storage system, automatic daylight-adjusting lighting dimmers and occupancy sensors, and a data center cooled much of the year with 100 percent outdoor air.[57]

Alterra Forestry Center, Wageningen

For the Institute for Forestry and Nature Research (IBN), Germany's Behnisch Architekten (see Chapter 5 for more of the firm's work) was tasked with providing a research facility that would integrate well with the natural world and also inspire forestry researchers. The 11,250–square-meter (121,000–square-foot) Alterra forestry center north of the university city of Wageningen was

completed in 1998 and illustrates Behnisch's combination of bioclimatic design and beautiful buildings (Figure 3.9). Constrained to be built on a standard building budget, the project aimed at maximum carbon dioxide emission reductions. The site introduced natural and human-made elements such as stone walls, groves of trees, hedges, berms, ponds, swamps, and water channels. Two indoor gardens provide a focus for the office workers and informal meeting areas. They also serve as the lungs of the building, providing fresh oxygen and absorbing excess carbon dioxide.

To keep costs down, the architects relied on prefabricated components such as a conventional greenhouse glass roof. By working with the manufacturer, the architect was able to redesign the conventional greenhouse supports so that no energy-intensive aluminum is used in the window frames, only galvanized steel. The project is built primarily with exposed concrete, with wood for the façades. Recycled cotton products make up the building insulation. Leftover construction site materials were used to create the external garden areas, reducing waste disposal requirements.[58]

Netherlands Energy Research Center, Petten

Dutch architect Tjerk Reijenga's work on a new housing project was discussed in Chapter 1. One of his major commercial office projects is the Netherlands Energy Research Center in Petten. In this project, completed in 2001, he designed a retrofit of an energy-inefficient 40-year-old, 40,000–square-foot (3,530–square-meter) building, by using 37 kilowatts of building-integrated photovoltaics on south-facing sunshades.[59] There are also 35 kilowatts of photovoltaics on the building roof. The energy goal of the project was to reduce primary energy demand by 75 percent. (Italian architect Cinzia Abbate of Rome was also involved in the design of the solar elements.) In addition to the renovation, a new building on the site has photovoltaic modules integrated with the glazed exterior of the building to supply shading and 42 kilowatts of peak power.

These examples from many countries show that environmentally appropriate architecture was well established in Europe in the mid-1990s and that the current strong move toward reducing carbon dioxide emissions will only improve the energy performance of already well-designed buildings.

CHAPTER 4

Green Buildings in the United Kingdom

The occasion for my first visit to the United Kingdom in quite some time was the 2008 Ecobuild conference in London, held at Earl's Court, an aging exhibition hall on the Underground's Piccadilly Line that was packed with more than 1,200 exhibit booths and a reported 30,000 people, all to check out the state of green building in the United Kingdom. I was amazed to see a similar attendance (28,000) at the U.S. Green Building Council's November 2008 Greenbuild show in Boston, but the United Kingdom's turnout is more remarkable for a country with only one fifth the population of the United States. This turnout provided a strong case that interest in green building was even stronger in the United Kingdom than in the United States.

The U.K. Green Building Council, formed under the leadership of Dr. David Strong and the CEO, Paul King, has in its first year of existence become quite influential in the national dialog about reducing the U.K. carbon footprint and pushing forward with green building on many fronts. A charismatic man in his fifties, Strong heads a group of consultants called Inbuilt, a division of a very large U.K. construction and renewable energy firm, Renewable Energy Systems (RES), with the purpose of carrying out "research, design and delivery of sustainable built environments."

BEAUFORT COURT, HERTFORDSHIRE

An early and important major green building project was a zero-emission structure that now serves as headquarters for RES and Inbuilt, a place called Beaufort Court in Kings Langley, Hertfordshire. In 2000 RES commissioned Studio E and Max Fordham Partnership to design a zero-emission building as a headquarters for their wind farm development business. The RES Group took on the task of converting the former Ovaltine Egg Farm into a sustainable headquarters. Among other striking features, the project aims to provide biomass fuel to feed a boiler by growing its own *Miscanthus*[1] crop on a 12-acre site. The project also features a 225-kilowatt wind turbine and a smaller photovoltaic array (with 3,200 kilowatt-hours of annual production) on the office building, as shown in Figure 4.1. For cooling, an 80-meter (264-foot) borehole is used to secure groundwater for cooling, using chilled beams as ceiling panels (see Chapter 6 for more on this technology).

Completed in 2003 as an exemplar of sustainable development, the 28,000–square-foot Beaufort Court is reportedly the first zero-net-carbon commercial office building in the United

FIGURE 4.1 At Beaufort Court, the key is the careful attention to building renovation and renewable energy systems, such that the entire operation is carbon neutral. *(Oak Taylor-Smith/Max Fordham LLP)*

Kingdom. This is a truly unique and pioneering project, one that should be replicated in each climatic region of the United States. Table 4.1 shows Beaufort Court's projected energy demand and energy production, as an example of the energy balance needed for a net-zero development. Table 4.2 shows actual energy production in 2007, with wind power making up 56 percent of total energy supply. You can see that even with 30 percent reduced production, mostly from reduced wind and biomass contribution, the actual energy production still exceeded consumption, illustrating the importance of reducing demand (through conservation and efficiency measures) before using renewable supplies in a project.

From discussions with Bill Watts of Max Fordham and Inbuilt's David Strong, I would say their approach to zero-carbon developments is worth emulating. It's both simple and elegant, something I learned in my science training that denotes a good theory. Einstein's theory of special relativity qualifies here; most high school students can understand it, but it's had amazing success for a hundred years. According to Strong, in the Inbuilt approach there are five steps to zero-carbon development:

1. Perform a complete site analysis to determine the annual availability of natural and renewable energy sources.
2. Design out as much energy use as possible, through active and passive measures.
3. Use cost-effective renewable energy systems to supply the necessary energy (note that the British consider biomass boilers a renewable energy system, even though there's not nearly enough in the United Kingdom to supply the entire country).
4. Use simple controls with an effective user interface.
5. Conduct a post-occupancy evaluation (POE) to ensure that you're getting the results you expect; if not, then fix what's not working. (This is a step largely neglected in the United

TABLE 4.1 PROJECTED ENERGY BALANCE AT BEAUFORT COURT.

	ELECTRICAL (MWH)	SPACE HEATING (MWH)
Building annual demand	115.0	85.0
Energy production		
Wind	250	—
Heat collected into storage	—	24.0
Solar electric and thermal	3.2	15.0
Pumping load	−4.5	—
Heat lost from storage	—	−12.0
Biomass: peak production	—	160.0
Net production	248.7	187.0
Potential electrical export	133.7	—
Potential surplus biomass heat	—	102.0

1 MWh = 1,000 kWh.

States and Canada, where many designers expect to walk away from a completed project, never again to return.)

Bill Watts was the principal for the project and provided a detailed analysis of the project in its third year. The overall use of energy was 80 kilowatt-hours per square meter, or about 7.4 kilowatt-hours per square foot, about half that of the most energy-efficient U.S. commercial buildings. The solar array and wind turbine output closely match the electrical energy loads, so that the building operated in its first two years at very close to zero net energy, without any real contribution from the biomass boiler. In an interview at his office in London, Watts told me about all the glitches in implementing the project's energy systems, illustrating both his intellectual honesty and the difficulty of attempting wholesale innovation on a single project in a very conservative building industry.[2]

TABLE 4.2 BEAUFORT COURT ACTUAL ENERGY PRODUCTION, 2007.

SOURCE	ENERGY (KWH)	PERCENTAGE OF TOTAL SUPPLY
Wind	165,942	54
Solar thermal	67,719	22
Biomass boiler	41,211	14
Borehole cooling (geothermal)	26,910	9
Photovoltaic electric	3,391	1
Total actual production	**305,173**	**100**

30 ST. MARY AXE ("THE GHERKIN"), LONDON

Foster + Partners designed London's first sustainably designed skyscraper, which is an instantly recognizable addition to the city's skyline. Completed in 2004, 30 St. Mary Axe was commissioned by Swiss Re, one of the world's leading reinsurance companies, and rises forty-one stories, with 76,400 square meters of offices and a shopping arcade. Generated by a radial plan with a circular perimeter that recalls Foster's Commerzbank headquarters building in Frankfurt (profiled in Chapter 5), the building widens in profile as it rises and tapers at the top, hence its local nickname, "The Gherkin."

The tower's diagonally braced structural envelope allows column-free floor space and a fully glazed façade, which opens up the building to light and views. Atriums between the six radial fingers of the building link together vertically to form a series of informal meeting spaces that spiral upward. Because it's more slender than a rectangular block of equivalent size, reflections are reduced and transparency is improved.

The office areas have a double-glazed outer unit with a low-emissivity coating and an internal screen of laminated glass to maximize daylight penetration and optimize views out. The cavity also contains perforated blinds to prevent solar gain and mitigate glare. The blinds enable most solar radiation to be intercepted before it reaches the office spaces, thereby reducing the large cooling load typical of conventional fully glazed office buildings.

Lightwells are clad with a combination of opening and fixed double-glazed panels with tinted glass and high-performance coatings to reduce the penetration of solar radiation. The darker visual appearance of the glass maintains the spiraling expression of the lightwells on the elevation. The dome at the building's apex, which houses the corporate hospitality facilities on levels 38–40, is similarly clad, topped by a 2.5-meter diameter lens, the only curved glass unit in the building.

The shape also creates external pressure differentials that Foster + Partners used for a unique natural ventilation system. Spaces distribute fresh air drawn in through horizontal opening panels in the façade while acting as a buffer between the external and indoor environment, thereby reducing temperature differences, noise, and pollution. These voids take advantage of the building's aerodynamic form.

During unoccupied hours in the summer, the windows can be left open to allow outdoor air to help cool the building overnight, reducing overall energy consumption. Fresh air supply systems are designed with heat exchangers to absorb either heating or cooling capacity before discharging exhaust air to the outside. The system reduces the tower's reliance on air conditioning and, together with other sustainable measures, means that the building is expected to use less than half the energy consumed by air-conditioned office towers.

Natural ventilation can supplement air conditioning for up to 40 percent of the year, reducing energy consumption and carbon dioxide emissions. When it is used, air conditioning comes via water-cooled refrigeration machines coupled with closed-circuit cooling towers that use no ozone-depleting refrigerant and offer a strong coefficient of performance. The evaporative cooling towers with plume elimination use waste condenser water heat.

The office lighting systems are controlled by a functional extra-low-voltage switching system, with flexibility for central or local control to suit the tenants' office layout. Unwanted solar gain is intercepted by the double-skin façade system and discharged into the lightwells.

A decentralized mechanical control plant offers the flexibility to supply and control ventilation not just on a floor-by-floor basis but also to each individual office finger. Because supply is closely matched with demand, energy consumption is lower than that of a central system for the whole building.

40 GROSVENOR PLACE, LONDON

Here's a very different type of building. Designed by international architecture and engineering firm HOK and completed in 1999, this 325,000–square-foot, six-level office building (Figure 4.2) in London's prestigious Belgravia neighborhood received a BREEAM Excellent rating.[3] In a neighborhood of homes and buildings more than 200 years old, the emphasis was on flexible, sustainable design.

FIGURE 4.2 At 40 Grosvenor in the heart of London, HOK Architects solved the challenge of providing daylight and natural ventilation in a building that had to match the Georgian-style neighborhood architecture. *(Peter Cook)*

Specific sustainable features include a high-performance façade of natural limestone and glass, in keeping with the neighborhood appearance. Originally built as a single-occupant corporate headquarters, the building was designed to be flexible enough to function as a multi-occupant space.

Because London is a very conservative office market, the focus was on passive design features rather than photovoltaics, enthalpy (heat recovery) wheels, and borehole cooling systems. The project team wound up selecting a combination of displacement ventilation (underfloor air supply) and chilled ceiling systems. Estimated energy consumption was 20 percent below that of comparable structures.[4] (Remember, this was designed more than 10 years ago.)

A southwest-facing atrium was an important energy design element, providing a buffer zone and not requiring any auxiliary heating or cooling except at a reception desk. The unconditioned atrium was designed to receive exhaust (heated) air from offices in winter and cool air from the same source in summer. However, in the London winter, the atrium was too cold and so additional local heating had to be introduced. There is also a projecting 40-meter-long brise soleil[5] at the fifth-floor level to provide shading for the full-height windows.

The underfloor air system gets a constant supply of 18°C (65°F) chilled water from a central plant on the roof and distributes coolness via underfloor plenums and diffusers to office occupants. Essentially a self-regulating cooling system, the chilled ceiling operates at a constant 17°C (63°F) from the building cooling water. In 2001, the building was named Best Commercial Workplace in Britain for its construction quality and flexible design.[6]

BRIGHTON AND HOVE CENTRAL LIBRARY, BRIGHTON

The Brighton and Hove Central Library and Jubilee Street Development in Brighton, Sussex consist of the 6,000–square-meter (65,000–square-foot) library, along with a hotel, residential development, offices, and retail shops (Figure 4.3). Finished in 2005, the library and other elements are models for sustainable design.

Brighton's Jubilee Library won the 2005 Prime Minister's Better Public Building Award. A £14-million ($28-million) private finance initiative (a developer-driven project for a public agency) designed by Bennetts Associates Architects in association with Lomax Cassidy & Edwards, the library is one of the United Kingdom's most energy-efficient public buildings. It reduces energy use and carbon emissions by about 50 percent. The building as a whole relies on local climatic conditions for daylighting and natural ventilation, and it can also recycle rainwater.[7]

The engineering of the building supports the architectural intention by allowing the structural mass to be fully used and integrated with the environmental control systems, thus reducing the library's energy consumption. The hollow walls surrounding the central library space contain air ducts from roof-level plant rooms that feed air through the hollow core units, thus conditioning it before it enters the perimeter rooms and main library space. In winter the warm air is circulated back to the plant rooms at roof level, and in summer the extract system is naturally driven by convection created when the three roof-mounted wind towers (air exhausts) centrally located over the main library are opened.[8]

The building service engineering design was by Fulcrum Consulting, whom we'll encounter in Chapter 6. The low energy use resulted from the innovative low-energy approach and excellent BREEAM rating, using a mix of the established thermal storage TermoDeck system and a wind-assisted displacement ventilation system.

The 2005 Royal Institute of British Architects (RIBA) Sustainability Award citation calls the engineering design a "Trojan horse for structural and spatial expression," a fittingly apt phrase for a project with the engineering so interwoven with the design intention. For this building, the projected energy use of 32 kilowatt-hours per square meter per year (2.95 kilowatt-hours per square foot) is about 78 percent lower than that of a benchmark building. The only exception to the remarkably low energy use is that fan power consumption for the TermoDeck system, which tends to run around the clock all year, is about three times that of a normal building, but it is still a low 6.1 kilowatt-hours per square meter per year.[9]

WESSEX WATER OPERATIONS CENTRE, BATH

Passive engineering is shown in the design of the Wessex Water Operations Centre in Bath, a project completed in 2001. The measured carbon dioxide production of the building is about 25 to 30 kilograms per square meter per year, about one third that of a typical U.K. low-rise office built at the same time, equivalent to about 5 kilowatt-hours of energy use per square foot, about one third that of a "good" building in the United States. By contrast, New Street Square, a high-rise office in London, will probably generate 40 to 60 kilograms per square meter per year, twice the production of Wessex Water, but will use only about half the measured energy (134 kilograms per square meter per year) of other nearby offices.

FIGURE 4.3 Part of a larger urban redevelopment project, the 2005 Brighton and Hove Central Library is a fine example of low-energy daylit design by Bennetts Associates Architects, cutting energy use by more than 50%. *(James Brittain/Bennetts Associates Architects)*

This project was the fourth in a series of major headquarters designed in the 1990s by Bennetts Associates that were intended to show, first, how architectural form had a critical role to play in the design of the workplace and, second, how sustainability was consistent with design at the highest level.

At the time, the nonprofit Building Research Establishment called the Wessex Water project the greenest commercial building in the United Kingdom. The building has been the subject of extensive post-occupancy assessment, which has validated the original strategy behind its environmental design.

Located on a steeply sloping site in a designated Area of Outstanding Natural Beauty, the building has a low profile. Most of the office accommodation occurs in three uniform wings in an "E" shape (in a plan view), with each wing facing the sun and looking over the roof of the one below.

Construction of the building was innovative in terms of embodied energy use and off-site prefabrication, resulting in a visual lightness that is a metaphor for the building's impact on its surroundings.

NEW STREET SQUARE, LONDON

New Street Square was designed for the large developer, Land Securities, and completed in 2008 (Figure 4.4). The project demolished an existing 1960s development and built in its stead five new buildings ranging from nineteen stories down to a two-story conference center, surrounding a new urban square. What's sustainable about it? According to one account, "The facade treatment also helps tick the box for environmental sustainability. The south-facing facades are clad entirely with brises-soleil to cut solar gain; those facing west get the same treatment, apart from where they are shaded by other buildings. On the east side the solar shading is limited to a glass frit and spandrel panels are used to create solid areas."[10] Having visited this project, I think the creation of social space in the square, accessed via an almost medieval-sized street, is a bigger part of the sustainability story, as is the flexibility of having buildings of multiple heights, which replaced the developers' original scheme of one huge, large-floorplate building. Some attention was given to the life-cycle assessment of the brise soleil materials, using a sustainability consultant who calculated the impact of material choices over a 60-year lifespan. The consultant evaluated three choices: aluminum and both coated and uncoated timber. Uncoated western red cedar came out as the best solution, needing no maintenance and gradually turning silver with weathering. It's refreshing to see sustainability considerations in a major office building focus on the materials rather than just energy use.

Another Bennetts Associates office project, a renovation completed in 2005 for the Hampshire County Council offices in Winchester, has a target of 39 kilograms per square meter per year of carbon emissions and a potential of only 22 kilograms per square meter per year if the waste heat from the information technology department can be recycled to help heat the building. This would represent a 75 percent decrease from the existing energy use. The point of all these

FIGURE 4.4 Completed in 2008 and designed by Bennetts Associates Architects, the New Street Square consists of 5 new buildings ranging from 2 to 19 stories, surrounding a new urban square, and was rated at BREEAM Excellent. *(Bennetts Associates Architects)*

numbers is that it's very helpful to benchmark buildings against a single standard and to show how energy use can be cut 65 to 80 percent in most projects, with good design and some clever engineering. (The Brighton Library, a facility that obviously gets a lot of use, produces about 47 kilograms per square meter per year of carbon dioxide emissions.)

CITY HALL AND GREATER LONDON AUTHORITY HEADQUARTERS, LONDON

Designed by Foster + Partners, the Greater London Authority Headquarters is one of the capital's most symbolically important new projects, completed in 2002. It occupies a prominent site on the Thames River beside Tower Bridge, housing an assembly chamber, committee rooms, and the mayor's office.

The 45-meter-high (160-foot) building, made with structural steelwork and a reinforced concrete core, was designed so that it has no real front or back. Based on an analysis of sunlight patterns throughout the year, its shape is derived from a geometrically modified sphere, with computer modeling techniques used to achieve optimum energy performance by minimizing surface area exposed to direct sunlight. The angle of glass front inclination varies from 81° to 31° from horizontal.

The building also includes a combination of active and passive shading devices. To the south, the building leans backward to provide shading for the naturally ventilated offices. In addition to operable vents for natural ventilation, an efficient cooling system makes use of groundwater pumped up from boreholes from the water table. Not only does this eliminate the need for chillers, but for most of the year the building also needs no additional heating. Overall, it uses only about one quarter of the energy consumed by a typical air-conditioned office building.

THE INLAND REVENUE CENTRE, NOTTINGHAM

Designed by Hopkins Architects, the Inland Revenue Centre houses 1,800 employees and is an early example of the British approach to natural ventilation using thermal chimneys. Air enters at the bottom and is removed at the top, with heat gain from the windows driving the circulation. Perimeter grills and fan coil heating units beneath the raised floors bring fresh air into the offices. As it heats up, it is drawn to stair towers powered by the heat gain through glass blocks. Fabric-covered dampers on the rooftops rise up 1 meter as needed to expel the heated air.[11]

NEW PARLIAMENTARY OFFICES, PORTCULLIS HOUSE, LONDON

Also designed by Hopkins Architects, the new parliamentary offices are a seven-story block built around an enclosed courtyard. In the Portcullis House building, components such as triple glazing, solar screens, and venetian blinds keep the building cool in summer and warm in winter. Ductwork is in the thick external walls, connecting to underfloor air distribution systems on each floor. An enthalpy wheel captures heat from the exhaust air and returns it to the incoming air stream in winter, and the opposite takes place in summer.[12]

NOHO SQUARE, LONDON

In the Noho Square project by Make Architects, completed in London in 2006, a 1.2-hectare (2.88-acre) existing Middlesex Hospital presented an opportunity to create an exemplary mixed-use urban block in central London. In addition to the efficiencies offered by creating a dense, mixed-used plan in the heart of the city, the building generates its own energy using a combined heat and power central system. Biomass boilers are used throughout, and green sedum roofs limit rainwater runoff.

PLANTATION PLACE, LONDON

Designed by Arup Associates, Plantation Place was completed in 2004. The fifteen-story development designed for financial, insurance, and trading firms occupies almost a complete city block. The streets around the site are narrow, and so the street-level façades are designed to be viewed obliquely. The upper façade is a clear glazed double skin; the outer glass protects the opening windows of the clear and opaque inner skin from wind and rain.[13]

At Plantation Place, there are two buildings: the 500,000–square-foot (46,451–square-meter) One Plantation Place, three quarters of which is leased to Accenture consultants, and the 160,000–square-foot (14,864–square-meter) Two Plantation Place. On the upper, fully glazed floors, unframed sheets of glass are held in place by clamps. The glass is angled at 3° from vertical, Arup director Michael Beaven explained to me, which has several benefits. First, its reflections are primarily of the sky, so clouds appear to drift across the building. Second, and more practically, the gaps at the top and bottom of each sheet encourage air circulation, providing a thermal buffer outside the building itself. This gives the top floors natural ventilation and reduces the need for air conditioning. An inner skin of standard, sealed double glazing and solid spandrel insulation provides the actual building perimeter, effectively providing a triple-glazed building envelope.[14]

The building tapers as it goes up, going from a 50,000–square-foot floorplate for the first six levels, to 30,000 square feet for floors 7 through 9, then to 14,000 square feet for floors 10 to 14. A sealed air-conditioned environment is provided only for the lower six floors of offices. The firm opened up ancient wells on the site to provide groundwater for a cooling assist to irrigate flowering plants and flush toilets. As a core-and-shell office building, it is configured for a wide variety of service company users, with data and wire cabling distribution through 6-inch-deep floors, along with passive and active chilled beams and chilled ceilings. All heating and cooling systems are water-based for carbon efficiency.

At One Plantation Place, the atrium changes shape as it rises through the changing floors. At ground level the atrium rises from the far end of the main entrance, lending a sense of spaciousness to the reception area. When it reaches the seventh floor, the atrium moves southwards to the edge, creating a direct sun path almost as far as the entrance on the north face. At each floor, the atrium is positioned where it gives the greatest benefit. On the larger floors—ground to sixth floor—it is in the center; from floors 7 to 9 its position creates U-shaped floorplates, and floors 10 to 14 need no atrium because they are narrow enough to receive daylighting in all office spaces. The atrium is sealed for the first six stories, then has operable windows as the building goes higher.

Located next door to Foster's "The Gherkin," Plantation Place received a Very Good rating under the BREEAM 2002 standard. Arup Associates has a unique approach toward the fit-out of this type of core-and-shell building, according to Michael Beaven. "We designed the building so it can respond to those users who want to engage with its environmental performance, and those who possibly don't. We work towards occupier engagement because without it even the most environmentally sensitive of designs will simply not deliver its promise."[15]

STRATFORD CITY, EAST LONDON

Started in 2003, Stratford City, another Arup Associates project, will eventually encompass 14 million square feet of commercial uses and as many as 400,000 homes. The project includes a district cooling system. BREEAM Excellent certification is required for all structures.

CORPORATE CAMPUS FOR SKY TELEVISION, LONDON

Arup is now designing a corporate campus for Sky Television, owned by News Corp. Scheduled for occupancy in 2010, the project will house 10,000 people. It will be the first naturally ventilated television studio in the world and will be powered with wind turbines. The firm will be exploring closed cycles with this project, trying to go beyond zero carbon to actually generate more energy than it uses and export that energy to a complementary load.

SCHOOL OF SLAVONIC AND EAST EUROPEAN STUDIES, UNIVERSITY COLLEGE, LONDON

Designed by Short and Associates,[16] the project was intended to provide natural daylighting and ventilation on a building site trapped on three sides by a chemistry building, an examination hall, and a row of Georgian terrace buildings. In addition, the building sits in the heart of Georgian-era Bloomsbury, which is fiercely protected by severe planning and historic conservation constraints. Climatically, it is close to the center of London's heat island, and therefore cooling is an important issue.[17]

FIGURE 4.5 This building from Short and Associates illustrates year-round natural ventilation, summer passive cooling, and extensive daylighting, providing a low-energy strategy in a city center at 50° north latitude. *(Peter Cook)*

The design solution was to provide a D-shaped plan that was formed through numerous tests, including compilation of weather data indicating that passive ventilation could maintain ambient temperatures and performance of natural lighting studies to ensure that the neighboring chemistry building would not lose too much natural light (Figure 4.5).[18]

According to firm principal and Cambridge professor Alan Short, "The building has a hybrid environmental strategy, naturally ventilated all year and passively cooled through the summer months by engaging downdraft cooling via a central lightwell through periods of summer peak temperatures. The London 'heat island effect' shows the city centre to be warming but this project demonstrates that it is possible to configure a low-energy strategy in a city center at these latitudes. This is the first known application of this low-energy environmental strategy in a city center in the world." Short and his colleagues exhaustively modeled and tested the strategy at the Institute of Energy and Sustainable Development at De Montfort University, Leicester, and the BP Institute for Multiphase Flow at Cambridge University.[19]

Natural daylighting is provided by a central lightwell that runs the full height of the building (seven stories) and also provides pathways for natural ventilation. (Figure 4.6 illustrates the designed airflow pathways.)[20] The stairwell also serves as a space for ventilating: Air flows along the façade to a ventilating parapet wall aligned in height with the adjoining Georgian terraces.[21]

In the summer, ventilation occurs when incoming air enters the lightwell (through a series of

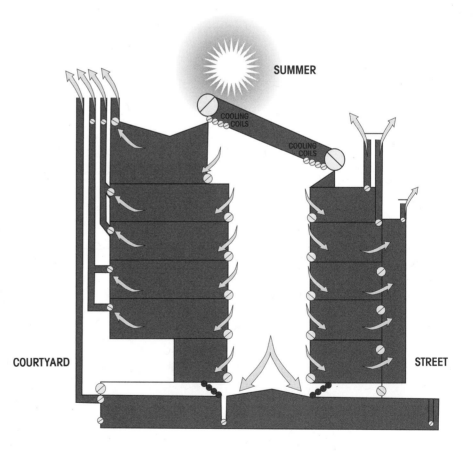

FIGURE 4.6 An extremely clever solution to cooling in central London, passive downdraft cooling pulls cooled air over chilled pipes into a central atrium and distributes it throughout the building. *(Redrawn with permission from Short & Associates)*

windows in the lightwell head). Air temperature drops as the air comes into contact with chilled water tubes located at the top of the lightwell; the chilled air sinks through the lightwell, providing a reservoir of cold air that supplies each floor. As internal heat gains warm the air, it rises and is exhausted through stacks located on the outside perimeter or the ventilating parapet.[22]

In the winter, the flow pattern is reversed: Outside air enters through low-level intakes at the street façade and at basement level, and air is drawn to a plenum between the basement and upper ground floors, where it is heated by batteries before passing into the lightwell. Heated exhaust air then exits through vents in the top of the building.

Completed in 2005 at a cost of £10 million, the 40,000–square-foot (3,600–square-meter) building won the RIBA Award in 2006.[23] Figure 4.7 shows how the energy use of this building compares with that of a standard building.

UNIVERSITY OF COVENTRY

For the Lanchester Library at this university, Short and his colleagues took on a project on a building site that is roughly square and is drastically sloping, bounded by a major ring road. Because of the traffic noise, the interior environment needed to be protected from noise, so operable windows were not a good option. The site had a square footprint; the problem is that square buildings are not well suited for natural ventilation because floorplates are too deep to move air naturally. So the design solution was to create a perforated square footprint, with each side measuring approximately 50 meters (165 feet).[24]

To promote natural daylighting and ventilation, five lightwells are carved out of the deep floorplates, with four smaller perimeter lightwells and a larger central atrium. The perimeter lightwells supply air at low levels through operable dampers to each floor, and the larger lightwell is used for air extraction. The lightwells run the entire height of the building.[25]

Natural ventilation is achieved by stack effect, with sixteen perimeter stacks and an addi-

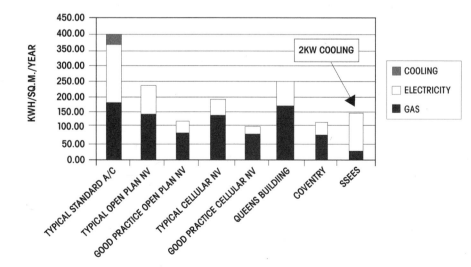

FIGURE 4.7 The School of Slavonic and Eastern European Studies (SSEES) building cuts cooling demand nearly to nothing while also providing a good reduction in heating energy use.
(Redrawn with permission from Short & Associates)

tional four directly connected to the top floor to prevent backflow of air into the floor. The incoming supply air, heated by equipment and people, rises to the top of each floor beneath the ceiling (the ceiling height is 4 meters [13 feet], so the heated air never interacts with people). Because of the difference in pressure between inside and outside, heated air is pulled up and out through the stacks and drawn out at the top of the central lightwell.[26]

For nighttime cooling, dampers are opened at predetermined set points, and heat accumulated throughout the day from people, solar gain, and equipment is flushed out. In the building, concrete floor slabs absorb the cooler air and store it for the next day's cooling. As the building builds heat the next day, the cool concrete slabs absorb the heat, keeping the building cooler longer throughout the day, an energy-saving strategy that eliminates the need for mechanical systems to run the entire day.

The key to the success of this project is creating enough openings inside the building so that air and light can move easily into every space. In this approach, the need for natural ventilation and daylighting dictates much of the architectural form of the interior. Completed in August 2000, the 10,000–square-meter (110,000–square-foot) building cost £35 million, including fit-out, and has received numerous awards.

NATURAL VENTILATION AT QUEENS BUILDING, DEMONTFORT UNIVERSITY, LEICESTER

At DeMontfort University in Leicester, in the early 1990s, Alan Short and Brian Ford were tasked with providing a new engineering teaching and research facility for the School of Engineering and Manufacture. The design brief called for "an innovative building of traditional construction and environmental sensitivity."[27] The engineering school wanted to challenge conventional wisdom in a creative and responsible way, using the best possible environmental design criteria.[28]

The building contains four stories, with classrooms, lecture and seminar rooms, teaching staff offices, and two auditoria for 150 people each. It accommodates as many as 1,000 students and 100 staff daily, along with as many computers. The central part of the building is divided by a top-lit concourse running the full height and length of the building.

The building is naturally ventilated by a combination of simple opening windows, with automatically controlled windows and vents at high levels. A series of chimneys provide automatic ventilation of the two 150-seat auditoriums. In each space, lighting is controlled by the occupant.

The building is made out of load-bearing red brick, with 100 millimeters (4 inches) of rockwool cavity insulation, with 7-inch concrete block on the interior walls.[29] Six inches of insulation is provided for the roof deck. For the most part, the windows are double glazed. Temperature sensors control the opening of the higher-level windows in the engineering workshop, and the lower-level windows are manually controlled and tilt inward.[30]

The energy-saving design concept relies on a highly insulated, thermally massive envelope[31] with a shallow floor plan, along with high ceilings that promote natural ventilation and daylighting. A central lightwell acts as a thermal and acoustic buffer zone. Carefully designed cross-ventilation and stack effect ventilation minimizes the need for mechanical ventilation and cooling. The entire building was designed to function without air conditioning. Accumulated heat is removed by cross-ventilation or by stack effect, promoted by the high chimneys. On summer evenings, ventilation dampers are opened to precool the structure for the next day. In the electrical laboratory wings, there is an enclosed and shady courtyard, facilitating a narrow floorplate of 6 meters (20 feet), also designed to cross-ventilate.

The stack effect from eight chimneys above the roof provides natural ventilation for the laboratory and teaching spaces in the central building, in combination with manually operated windows at the perimeter. A shallow section (18 feet) of the two entrance wings promotes cross-ventilation through low- and high-level openings to create up to 50 percent openings to the entire façade. The complexity of the passive ventilation strategy demanded automatic control of low-level inlets and stack or ridge exhaust ventilators in the majority of areas.

THE HELICON, LONDON

Completed in 1997 and designed by the U.K. firm of Sheppard Robson, the £33-million ($66-million) Helicon is another good example of a double-skin building in an urban setting.[32] There is a Marks & Spencer retail store for three of the nine aboveground floors. Above the 16,500 square meters (170,000 square feet) of retail space and access, the remaining six floors provide 11,500 square meters (124,000 square feet) of speculative offices. The architectural concept was to provide maximum transparency for the building while allowing adequate solar control without resorting to tinted and reflective glasses (Figure 4.8).

FIGURE 4.8 Helicon is a delightful combination of low-energy shops and offices on a tight site in London, by Sheppard Robson Architects. *(Sheppard Robson)*

According to the architects, "the Helicon was the first U.K. speculative office building to incorporate chilled ceilings, displacement ventilation and an active double-skin façade."[33]

The six office floors are arranged around an atrium with setbacks inside and out to provide terraces and accessible outside spaces. The first three floors and two basements provide space for shop floor, storage, and delivery access for the retail units.

The double-skin glazing can be naturally ventilated with automatic openings to induce a stack effect to dispel unwanted solar gain. In the cavity between the two layers of glazing, the venetian blinds are lowered and tilted automatically to respond to outside light, solar intensity, inside light levels, and inside temperature. On the east and west façades, there is triple glazing, which creates a cavity that contains solar control blinds.

The double skin consists of an outer pane of frameless single glazing and inner double-glazed panels. The entire system was designed to act as a thermal chimney with automatically controlled vents and tilting blinds. To control unwanted solar gain, the atrium roof is glazed with 50 percent reflective glass.[34]

The basic energy concept was to cut conventional energy use for this type of building by about 50 percent by relying on solar energy control through the façade, maintaining internal comfort by minimizing solar gain. There is also a displacement ventilation system that works in conjunction with chilled ceilings. The entire scheme relies on minimum fresh air provision, with heating and cooling provided within the space instead of having to condition a large volume of makeup air. During the winter, the double-skin system on the east and west façades is kept closed to act as a thermal buffer, reducing heat loss.

Because of the need for almost continuous cooling, the chilled ceiling system makes internal conditions feel more comfortable, using a radiant cooling effect. The chilled ceiling panels are integrated into perforated metal ceiling tiles that account for around 36 percent of the ceiling area. The double-skin system on the east and west façades can be automatically opened with low- and high-level openings to produce a stack effect that takes away unwanted solar heat gain in the cavity, whenever internal temperatures exceed 28°C (82°F).

The five-story double-skin system allowed the internal environment to be designed without the variable air volume systems typical in office developments. Despite a reported 15 percent increase in the initial cost, the need for less heating, ventilation, and air conditioning plant is expected to cut annual operating costs by 16 percent.

In the office spaces, air is fed into a pressurized floor plenum and supplied into the space through floor-mounted circular grilles at 18°C (64°F), warmer than the standard 55°F from overhead diffusers. As air circulates through the space, both people and machines warm it; the heated air rises to meet the chilled ceilings. Then the air is exhausted through the double-skin cavity to higher levels in the building.

The daylighting goals were met by full-height glazing that provides daylight to the deep floorplates of the retail areas. Stepping back the office floorplates to increase daylight levels at the base of the atrium maximizes daylight gain into the office areas. Solar control is provided by aluminum louver blades, which are automatically adjusted to control solar gain and glare. Through a lot of testing, the blades were designed to be 14 percent perforated, with a minimum solar reflectivity of 70 percent. The louvers can be tilted up to 70°, according to solar conditions.

WOLSELEY SUSTAINABLE BUILDING CENTRE, LEAMINGTON SPA

Wolseley is a "building merchant," or building product distributor, one of the largest in the world, with more than 500 outlets in the United Kingdom alone. In recognition of the growing interest among their customers (mostly contractors, building operators, and facility managers), the company decided to build a £3.2-million ($6.4-million) showroom as an ecologically conscious building, showcasing many of the green products it sells, such as water-free urinals and dual-flush toilets; photovoltaic and solar thermal systems; insulation products, including Thermofleece sheep's wool insulation; a biomass boiler using wood pellets; wall products such as drywall with phase-change materials in the gypsum; ground-source (geothermal) heat pumps; krypton-filled, triple-glazed windows with a self-cleaning nanotechnology coating on the exterior; floor coverings, including linoleum, a hard floor with 30 percent recycled glass, and one with recyclable carpet tiles; pavers and systems for rainwater infiltration and recycling; and more than 150 other products, large and small. Designed by ECD Architects,[35] this is a small gem that is well worth visiting.

Shown in Figure 4.9 and opened in June 2008, the Wolseley Sustainable Building Centre has a simple story: Build the place right in the first place, with a long east–west axis, put in sun shades and overhangs to cut solar gain (in this case, the sun shades have photovoltaic panels on the top), and have operable windows allowing plenty of cross-ventilation. I built a passive solar home in California nearly 30 years ago using the same principles.

We discover good design over and over again, but each incarnation is a little better. Now we have ground-source heat pumps to dramatically reduce electricity use for heating and cooling, low-flow toilets that use about one third the water of traditional toilets, and far more efficient glazing and insulation systems. There are also wall-mounted meters that record the current power output and total energy production from the two photovoltaic systems serving the building. This is a

FIGURE 4.9 The largest building products distributor in the United Kingdom, Wolseley built a model green demonstration building so that contractors could see how to use and install a wide range of green products. *(Timothy Soar Photography)*

good reminder that what gets metered gets managed. More of our buildings need real-time, highly visual meters and monitoring devices to allow careful management of energy use.

There are some nice commercial touches also. The small flat-screen panels not only tell the story of the building and the various products but also allow you to access information on any product you wish, just by entering your four-digit customer code. By the time you get back to your office from visiting the showroom, if the system works as advertised, you'll have electronic files of product literature on all the products that interest you. You won't need to lug glossy brochures all the way back to the office, then find a place to file them. And a salesperson will soon call asking about specific project placement for each product.

Celebrating the opening, Nigel Sibley, U.K. managing director for the firm, said, "Wolseley is committed to helping the industry reduce the environmental footprint left by developers and occupiers alike. Both regulation, such as the Code for Sustainable Homes, and market forces are driving the construction industry to embrace sustainability. Wolseley has made a significant investment that reflects our belief that sustainable products will move from 'niche' to 'norm' in the construction industry."

It pleases me to imagine that in just a few years, I will be able to visit dozens of similar showrooms around the world, organized and promoted by similarly large companies, but this is one of the first I know of from an established building product distributor, which involves really trying to "walk the talk" and show in real time and in real practice how these products work and how to use them. I think that £3.2 million is a real commitment. Hats off to the chaps from Wolseley!

THE GREEN OFFICE AT THORPE PARK, LEEDS

The highest BREEAM-rated building to date, with an Excellent rating and a design score of 87.55 percent, is a 4,000–square-meter (43,000–square-foot), £6-million ($12-million) office building in the United Kingdom, completed in 2006, called Thorpe Park in the city of Leeds. Developed by Innovate Property, this is a speculative office building rated according to the BREEAM Office 2005 system.[36] Carbon emissions are 80 percent lower than those in a conventional building.

Designed by Rio Architects and located on a 2.8-acre site at Thorpe Park in Yorkshire, the project consists of a three-story, 43,000–square-foot building. Consisting of two 14-meter-wide wings on either side of a full-height central atrium, the floor space was designed to provide maximum flexibility for occupant fit-out.

The design principles for this building will sound familiar to anyone who's been reading this book or who is familiar with the LEED rating system:

- Mechanical ventilation is enhanced using a patented TermoDeck system that distributes and tempers the air supply to the floorplates through a labyrinth created from the hollow cores.
- The building is extremely well insulated, reducing the loss of energy through the envelope dramatically.
- The building is designed according to passive solar principles, using the early morning sun to warm the building but excluding the midday sun to avoid overheating.

- The thermal mass of the concrete frame is used as a giant storage heater in winter to recover the heat from people and computers.
- In the summer the concrete is used like an ice store, chilled overnight to keep the building cool during the next day.
- The large windows provide plenty of natural light, avoiding the need for electric lighting for most of the year.
- The toilets use a vacuum system, like aircraft toilets, to reduce the water used from 6 liters (1.6 gallons) per flush to 1.2 liters (0.3 gallon).
- Rainwater from the roof is collected for use in flushing toilets, which, coupled with the extremely low flush volumes, means that no potable water is used for sewage conveyance.
- The landscaping is ecologically sensitive and uses native planting and wetland areas to encourage wildlife habitats. The indigenous and protected bat population can take advantage of bat boxes built into the bordering treeline.
- The surface water runoff and excess rainwater are drained into the landscaping or recycled back into the building's water system.
- The roof has been seeded with native plants to further augment the natural habitat and to encourage bird and insect life.
- The parking lot is paved with a Formpave system. This allows rainwater to permeate the surface and return to the water table and the wetland areas.
- The site has been designed so that no rainwater is discharged to a stormwater outfall but is instead managed on site.
- Extra bicycle lockers and showers complement the local green transport initiative.

What can we learn from the U.K. experience with green building? First of all, U.K. architectural and engineering design is about 10 years ahead of most of U.S. design, with its focus on natural ventilation, ground-source heat pumps, double-skin façades, building-integrated photovoltaics, building shell–integrated cooling, and a number of other sensible, cost-effective, low-energy approaches. Second, the focus on building labeling for energy use and post-occupancy evaluations is a trend that we should adopt. But there's much here we can learn from and improve upon, particularly in U.S. climatic regions similar to those in the United Kingdom.

CHAPTER 5

Sustainable Buildings in Germany

Sustainable design in Germany is far more integrated into the cultural and economic fabric, with legal requirements for daylighting and fresh air, an approach of designing buildings to last for a very long time, a focus on low-energy design, and an innovative approach to integrating engineering into building design from the beginning. Now, let's take a look at what our friends in Deutschland have been up to the past 20 years.

LUFTHANSA AVIATION CENTER, FRANKFURT

The Lufthansa Aviation Center, designed by Ingenhoven Architekten, is a magnificent building, located at the Frankfurt airport and situated between an airport frontage road, a main high-speed train line, and a busy highway (Figure 5.1). When I toured this office building in April 2008, what impressed me the most, beyond the sheer size (seven stories and ten wings)—about 70,000 square meters (750,000 square feet)—was the quality of detailing and the quiet of the comfort system. The only disturbing feature was a series of separately ventilated smoking stations on the ground level (still a feature of European culture) that tried but did not succeed in containing all smoke.

The project is designed like a comb, with a long central core and office wings that come out at right angles. Between the office wings are glass-enclosed but unconditioned gardens. The building has more than 500,000 square feet of glass, and all offices are within a short distance to daylight (per German standards).

The comb-like building plan of the Aviation Center encloses landscaped gardens as buffer zones, insulating the building against emissions and noise. Plants chosen from five continents symbolize Lufthansa's global connections. All of the 1,850 office workplaces have views into the glass-roofed gardens and can be naturally ventilated. The open central passage on each floor connects all the different areas. On completion of the second construction stage in the next decade, this building will accommodate 4,500 employees and include building wings housing twenty-eight gardens.

The current building has an outer layer of single glazing protecting the nine gardens. Each garden represents a part of the world Lufthansa flies to, including Japan, South Africa, and southern California, for which there is a beach volleyball court. The building contains magnificent commissioned artwork, especially in the gardens.

The project also meets a variety of ecological criteria, including 100 percent of the wood from Forest Stewardship Council–certified sources and no use of polyvinyl chloride anywhere in the building.

Principal Christoph Ingenhoven says, "From the beginning, we wanted to have what was technically possible: beginning with the gardens, which serve as climate buffers and improve the microclimate, through thermal activation of the constructed mass, and extending up to the employment of wood. Also the non-tinted glass, the high daylight yield and the correspondingly reduced need for electric lighting contributed to the building using only a third of the energy of a comparable structure."[1]

As a result of this location, the building was designed to meet strict height restrictions and constructed in a manner that offered lots of light and air, yet was not affected by the noise of planes, trains, and automobiles.

The building is designed for a high level of comfort and energy efficiency, with estimated energy use one third that of a conventional German office building. Chilled and hot water are provided by the airport's central plant. Ventilation air for the building is brought in through several large inlets located at ground level. This air is brought through a tunnel located 30 feet below the building, used to capture ground temperatures as a source of preheating in the winter and precooling in the summer.

Conditioned air is then brought in under the floor in a displacement-type delivery. The exterior walls of the office wings use a double façade that is open at the top and bottom. This façade provides for improved insulation and for acoustic and wind isolation. The interior portion of the façade is triple glazed, and the exterior portion is single glazed. Between the two walls of the façade are blinds that are mechanically controlled based on sun intensity and location. These are used to capture solar gain and to keep it from infiltrating the interior of the building when necessary. A second set of roller blinds is provided for all interior windows. These are manually controlled by the building occupants and are used for glare control and privacy.

Between the office wings are enclosed gardens. The exterior walls of the gardens have a single façade and mechanically operated external windows. The windows and vents mounted at the ceiling are used as part of an automated sequence to naturally ventilate the atriums and to control the temperature. The office wings have operable doors that open into the atriums for natural ventilation of the office areas. The building also features automated lighting control with daylight harvesting.

COMMERZBANK HEADQUARTERS, FRANKFURT

One of Foster + Partners' most recognizable projects is the headquarters for Germany's third largest bank, Commerzbank, located in the banking capital of the country, Frankfurt (Figure 5.2).[2] This building was completed in 1997 and still stands as the tallest structure in Europe, towering about 300 meters above Frankfurt. As one approaches it from one of the many streets in the neighborhood, it's difficult to see how tall it is. The podium of the building is a very user-friendly two stories, and that dominates the streetscape. This building is recognized by most as the first sustainable skyscraper, although the RWE Tower in Essen, completed about the same time by German architect Christoph Ingenhoven, can certainly lay claim to equal recognition.

The basic plan of the building is triangular, with elevators at each apex and the middle of the building open for views to sky gardens at nine locations. This is the first European building to integrate gardens into the very fabric of the building and to elevate them above the main floor. After all, winter gardens are very common in European buildings, typically in open central atriums, but Foster took this idea literally to new heights.

Also unique is that the views to the interior showcase the gardens for the clerical workers in the building, providing them with a view of greenery and daylight and a view to the exterior through the glazing behind the gardens. The exterior offices serve the executives, with views of the Frankfurt skyline, and have integrated natural ventilation through the façade and solar control with exterior-mounted shading.[3]

The building provides 70,000 square meters (770,000 square feet) in sixty stories, a formidable structure by anyone's reckoning. The gardens are four stories tall and are placed three on a side around the building to serve several floors each. The building's three corners are rounded to provide more space for essential services. The building has operable windows, but these automatically close when there is a need for air conditioning. The central atrium serves as a thermal chimney for natural ventilation of the offices.

FIGURE 5.2 This mid-1990s building by Foster + Partners in Frankfurt, Germany's financial capital, is still the tallest building in Europe and one of the greenest.
(Ralph Richter, Commerzbank AG)

The building has three layers of glazing to provide for natural ventilation and solar shading devices. Chilled ceilings are used throughout for basic air conditioning, with special dew point controls to prevent condensation. The natural ventilation provides night flush cooling of the building to exhaust warm air built up during the day.[4] As in most European office buildings, perimeter heat in the winter is provided by radiators.

EUROPEAN INVESTMENT BANK, LUXEMBOURG

The small country of Luxembourg borders Germany, and this project was also designed by Christoph Ingenhoven, so I've included it here. In April 2008, I toured the nearly finished European Investment Bank (EIB) headquarters building in Luxembourg city (the largest city in a country of less than a half million people) with project architect Ben Dieckmann. The EIB, shown in Figure 5.3, is one of the largest government banks in the world and employs people from throughout the European Union. The building site is a steeply sloping hillside, with a panoramic view of the woods nearby from one vista and also the downtown area of the city from the front of the building.

The building follows a similar concept to the Lufthansa Aviation Center in Frankfurt, with plenty of daylight, an overall glass covering, and gardens throughout. Opened in the fall of 2008, the EIB building covers some 70,000 square meters (about 750,000 square feet). It is a really spectacular and beautiful building in an otherwise ordinary group of institutional office buildings.

This is the first building in continental Europe to be certified "Very Good" by the United Kingdom's BREEAM standard. The EIB finances European Union projects and is one of the most influential banks in the world. Its new building is located next to the original bank headquarters, designed by Sir Denys Lasdun and built in 1980 on Luxembourg's Kirchberg plateau.

FIGURE 5.3 Completed in 2008 by Ingenhoven Architekten, this extension of a 1980s building by Sir Denis Lasdyn puts Luxembourg on the map of the continent's green buildings, with lots of daylight and winter gardens in a cloudy central European climate.
(Ingenhoven Architects, Düsseldorf)

A vaulted double-glass sheath spans over the V-plan of the new office building, which is bound together by atriums and winter gardens. The halls function as climate buffers and are an important part of the energy concept. Over seven stories, the flexibly planned and communication-friendly building integrates all functions of the headquarters and workstations for about 750 bank employees.

The climate is typical of this part of Europe, as Luxembourg lies between Germany, France, and Belgium, in a mostly industrial region. There are about 30 inches of rain per year; the average summer temperature is 63°F, and the average winter temperature is about 32°F.[5] (This is similar to the weather in the Pacific Northwest of the United States.) In this climate, natural ventilation with 100 percent outside air is feasible much of the year.

As a result of the design features, the energy use is projected at 71 kilowatt-hours per square meter per year (6.6 kilowatt-hours per square foot per year), an excellent result for the office portion. (This projected energy use excludes the data center, which tends to be a very large energy user.)

The ventilation system is based around desiccant cooling, a system that cools the air by using heat and water as energy sources. Incoming fresh air is dried by a desiccant wheel (with a resulting increase in temperature) and is then cooled by a thermal wheel system. Finally, the incoming air is humidified to a comfortable level in a washer. The exhaust air is humidified by the washer and cooled, passing its coolness to the incoming air. The exhaust air is then heated to lower its relative humidity; finally, the exhaust air passes through the sorption wheel, absorbing the humidity taken from the wheel by the incoming air.

In this way, water and air provide the cooling, with electrical energy used only by auxiliary equipment such as pumps and motors. About twenty-five of the forty air-handling units provide this double function.[6] Total power demand for the ventilation system is about 513 kilowatts. For the overall building, the power demand is 2,084 kilowatts, about one quarter of which is for the computer room.

Fresh air is provided to all office spaces during the day at constant volumes, with natural ventilation most of the year. Just enough ventilation is provided for good indoor air quality. Because cooling energy transport with water is much more energy- and space-efficient than with air, the cooling is separated from the ventilation system, and this building is cooled only as needed. (Most office buildings in the United States are overventilated because the ventilation and cooling systems are combined.)

The building has a double-glass façade on the outer skin, with a single-glazed façade for the occupied spaces, a unique design that allows the double-skin to buffer the overall temperature, with the single-glazed façade offering privacy and glare control. For example, to reduce the air-conditioning load, sun shading is provided on the single façades, with an external textile screen; on the double façades, aluminum sun blind lamellas are provided within the façade. The sun shading can be both user controlled and centrally monitored, to control solar gains. To prevent glare, the angle of the lamellas can be controlled to provide daylighting without getting direct sun into the workspaces.

The building also uses two cooling towers to provide chilled water at 14°C (57°F), which connects to a 15–20°C chilled water net in the building. The thermal mass of the building is activated through an aluminum–plastic composite pipe to create chilled floors that take away heat during the day, reloaded with chilled water at night. When outside temperatures are below 12°C (54°F), about 70 percent of the year, free cooling is provided to the thermal mass. (This is different, and more effective, than "night flush cooling" to take away excess heat generated by daytime activity.)

NORDDEUTSCHE LANDESBANK, HANNOVER[7]

A photo of this remarkable building, designed by Behnisch Architekten, graces the cover of this book. Completed in 2002, the 75,000–square-meter (807,000–square-foot) office building occupies an entire city block and serves as an important element linking the various activities that define the neighboring quarters of the city: retail, commercial, residential, cultural, sport, and leisure. Through varying heights the building integrates itself into the existing fabric of the city.

In accordance with local urban planning guidelines for four- to six-story buildings, the shallow-plan perimeter building is aligned with the existing streets, complementing the pattern and scale of its surroundings. From the exterior it resembles the traditional city block, and a large public courtyard lies in the middle, protected from the traffic noise of the busy streets. This courtyard is characterized but not dominated by the daily operations of the bank itself and further enlivened by shops, restaurants, cafés, large reflecting pools, extensive landscaping, and public art.

A 70-meter-high building rises from the courtyard. Air conditioning was considered redundant, with reliance placed instead on groundwater, along with sun, wind, and mild outdoor air temperatures (less than 5 percent of the year above 22°C [72°F]); this reduces operating costs and initial costs. When needed, active cooling is provided by 18°C (64°F) water sent through a network of polyethylene tubes in the concrete ceiling.[8] In winter, 30°C (86°F) water is pumped through the same tubes for heating.

The movable blinds protect against both sunlight and glare, without darkening the offices too much. The uppermost slats are angled independently of the rest so that daylight is redirected to the reflective ceiling and into the building depths. The walls along the corridors are glazed, increasing natural light levels.

These various measures, along with connection to a local district heating system and a network of solar panels, reduces annual carbon dioxide production by about 1,900 metric tons per year.[9]

Most of the building is naturally ventilated, with windows providing ventilation and the exposed superstructure providing thermal mass and temperature balancing. Areas of double façade provide protection against noise and vehicle emissions while serving as a duct transferring air from the central courtyard to the individual offices. The large areas of water in the courtyard reflect daylight into the offices and temper the microclimate. There are also generous roof gardens.

RWE TOWER, ESSEN[10]

Designed by Ingenhoven Architekten, the RWE building is 535 feet tall, the tallest structure in this part of Germany and is round in plan view, with thirty stories rising from a one-story pedestal. Mechanical equipment is located halfway up the building, so it's not necessary to fix things on the roof. As a round building, it has the smallest amount of skin for the volume enclosed.

The building was the first high-rise in Germany designed in a wind tunnel. Ventilation flaps at the bottom help relieve pressure differences between inside and outside, making it easy to open windows and doors. With operable windows, there is also a sunscreen to protect occupants from unwanted solar exposure.

There is a double-glass façade with a 20-inch (50-centimeter) space between the two glass walls to allow for a ventilation corridor and solar protection screens. Air from the outside passes through to the inside without causing drafts. The building is naturally ventilated about 70 percent of the time.

Above the entrance to the building, on the south, there are about 19 kilowatts of building-integrated photovoltaics with single-crystal photovoltaic cells. The building features night flush ventilation, use of the building envelope for thermal storage and cool energy transmission, and daylighting of 70 percent of the floor area on average.

OZEANEUM, STRALSUND[11]

Designed by Behnisch Architekten of Stuttgart, the new museum and aquarium building was built on the historic waterfront of the port of Stralsund, a World Heritage Site. Completed in 2007, the Ozeaneum (German Oceanographic Museum) has become a major tourist attraction on Germany's Baltic coast. The total building area of the aquariums is 17,300 square meters (186,000 square feet); each aquarium has different temperature levels according to the region of the ocean they represent, and the water needs to be cleaned and currents induced without using too much energy.

Shown in Figure 5.4, the Ozeaneum building relates to the sea rather than to the buildings of the old town. It is conceived as an open house that can be "flooded" from all sides by daylight and visitors, in a manner akin to that of water swirling around stones on the seabed. The building is divided into four sections, each of which is devoted to a particular exhibition theme.

The design program seeks to maximize daylight in the atriums and to use radiant heating and cooling whenever possible. Pumps are optimized for low energy consumption. At this latitude of 54° north, there are only 34 days per year above 25°C (77°F), so the outdoor environment contributes significantly to the interior cooling program.[12]

FIGURE 5.4 This aquarium complex, designed by Behnisch Architekten and laid out like stones on the seabed, creates an elegant low-energy solution to provide diverse marine environments. *(Johannes-Maria Schlorke)*

FIGURE 5.5 Designed by Ingenhoven Architekten, Uptown Munich is the tallest office building in Bavaria's capital, with a unique approach to bringing natural ventilation in through the windows that uses "portholes" operated by mechanical actuators. A planted mature pine forest and four smaller buildings create an urban village at the edge of the city. *(Jerry Yudelson)*

UPTOWN MUNICH OFFICE TOWER, MUNICH

I visited Uptown Munich in April 2008 as a guest of the Hines development firm and got a chance to visit the thirty-eight–story tower, designed by Ingenhoven Architekten and leased to the O_2 wireless company. From the top of the tower, the tallest building in Munich, there is a great view to the south of the Bavarian Alps. Most interesting to me was how the architect carried natural ventilation into each floor using a custom-designed "porthole" (Figure 5.5) with an actuator arm concealed in the ceiling. As temperatures rise, the actuator arm pushes open the porthole, allowing fresh air to enter the offices. Along with the natural ventilation system, bright solar glass and ventilated interior-mounted solar protection systems help to keep the all-glass façade from overheating.

Completed in 2004, with 85,000 square meters (915,000 square feet), this project is also a modern urban village with four seven-story high-rise office buildings connected by a central walkway. There is also an "instant forest" of 60-year-old pine trees, 10 to 12 meters tall, imported from a nursery in northern Germany and arranged in a sandy forest floor, providing a nature park that buffers the offices from a very busy ring road adjacent to the site.[13]

MAIN TRAIN STATION, STUTTGART

Ingenhoven won the prestigious Holcim prize in 2006 for the winning design for the Stuttgart main train station, particularly with his concept for a zero-energy project (the project was originally awarded to the firm in 1996). The project is expected to be completed between 2016 and 2018, but the current economic crisis may delay completion. Much time has been spent digging a railroad tunnel under the town so that trains won't have to come in and go out the same way but will be able to pass under the city and directly through the station.

The further development of the European high-speed railway network included renovation of Stuttgart's main railway station. At 185,000 square meters (2 million square feet), it is southern Germany's biggest town planning infrastructure project and the first part of the greater Stuttgart 21 program that includes new inner-city development over the buried tracks. A minimalistic concrete shell will span the platforms, and the top of the plaza will connect inner-city pedestrian zones with the historic Schlossgarten park. Twenty-eight "light eyes" will bring daylight and natural ventilation into the station. No energy is needed for heating, cooling, and lighting, making the station a zero-net-energy building.[14] The basic ecological concept makes use of natural physical cold and heat storage mechanisms of the earth, making heating and air-conditioning systems superfluous. Ventilation of the station is through the light eyes, which can be opened, and through the air movement induced by trains moving through the station.

The light eyes are evenly distributed above the platforms, guaranteeing that the station hall has an adequate supply of natural light for up to 14 hours a day. The vaults and openings in the hall permit an even distribution of natural light. Light-colored, reflective surfaces ensure that the hall is pleasantly lit even in dull weather. The results of lighting model studies performed to date have been incorporated into the form-finding process. At night, the underside of the shell structure is used to reflect the artificial lighting. To reduce CO_2 emissions, the station lighting is powered by renewable electricity supplied by the local electric utility or by photovoltaic cells located on the northern station building.

THERME, BAD AIBLING

I had an opportunity to tour this project, about 60 kilometers southeast of Munich, during a visit to that region in April 2008. In this renovation of a working but somewhat run-down spa, the architecture and engineering needed to be exceptionally well integrated to provide tight environmental control of a warm, humid environment (the inside of a bathhouse) without any noticeable discomfort to the bathers from moving air.

This nearly 11,000–square-meter (118,000–square-foot) project is visually intriguing, with five domes set into the existing baths and housing various pools and treatment areas. Each dome offers a unique mood, from totally quiet to quite lively; each has different colors and visual themes (Figure 5.6). During my visit, I passed up a chance to take the mud bath, although it was tempting to do so. I also visited the equipment room below the main bath area. I was amazed at how extensive it was, until I reflected on the fact that this project is constantly moving water and air, with very tight controls.

In responding to the complex demands of water quality, indoor environment, and privacy, the various indoor pools and treatment areas are accommodated in separate cabinet-like units. These are united by an undulating pool deck that extends from the changing areas through a generous winter garden out toward the outdoor terraces. The winter garden provides visitors various bathing possibilities in a quiet and relaxed environment and affords access to both cabinets and the outdoor pools and sauna areas. The deck is sheltered by a low-lying timber roof. Extensive glazed roof lights provide variable daylighting conditions throughout the winter garden.[15]

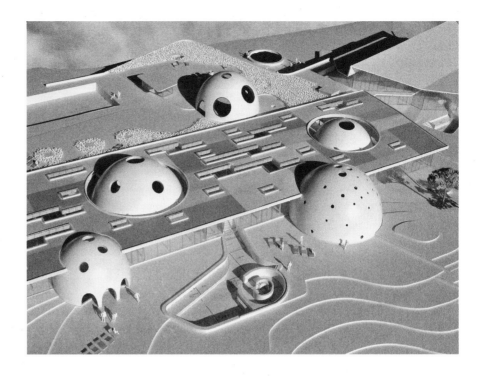

DEBIS TOWER AT POTSDAMER PLATZ, BERLIN[16]

The Debis project is part of Potsdamer Platz, a once vibrant area, desolate until the 1990s because the Berlin Wall was located there. Italy's Renzo Piano Building Workshop was commissioned to design eight buildings, including two new corporate headquarters. The Debis Building houses the headquarters of the property, financial service, information technology, telecommunication, and media service divisions of Daimler-Benz, which had taken on the mission of helping to rebuild Berlin.

Completed in 1997, the building contains 45,000 square meters (500,000 square feet) of office space, rising from a six-story broad lower platform to a narrow twenty-one–story tower. A 14-meter (46-feet) wide atrium runs 82 meters (270 feet) from north to south down the center, providing two overlooking office wings (this follows the German regulations requiring a 2 percent daylight factor at workstations).[17]

In terms of design challenges, the east, south, and west elevations have the highest exposure to solar gain; to handle this problem, a glass wall is offset from the main wall, made of glass panels that open to 70°. Sensors control this glass panel system to allow ventilation in warm weather. The building's inner skin incorporates upper and lower panels of insulated glazing. The upper windows open automatically at night in warm weather to ventilate the interior and remove the heat built up inside the building during the day.

The natural ventilation approach keeps the building comfortable for much of the year, along with the double-glass skin. Equally important for an office building, the second skin provides a noise barrier in both natural ventilation and sealed modes. The inner skin consists of a strip window façade with double-glazed, low-e coated glazing in aluminum frames. The external façade is 70 centimeters (28 inches) in front of the inner skin.[18]

The heating system operates with perimeter fin tube heaters, providing individual temperature control in offices. Heat recovery wheels are used to recover heat from the exhaust air stream in winter, reducing the need to heat the incoming air. For supplemental cooling in warmer weather, the building uses chilled ceilings. To promote personal comfort, the building provides operable windows, narrow floorplates that give good daylighting to all workstations, and external blinds mounted just outside the inner skin to control glare. Overall, the project is expected to rely on electric lighting less than 40 percent of the year in this cold northern city, quite an achievement.

In summer, the natural ventilation system will work until the outside air temperature exceeds 30°C (86°F). In the winter, when outside temperatures fall below 5°C (41°F), a supplemental heating system kicks in. The designers expect natural ventilation to be adequate for the entire building about 40 percent of the year, and the climate management strategies are expected to reduce overall energy use by 40 percent.[19]

PRISMA NÜRNBERG

In the spring of 2008, I visited one of Herbert Dreiseitl's projects in the city of Nuremberg, Germany. Under about a third of an acre of glass is a peaceful enclave, full of plants, water, and light, as shown in Figure 5.7.

Completed in 1997, Prisma ("prism") Nürnberg combines the elements of managing stormwater, collecting and treating rainwater, admitting daylight, and creating a pleasing indoor environment that sits between a commercial block with thirty-two offices, nine stores, and a coffeehouse alongside a busy street and a residential block with sixty-one residential units and a kindergarten one street in. As you step into the space between the two blocks, you enter into a semitropical paradise, surrounded by plants from South America and Australia, with the sound of running water from five 5-meter-high waterwalls placed along a city block. The 15-meter-high (50-feet) glasshouse contains 15,000 cubic meters (532,000 cubic feet) of space and rises over a series of water features with 240 square meters (2,583 square feet) of water surface area.[20]

The falling water draws down fresh air pulled in from a slit in the wall, with moist air (welcome in a dry winter cli-

FIGURE 5.7 Prisma Nürnberg illustrates Atelier Dreiseitl's approach at its best, fully integrating light, art, and water while treating stormwater and moderating the cold outdoor climate.
(Atelier Dreiseitl)

mate) blown gently into the space at a speed of about 10 feet per second. The system cools the building in summer (with the water between 64°F and 68°F) and heats it in winter.[21] Layers of colored glass provide an artistic backdrop for each waterwall, which is lit up at night.

Stormwater is collected from the roof of the glass building, a 65,000–square-foot catchment area, and is stored in a 64,000-gallon tank, is pumped up to the surface, and flows along a 110-meter watercourse, never more than a foot deep. There are actually two separate cycles in the building. The first cycle irrigates the plants in the greenhouse and creates an interesting waterscape of creeks and ponds. The second pumps water in between 5-meter-tall glass walls. In this process, air is purified and cooled. The remaining rainwater recharges the ground under the building.

NEW GERMAN PARLIAMENT, REICHSTAG, BERLIN

Designed by Foster + Partners and completed in 1999, the reconstruction of the German capitol took some cues from the old Reichstag, but in other respects it is a complete departure. Within its masonry shell it is transparent, opening up the interior to light and placing its activities on view.

The building's energy strategy starts with using refined vegetable oil for heating. Surplus heat is stored as hot water in an aquifer 300 meters below ground and can be pumped up to heat the building or to drive an absorption cooling plant to produce chilled water. The Reichstag's modest energy needs allow the building to perform as a power station for the new government quarter whenever its demands are less than its power production.

Natural ventilation in the chamber uses fresh air drawn up through the chimney effect. Heat exchangers recover and reuse warm air not expelled through the dome. "Intelligent windows" consist of a manually operated inner layer and security-laminated outer layer that draw in fresh air via ventilation joints. Renewable vegetable oil biofuel burned in a co-generation plant also produces clean electricity, reducing annual carbon dioxide output by 94 percent. Surplus heat stored in the aquifer provides hot water for heating. Cold water is stored below ground to provide cooling via chilled ceilings in hot weather. Photovoltaic panels cover 300 square meters (3,200 square feet) on the roof.

Processed heat is discharged from the co-generator and stored in the underground aquifer. Groundwater is pumped up at its natural temperature of 20°C (68°F) and then heated up to 70°C (158°F) using the waste heat of the co-generator. In winter the process is reversed, with warm water from the aquifer pumped back up to the building for heat supply at a low temperature (going from 65°C to 30°C [149°F to 86°F]) via heat exchangers.

The warm water from the aquifer not only heats the air and the underfloor heating system directly or indirectly via heat pumps but also drives a chlorofluorocarbon-free absorption cooling machine. Additional heat is also provided directly by hot water from the combined heat and power generator.

Large air ducts built 100 years ago naturally ventilate the plenary chamber. Fans take the air very slowly into a pressurized floor beneath the chamber. From there, the fresh air is released into the chamber as low-velocity ventilation. The warm exhaust air rises through openings in the dome's daylight cone and is released outside.

Operable windows, combined with a second outer glazing layer, allow natural ventilation to most rooms. Between the layers of windows, there is a solar shading device. Up to five times the room's air volume can be exchanged per hour.

The dome of the plenary chamber is an essential part of the daylighting system. Its cone-shaped mirror blocks direct sunlight while allowing in diffused daylight. The building's inherent thermal mass provides a comfortable base temperature range, reducing heat load peaks by about 30 percent. Mechanical ventilation supplements the natural ventilation system but is used only sporadically, for short periods. One hundred photovoltaic solar modules on the Reichstag's roof provide a peak output of approximately 40 kilowatts, sufficient to drive the exhaust air ventilation system of the plenary chamber and operate the shading devices in the dome.

GSW BUILDING, BERLIN

Finished in 1999, the central administration building of the GSW housing property association in Berlin was designed by Matthias Sauerbruch and Louisa Hutton. The double west wall of the twenty-two–story, 11-meter (36-foot) slab block that spans the two main low-rise blocks creates a thermal flue. The building plan is narrow to maximize daylight use and natural ventilation; the façade is carefully shaded to reduce solar heating in summer, and a wind roof assists natural ventilation.[22]

The east façade has triple-glazed windows with blinds between the panes, a typical European design innovation for solar control. On the east façade, there are louvered metal panels that allow fresh air to enter, independent of the window operation.

The energy savings concept features fresh air flowing from below into a 1-meter-wide space beneath the façade and rising upward, pulling air out of the offices and contributing to achieving an energy-saving effect of about 40 percent. The west façade induces vertical airflow by using stack effect ventilation, relying on the thermal buoyancy of the warm exhaust air. In winter, the mechanical ventilation system feeds back heat from exhaust air to the central plant to partially heat incoming air.[23] According to one writer, "The 22-story main building and two low-rise pedestals are slightly concave, and perhaps the best feature is the double-glazed, energy-efficient facade, which covers the surface in flickering iridescence."[24]

FREE UNIVERSITY, BERLIN

Foster + Partners' redevelopment scheme for the Free University, which occupies a central role in the intellectual life of Berlin, with more than 39,000 students, consisted of a 2005 retrofit of the campus's early 1970s Modernist buildings and a new library. The main original structure was made of concrete with two central cores and retained strong thermal properties. Its original façade was distinctive, but the exterior of Corten steel had decayed by the late 1990s and was replaced with a new bronze cladding.

Steel-framed with double-layered vacuum metal panels, the building's four floors are naturally ventilated. The natural ventilation uses a skin cavity that relies on heat recovery for up to 60 percent of the year. The window system includes an inner membrane of translucent glass fabric panels and translucent ethylene-tetrafluoroethylene elements that filter daylight through scattered transparent openings. All told, the design achieves a 35 percent reduction in annual energy use.

TRUMPF INTERNATIONAL, DITZINGEN

Trumpf International, in Ditzingen, provides high-precision laser cutting systems used in manufacturing. Part of the company's corporate campus, this office building is approximately 8,000 square meters (87,000 square feet). The project provides an open office space to provide a collaborative environment. The site faces a major highway, and noise was a big concern.

The building uses a double façade to provide both improved energy efficiency and acoustic isolation from road noise. The exterior wall of the façade is fixed glass with operable windows in the interior wall. The top and bottom of the façade are open, allowing ventilation. The heating and cooling plant is fairly conventional. The chiller uses an air-cooled condenser with a water spray on the outside surface. Radiant tubes embedded in the structural slab that forms the ceiling provide space heating and cooling. Piping was stubbed out for the future addition of radiant panels if capacity needs to be added. Ventilation is provided by air handlers that also provide humidification and dehumidification. Displacement ventilation is used, with air delivery coming in from under the floor. The result of this design is a very quiet and comfortable building with dramatic architecture.[25]

German sustainable design practice is remarkable, and the work of good architects and engineers is significant. This chapter highlights only a few of the architects who really stand out. (The engineers get their chance in the next chapter.) Because Germany is a cold northern country, because of a tradition of high-quality engineering, because architects really understand building physics, and because of the strong regulatory role of government, I found that many of the German projects have a level of precision and detailing that is often lacking in U.S. projects. This is particularly evident in façade design and construction practices and with corporate, public, and institutional clients who support low-energy designs with great daylighting and natural ventilation, even with their higher initial costs. Because much of the German experience is not published in English, there's less information about German projects than there is of work in the United Kingdom, hence the importance of field visits and direct observation of realized projects so that North American architects and engineers can see what our European friends have been doing for the past 20 years to advance the frontiers of sustainable design and construction.

CHAPTER 6

Green Engineering in Europe

American and Canadian engineers can learn a lot from the European experience with green and sustainable design. For quite some time, North American building engineering, especially for offices, has been using air conditioning for both ventilation and space conditioning, resulting in excessive energy use and decreased comfort. Furthermore, most engineers have abdicated any role in architectural design, preferring to just add more air conditioning (and more cost and energy use).

Human comfort is based not just on temperature and relative humidity but also on radiant temperature (the apparent temperature of surfaces), airflow, clothing, and even the ability to exercise control over temperature and airflow. We have provided comfort in our buildings but at an energy and cost penalty, because most buildings are overdesigned and overventilated. The last thing any design engineer wants to get is a call saying that the building just completed is too hot.

At the same time, American workers have become accustomed to a carefully controlled environment, 73°F plus or minus 2°F, so that they can wear indoors whatever they please, no matter what the weather outside: wool suits and ties in summer, miniskirts in winter. This attitude would surprise most Europeans: They expect to wear warm, heavy clothes in winter and cooler, lighter clothes in summer. As a result, European designers have tended to rely more on radiant space conditioning, with a broader range of temperatures, typically with the opportunity for office workers to open the windows when the weather's nice outside.

With this background in mind, let's take a look at some current developments in European engineering. With a colleague, Paul Ehrlich, a professional engineer, I undertook a study of current developments in green engineering.[1] I also spoke with the presidents and partners of a number of German and English engineering firms to get a broader perspective on their approach to low-energy design. One of the firms was Transsolar of Stuttgart, Germany, whose work is featured in this chapter. Another was Max Fordham Partnership, a sustainable design firm, and the engineers behind the Beaufort Court development presented in Chapter 4. Bill Watts is principal at Max Fordham and is part of a large group of U.K. engineers trying to get buildings quickly to the zero-carbon stage by focusing on integrated systems and structure along with carefully crafted renewable energy schemes.

One of the first things I noticed is that building service engineers and climate engineers in Europe appear to have a different relationship with architects than most mechanical and electrical engineers in the United States. There is more of a partnership of equals and less of a subordinate or sub-consultant relationship. Partly this is cultural; partly it is a result of lower architectural and engineering design fees in the United States, partly the result of the specialized training and experience of the respective parties.

One engineer, Patrick Bellew, president of Atelier Ten in London and one of the United Kingdom's best-known mechanical engineers, told me that engineers in the United Kingdom get almost one third more in fees; factoring in lower wages there, engineers have about twice as much time to spend on a project than in the United States. Inevitably, this extra time is reflected in greater time to study climate and other factors before beginning the design and to participate in more iterations of architectural design.

In the United States, the prevailing attitude in many building engineering firms (and I worked for two of them from 1997 through 2005) is, "I only get paid to design the project once; when the architect has a final design concept, then we'll start our engineering work." As a result of this attitude, there is less integrated design and more of a serial design approach, resulting in more separate systems with greater energy use and higher initial costs. There are also some cultural factors at work; basically, building engineers seldom study architecture, whereas all architects have to take at least one course in building systems. I address alternative approaches to achieving a more integrated design process in a recent book, *Green Building through Integrated Design*.[2]

I also interviewed Andy Ford, director of Fulcrum Consulting, one of the United Kingdom's premier engineering firms.[3] In Chapter 4, their work is profiled in the discussion of engineering systems at the Brighton and Hove Library. Ford says,

> In terms of buildings, right now we're looking at long-term thermal storage, especially interseasonal thermal storage and ways of applying it directly to building construction. That covers normal ground-source heating and cooling. We're looking at how heat flows through the ground, how to replicate what happens naturally (the sun shines on the surface and it conducts heat into the ground), how to enhance that and control the temperatures you get within the ground better so you can then use them to heat and cool buildings. Where we're going at the moment is using pipes, earth tubes and ducts, and direct access by drilling boreholes (wells) and probably most actively pursuing aquifer thermal energy storage (ATES) because it's applicable to very large-scale schemes, and the efficiencies are much higher than other methods. We're looking at interseasonal storage of heat—storing winter's cold for use in the summer and summer's heat for use in the winter, basically.

However, as engineers, Ford and his team are very focused on practicality and deliverability of solutions while keeping things as simple as possible, without using lots of equipment.

What would happen to sustainable engineering design if more engineering firms hired outside their specialized discipline and brought on board scientists of various stripes? I'm guessing that the field would rocket in importance and influence.

EUROPEAN SYSTEMS ALREADY IN USE IN THE UNITED STATES AND CANADA

There are already good examples of European trends taking root in the United States. A good example is the use of underfloor air distribution systems (displacement ventilation approaches). These systems have lifetime economic benefits, including energy savings, better indoor air quality, and lower costs of office churn (changing workstations). They use much less fan energy than conventional overhead ductwork because air is delivered through an underfloor space at very low pressure.

I first became acquainted with these systems in 1997, when a mechanical engineering firm at which I was working designed some of the first such systems in the United States, in Portland, Oregon. At that time, almost all the information on such systems came from Germany; in fact, the manufacturers of the floor diffuser boxes were from Germany. Since that time, hundreds of such systems have been installed in large-floorplate, open-plan office buildings in the United States, despite their higher net first cost of $4 to $7 per square foot.

As another example, a Portland, Oregon–based building engineering firm designed what was (through 2008) the largest LEED Platinum-certified building in the United States (about 412,000 square feet), located in Portland. This project set out to exceed the American Society of Heating, Refrigerating and Air-Conditioning Engineers (ASHRAE) 90.1-1999 energy consumption standard (in effect for LEED projects when the design began) by 60 percent. The principal engineer for the firm, Andy Frichtl, looked at many different approaches to space conditioning and ventilation; he chose as one of several solutions to specify a large number of chilled beams to provide radiant cooling. (Remember, this is in a climate without any significant humidity issues in design.) The chilled beam technology that he found and specified came from Germany. It provides a chilled surface, so that the body perceives a cooler radiant temperature and feels comfortable without relying just on chilled air ventilation.

TRANSSOLAR AND THE NEW SCIENCE OF CLIMATE ENGINEERING

If I had to single out one of the two or three most important developments in Europe over the past decade, something that could dramatically affect how North American architects and engineers approach sustainable design, it would have to be the development of climate engineering as a practical science. And that development can be attributed directly to one person, Matthias Schuler of Transsolar, a climate engineering firm founded in 1992 based in Stuttgart, Germany, with offices now in Munich and New York.

Of course, other engineers have been thinking along the same lines, such as our English colleagues Patrick Bellew, Andy Ford, Bill Watts, and Guy Battle, as well as Michael Bauer and Peter Mösle of DS-Plan (also in Stuttgart), but Schuler has had more international influence.

Transsolar says, "The purpose of climate engineering for building is to ensure the highest possible comfort for occupants with the lowest possible impact on the environment."[4] In particular, Transsolar seeks to go beyond just energy conservation considerations of the building envelope "towards a more holistic design recognizing the interdependence of comfort issues and integration of all building systems and components, by addressing simultaneously daylighting, natural ventilation, air quality, air temperature, acoustics and the well-being of individuals working in the building."

In much of Europe, Germany in particular, much attention is paid to what's called building physics, seeing the building as an active system of constantly shifting internal loads, external loads such as outdoor air temperature and solar gain, and moisture moving into and out of the spaces and interacting constantly with all the materials in the space. Looking at the building as a complex system requires complex modeling tools as well because there are indirect and synergistic effects going on all the time. Within the next 5 years, I think architecture and engineering schools will recognize not only the importance of buildings in managing climate change but also the central role of building physics in the curriculum.

What Schuler and his partners have done is simple and ingenious. They've taken building service engineering (we would call it mechanical and electrical engineering) away from specifying heating, cooling, and lighting systems and back into the full range of "design for comfort" considerations. For example, most engineering systems are specified today using three variables: air movement, relative humidity, and air temperature. The standard approach considers comfort to be achieved when temperature and humidity are located inside a specified range on a psychrometric chart.[5] Air movement is regulated to meet minimum ventilation codes for fresh air supply. Most often, the amount of cooling needed in a modern office building provides adequate ventilation air as well. There's nothing wrong with this approach; it does work, and it provides rapid responses to changing internal loads and a reliable supply of fresh air. The problem is that it is very expensive in both equipment and energy use. In fact, it's impossible to design a low-energy building using mechanical systems alone. And using mechanical systems alone locks in today's technology for at least 25 years, the approximate economic life of the equipment.

Schuler says that, instead, we should start with a person's physiology and psychology and consider how the body responds to surface temperatures, operable windows, direct and indirect solar gain through windows, and so on. We can consider radiant heating and cooling first, exterior fixed and movable shading, stack effect natural ventilation, operable windows, façades that admit fresh air directly, and so on. Looked at another way, mechanical heating, ventilation, and air conditioning (HVAC) systems are a symptom of design failures elsewhere in the building rather than the first place to start with engineering design.

His philosophy is expressed in this statement: "Sustainability in buildings is not limited to merely minimizing the energy requirements for heating and cooling but should consider the entire scope of user comfort, i.e., from a thermal, visual and acoustic perspective." Doing this entails early engagement of the climate engineer, preferably as part of the competition team. Schuler says, "We realized right from the start that it is only by exerting early influence on the architectonic design that noteworthy impact on the future energy consumption and user comfort of the planned building can occur."[6]

I met with one of Transsolar's principals, Helmut Meyer, one afternoon in 2007, in a conference room of the Behnisch Architekten firm. Even this meeting place was emblematic of the close working relationship between the two Stuttgart-based firms. In fact, David Cook, one of the Behnisch partners (and the author of the Foreword to this book), told me that their collaborations are the essence of integrated design. When Behnisch gets a new commission, says Cook, they invite Thomas Auer (a Transsolar partner) over to have a cup of espresso in the kitchen (or on the back deck in good weather) and communicate the basic design approach to him. Then a few days later, Transsolar comes back with a few engineering concepts that work with that particular design concept; from then on, it's an iterative process in which the building systems and architecture are developed in tandem, not in sequence, as is the case with most U.S. projects.[7] Transsolar's approach is not just to give the architect a blank sheet of paper but also to create a climate of discussion and to define the design parameters from the beginning. That way, the architectural designers stay informed about the building physics through the early design process rather than producing a design that is really expensive to build and operate. In my view, when architects and engineers work together as equal partners in this way, great things can be achieved.

In a 2008 interview, Meyer explained further the firm's approach:[8]

Typically the design process here in Europe is kind of like reinventing the wheel. Projects start from scratch. There's the impression that you are doing something completely new. In the U.S., the approach for quite a lot of projects is using the same principles for the production of many similar buildings. Therefore, I think the intent of the design process is different. Of course, the money which is spent on the design process is also typically higher in Europe than in the States. But I think, overall, project costs are really comparable.

I have the impression that the market is much more competitive in Europe. Maybe it's because of the shorter distance between cities. For example, here there are typically five, six, seven, or eight façade manufacturers in competition and that never happens in the U.S. There are one or two manufacturers that control the market. In Europe, if I couldn't find a German façade manufacturer meeting my requirements, there's an Italian one, a Turkish one, and so on.

Transsolar believes that most U.S. buildings are overventilated because the ventilation and space conditioning systems are the same. As a result, quite a bit of bad air is recirculated to avoid losing so much of the coolness to the exhaust air stream. Transsolar prefers to use water as a heat transfer medium, instead of air, because a pound of water will hold 1,000 times as much energy as a pound of air for the same temperature difference (ΔT in engineer-speak).

Transsolar also believes in individual temperature controls wherever possible. Meyer pointed out to me that an automobile is a good example of awful thermal conditions—in the winter it's terribly cold until it gradually warms up, and in the summer it's beastly hot until the air conditioning kicks in—that we willingly put up with because we have control over the temperature settings. The same is true in buildings; if we want workers and other occupants to accept lower temperatures in winter and higher temperatures in summer, for example, then we must give them control over the environment through individual temperature controls, operable windows, and other means.

Transsolar also practices thermoactive slab cooling wherever possible, using radiant cooling, along with operable windows and a small radiator for cold winter days. Displacement ventilation, which provides a single pass of air through a space from below, is used to provide enough ventilation air, even in a building without operable windows. The firm believes in using active slabs that provide both radiant space conditioning and thermal energy storage. The only real drawback of this system is that it has to be operated well because it won't respond as quickly to changes in sunlight, outside temperatures, and internal loads as a standard overhead-ducted air-conditioning system.

Transsolar says that the greatest advantage of a thermoactive slab is that it can use high-temperature water for cooling and low-temperature water for heating. As a result, it's easier to operate the system with natural energies, particularly ground-coupled heat exchangers. During cooling, the heavy reliance on the thermal mass of concrete slabs provides a thermal lag that off-sets peak cooling loads, so that the size of the cooling equipment can be reduced and operating efficiency improved (because the system is operating for less time at partial loads).

Some of the basic design principles involved are deceptively simple, but it's hard to convince clients of their merits:

- No deep plan floors are included because they don't give good outdoor views or daylighting.
- Everyone has to have adequate daylighting; a daylight factor of 2 percent is minimal. If windows are 5 feet high, then the interior office depth can't be much more than 25 feet from the windows, far less than in most U.S. office buildings.
- Double-skin façades are useful where they can serve a variety of functions, such as providing natural ventilation, improving climate control, protecting exterior shading, and providing acoustic buffering.
- The use of HVAC is reduced by the use of radiant slabs; this also means there is no need for suspended ceilings in buildings (in fact, they work against this system), but it does mean floor coverings can be normal carpet, for acoustic control. In this case, there may be perimeter decentralized heating units because these zones are likely to be cold in winter.

There are a lot of subtle variations to Transsolar's approach. One favorite new project of mine is a 690,000–square-foot, twenty-two–story headquarters office for Manitoba Hydro in Winnipeg, Canada designed by KPMB, Toronto. The annual temperature swing in Winnipeg is nearly 75° Kelvin (135°F), from –40°C (–40°F) in winter to 35°C (95°F) in summer. Winter air is completely dry, and summer air is humid (think Minneapolis in the United States). It's also a very windy region; Winnipeg has been described as the windiest large city in North America. Quite a challenge for climate engineering! Thomas Auer's proposed solution is a twenty-two–story thermal chimney integrated with the architecture on the north side of the building to promote natural ventilation, as shown in Figure 6.1. On the south side is a six-story chain of nearly 300 flat Mylar strips, with water running down them. In the winter, the water evaporates inside the building, adding moisture to the dry air to make it more comfortable. In summer, the water is cooled, adding cooling to the building and condensing water from the humid air to reduce humidity, also making the interior more comfortable. And it's an art feature as well.

At Harvard University, for the Allston Science Complex, research labs that need tight environmental controls take up 50 percent of the total space. In this case, the design approach is to slow down the air movement, to reduce pressure drops in the ventilation systems that use more energy. The project will also use an enthalpy wheel, a technology that allows outgoing air to give up much of its heat or coolness to incoming air (depending on the season), saving as much as 50 percent of air-conditioning costs.

For the bioscience complex (expected completion 2010), with a gross floor area of about 1.1 million square feet (100,000 square meters), Behnisch Architekten and Transsolar are teaming up to redefine the environmental performance of a state-of-the-art lab, with a goal of reducing primary energy consumption by more than 60 percent compared with a reference standard lab building. Progressive design standards at this lab include

- Use of geothermal sources, or ground-coupled heating and cooling
- Tempering of incoming air through a supply air duct in the ground
- Natural ventilation
- Advanced methods of heat recovery and reuse, including returning air from offices for use in the laboratories (to reuse the already cooled or heated air)
- Roof gardens
- Interior winter gardens
- Rainwater recovery and reuse
- Specific wind and solar integrated strategies
- Sophisticated façade systems
- Daylight enhancement systems
- Wind turbines for power production

Speaking of the design process for the Harvard lab, Meyer says,

FIGURE 6.1 Manitoba Hydro's climate engineering by Transsolar aims to reduce energy use by 60% in one of the harshest urban environments in North America. KPMB's design creates a productive work environment for nearly 2,000 employees of the provincial utility company. *(Gerry Kopelow/Photographics, Inc.)*

We started by shadowing laboratory researchers, and out of that we defined an idea to separate the lab space itself from office space, which allows us to reduce air changes in the workspace through a zoning approach. We introduced enthalpy wheels for total energy recovery. It was not possible to use them for lab exhaust due to the pollutants in the exhaust air. However, in the past couple years, coatings for enthalpy wheels were introduced that minimize the risk of reintroducing contaminants into the makeup air. We reduced the number of air changes in general to the hygienic minimum [which saves lots of energy]. We have natural ventilation for the workspaces, a high-performance façade, and exterior shading for solar and glare control. The building is aiming for LEED Gold.

Many of the systems listed here are already in use individually or in groups for various high-performance projects around the United States and Canada. What makes Transsolar's work unique and valuable is the tight integration with the architectural design and with each other, all based on careful studies of the local climate conditions. After all, we are talking about climate engineering first and foremost.

Schuler believes that the rapidly growing concern about climate change and the need to minimize energy use in buildings will have a dramatic effect on how architects approach sustainable building. He believes that the planning team should set "the target of a sustainable building as a basic requirement" for any project, which will then result in "improved comfort and reduced energy consumption." In 2003, he said that "the architecture of today should accept the fact that limited energy resources and climate protection are now a fact of life, as is the case with fire protection or universal access issues, and use this as a basis for creating new ideas."[9]

SCHÜCO E-SQUARED FAÇADE CONCEPT

Another example of European technology that is making its way into U.S. practice is building-integrated photovoltaic (PV) panels, which were pioneered by another German manufacturer of building façades, Schüco. Based in Bielefeld, Germany, near Düsseldorf, using its "E-Squared" technology, Schüco marries efficient building façades with amorphous silicon PV cells to provide both glazing and energy production. An early example of the Schüco approach was the Solar Office at Doxford, England, highlighted in the Introduction. In the Schüco E-Squared façade concept, PV panels are integral with the façade but married with solar shading and other climate control and comfort systems. You can see the results in Figure 6.2.

Architect Stefan Behnisch thinks that façades are destined to play an increasingly important role in sustainable design solutions. He says,

> Planning more sustainable buildings certainly has an impact on the form and façade of buildings, but it also impacts on several other aspects. It affects the materials used and the opening vents, to name but two examples. The use of suspended ceilings is also certain to disappear over time. The thermal mass of the building is needed to stabilize the interior climate conditions. This affects not only the height of a building—it markedly reduces the volume, but also the appearance in the façades. Moreover, buildings will have to be oriented more towards the direction of the sun in future, i.e. south-facing façades will definitely be more closed than north-facing façades. Daylight control systems can then be used to light from the north deep into the building.[10]

So products such as the integrated PV–solar shading–glare control–natural ventilation façade are going to be more a part of building design in the future.

Here's what Schüco has to say about the technology behind the E-Squared façade:[11]

FIGURE 6.2 Schüco creates well-functioning façades that provide photovoltaic power, solar control, and natural ventilation. *(Schüco International KG)*

The Schüco E^2 Façade is a new façade system that saves and generates energy at the same time. This is made possible by incorporating intelligent building technology into the façade. The integration of photovoltaics, solar thermal transfer, thermal insulation, solar shading and decentralized mechanical ventilation with heat recovery provides consistent automation for floor-to-ceiling glazing. The result is maximum energy efficiency, economical building construction, a high-quality appearance and optimum comfort levels. At the same time, the functional units in the façade are a design feature of a new architectural style.

The aim is to achieve the best energy balance with maximum comfort for a wide variety of opening types. The façade profiles accommodate all the service and wiring systems and provide intuitive operating devices that have been integrated into the façade mullions.

Peter Mösle is a principal engineer of leading engineering firm DS-Plan in Stuttgart and a co-author of their 2007 book *Green Building: Concepts for Sustainable Architecture*.[12] Mösle expects that life-cycle operating costs will become increasingly important for real estate. Rising energy costs are a reason green technologies will become ever more important. DS-Plan's designs share many common approaches with Transsolar's; after all, they're in the same city.

TECHNOLOGY OVERVIEW[13]

My research into European techniques had two goals: to give North American engineers and contractors a heads-up about future technology changes and to encourage them to go to Europe and see for themselves how these systems work. We also found that some of the leading engineers from the United Kingdom have already set up shop in the United States (because language is not a barrier) and are actively including these approaches in their U.S. projects. These firms include Arup, the largest building engineering firm in the world (with ten U.S. offices) and Atelier Ten, a leading U.K. firm with one office in New York. Transsolar has also designed a number of high-performance projects in the United States and Canada.

In this section, I'll present selected European building system technologies and their status or potential for adoption in North America. I'll describe each building system technology conceptually and provide some considerations for design and application. I'll also include some brief descriptions of challenges and impediments to adoption in the North American markets. There are many more, of course, but the two core technologies about which you may not know enough are radiant heating and cooling systems and active façades.

Radiant Heating and Cooling

Radiant heating and cooling systems rely exclusively on the distribution of hot or chilled water throughout a building structure, as opposed to more conventional systems that rely on the distribution of cool or hot air using ducts. As the name suggests, radiant systems directly heat or cool the occupants through radiant heat transfer, as opposed to convection (air movement). Depending on the type of radiant system applied in a given building, the systems may also take advantage of the thermal mass of the building structure.

In the United States, radiant systems are used almost exclusively for heating and are becoming increasingly common in residential and selected commercial projects. In Europe, radiant systems are in broad use for both residential and commercial applications and for both heating and cooling.

Concept

Radiation is the most significant heat transfer mechanism between the human body and its surroundings. Other means in order of magnitude include convection, conduction (direct transfer), and perspiration (evaporative cooling). Therefore, radiant systems provide the best environment for human comfort. In both radiant heating and cooling systems, the preferred installation location is overhead in or on the ceiling, where it mimics the overhead sun and clear night sky effect that we know well and to which our bodies are quite accustomed. For example, I like to sit outside my desert home after a hot day and feel the coolness of the night sky.

The most important caveat for using radiant cooling and heating systems is that they do not provide ventilation, and a complementary outdoor air system typically is needed for ventilation purposes. Furthermore, radiant cooling systems provide only sensible temperature control and do not account for latent temperature, or humidity, control. In the case of radiant cooling systems, the potential for surface condensation (particularly in warm, humid climates) presents a significant concern, and depending on climate, humidity management may require a separate, complementary system to control moisture levels.

Energy and Cost Benefits

There are great energy benefits from using radiation for heating and cooling. Water has a much higher heat capacity than air. A pound of water will hold 1,000 times as much energy as a pound of air, and it takes far less energy to move a small amount of water around in tubes than to blow huge volumes of air to transfer the same amount of heat or coolness. As a result, the fans needed for ventilation can be smaller and their cost and energy use much smaller. The main drawback is that these systems do not respond instantly to changes in the environment, so they must be managed more carefully. Figure 6.3 shows the basic concept of radiant heating and cooling.[14]

There are three common physical means of facilitating heat transfer between the water and the building occupants:

Panels and Beams

Metal panels or beams containing tubing are surface mounted, embedded on floors, walls, or ceilings, or suspended from ceilings. Figure 6.4 shows a typical chilled beam, integrated with fire sprinklers and lights.

Slabs (Embedded Tubes)

Plastic tubes are embedded in the structure to provide a conduit for water, and the structure acts as thermal storage and radiant surface. This is typically done with a high–thermal density concrete slab (sometimes called an active slab) in the floor or ceiling. Tubes can also be run below other flooring materials, including wood floors and carpet, using special subfloor or insulating panels. This option is less effective because there is more insulation and less mass than when a concrete slab is used.

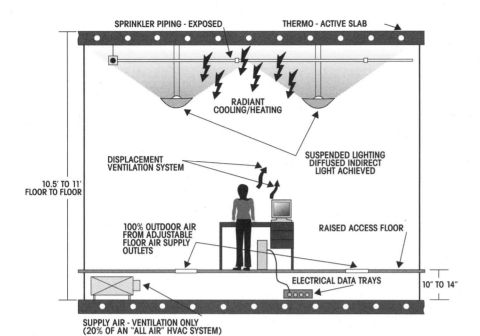

FIGURE 6.3 European designs make far greater use of radiant heating and cooling, an approach just beginning to be adopted in North America. *(Geoff McDonell/Consulting–Specifying Engineer, redrawn with permission)*

FIGURE 6.4 Chilled beams can integrate cooling with lights and sprinklers to provide a fully integrated climate control system in office buildings. *(TROX Multi-Service Chilled Beam)*

Capillary Tubes

In this approach, mats containing small, closely spaced tubes are embedded in plastic, gypsum, or plaster on walls or ceilings. The end result is similar to a slab. This type of installation is more common in smaller installations, including homes.

In all three methods, a mechanical system is responsible for cooling or heating the water. Such systems may include a chiller or chiller plant; heat pumps, including ground source (geothermal) heat pumps; a boiler or boiler plant; a cooling tower; or even well water, river or lake water, or other groundwater sources.

Benefits

Radiant heating and cooling systems excel in energy efficiency and human comfort.

- Because nearly half of the heat transfer between human beings and their surroundings occurs via radiation, radiant heating and cooling systems provide superior human comfort.
- Radiant systems are nearly silent, especially compared with noisy air movement in poorly designed systems.
- Decoupling sensible temperature control from ventilation allows improvement in indoor air quality, with elimination of air recirculation.
- Radiant systems generally use less energy than forced-air systems (with one reference estimating a 30 percent average savings, and a range of 17 percent to 42 percent potential energy savings in North American climates).[15]
- A building constructed using thermoactive slabs may consume up to 70 percent less energy than an equivalent conventional building with an all-air system.[16]

Challenges and Impediments

Radiant heating and cooling systems present a variety of challenges and impediments when it comes to use in commercial buildings in the United States:

- The design community of architects and engineers in the United States is not familiar with radiant systems, especially radiant cooling systems. Engineers are reluctant to venture into unfamiliar territory or put their stamp of approval on unconventional methods.
- Likewise, the construction community is not as familiar with radiant systems, and current methods of building construction are deeply embedded. This may make it harder to get reasonable bids for installing such systems.
- Humidity management and surface condensation potential present complexity and unfamiliar territory, especially in warm, humid climates.
- An integrated design approach is necessary, requiring coordination and collaboration across building design disciplines and trades. This runs counter to the conventional approach in the United States.
- Common energy modeling and building design tools do not all account for radiant heating and cooling systems. This makes it more challenging to meet state energy codes and to achieve credits in systems such as LEED.
- There is a common perception that radiant systems are more expensive from a first-cost perspective. Especially because some of the important suppliers of radiant systems manufacture products in Europe, it can be costly to import these products.

Active Façades

An active façade is any side of a building whose optical and thermal properties may change dynamically in response to local climate, occupants' preferences, or ambient lighting.

Active façades may also be adaptations of static façades or incorporate features of static façades, as shown in Figure 6.5. These static façades and their features include

- Double façades, ventilated and unventilated
- Daylighting, using sunlight redirection, light shelves, or overhangs
- Solar control, using selective glass
- Integrated electrical generation using PV cells

Lastly, a building automation and energy management system typically initiates and coordinates action of the active façade.

Concept

As described earlier, various mechanisms are combined to produce a building façade that changes its optical and thermal properties dynamically in response to various inputs. Common applications take forms that include

- Single façade with external light-deflecting sun shades
- Single façade with integrated shade or blinds
- Double façade, ventilated, with interstitial shading (Figure 6.6)

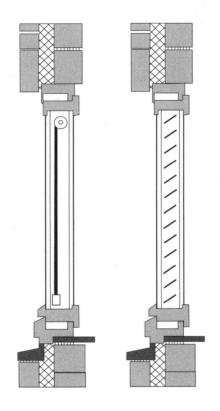

FIGURE 6.5 Single-façade buildings with integral solar control can reflect sunlight away while still admitting enough light for daylighting.

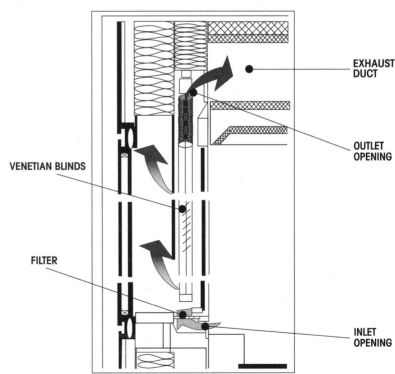

EXHAUST DUCT

OUTLET OPENING

VENETIAN BLINDS

FILTER

INLET OPENING

FIGURE 6.6 Double-façade buildings provide natural ventilation as well as solar and glare control solutions.

Benefits

The application of active façades is often driven by the desire to produce naturally lighted spaces in a building while minimizing solar thermal loading and glare. This desire is sometimes compounded by rating systems and building codes that impose minimum requirements for daylighting. Benefits of active façades include positive impacts on energy use and occupant comfort. Active façades provide a number of benefits, including

- Solar control, admitting or deflecting heat
- Daylighting control and natural lighting
- Glare reduction
- Reduced energy consumption through active load management or integration with demand response

Application

Active façades often include combinations of technologies. For a given building design, the combination usually is somewhat unique. Such combinations may include

- Double façades, with or without ventilation
- Interior shading (automated)
- Exterior shading (automated)
- Integrated PV cells
- Switchable glass (electrochromic, photochromic, or thermochromic)

Somfy is a French manufacturer of dynamic façades. I first encountered them in the fall of 2007 when I was invited to give a talk to a conference for architects in Frankfurt that Somfy sponsored. At that time, they were retrofitting Foster's Commerzbank building with external

FIGURE 6.7 Equally important with daylighting in buildings is keeping the sun out when you don't want it and controlling glare, solutions provided by Somfy's dynamic façade systems. *(Somfy)*

computer-controlled shutters. Somfy provides dynamic façade controls in the form of movable shades and shutters to many commercial and residential buildings. Figure 6.7 shows how this type of solar control allows office workers to have both daylighting and glare control at the same time.

In Europe, many factors are driving changes in façade design and the use of active components:

- Many European architects are designing projects with a high percentage of clear glass. The use of shading is needed to reliably cool the interior spaces.
- In Germany there are strict work rules that require all office space to be located in close proximity to daylight from a window or a skylight. As a result, offices typically are designed with a large amount of glass. Often this goes further to include operable windows or other forms of natural ventilation. The use of an active façade allows natural ventilation even for projects that may have extreme wind loads or high levels of ambient noise.

Challenges and Impediments

Active façades present a variety of challenges and impediments when it comes to use in commercial buildings in the United States and Canada:

- Active façades are not a mainstream building technology, and the design community of architects and engineers in the United States is not generally familiar with them.
- An integrated design approach is necessary, requiring coordination and collaboration across building design disciplines and trades. This is counter to the conventional approach.
- In the United States, engineers with façade expertise are not involved early enough in the design process (by architects).
- Some of the technologies used can be quite costly. For example, double envelopes or switchable glass is costly compared with more conventional façades or glass.
- Developers in the United States often demand less than a 3-year payback on building systems based on energy costs alone, whereas their European counterparts take a longer-term approach.
- In many European Union countries, there are codes that require access to adequate amounts of daylight and fresh air. This is generally not the case in the United States.
- In the United States and Canada, no single engineering discipline is responsible for shading and blinds. Consequently, this item is often neglected. In Europe, it is often the mechanical engineering discipline that is responsible for solar control systems, including shading and blinds. A new profession of façade engineering is developing that may rectify this situation over time.

Control Implications

The controls of active façade systems typically have both manual and automatic elements. On many systems the occupants are able to manually open and close windows on the inner façade layer. Because these windows are protected by the outer façade, there is little impact from weather or risk of noise intrusion. Some approaches also use active control elements such as systems to automatically open and close windows, vents, and dampers based on temperature, weather conditions, and emergencies such as fire.

The blinds used in active façade systems also require control. On many installations the blinds used either on the exterior of the building or within the layers of the façade are controlled in an automated fashion based on the position of the sun and the amount of sunlight present. On a sunny day, it is not unusual for "big brother" to have the blinds closed for several hours a day. This allows a dramatic reduction in solar gain but requires coordination and training for the occupants to make them comfortable with this concept. Often the user is allowed to override the automatic operations of the blinds or to control a second set of blinds that are provided solely for glare control. The control of blinds is typically done independently of the control of interior lighting.

WHAT'S ON THE HORIZON?

What we've presented here is just a sample. As an example of an approach that can be used in colder climates, consider the Swedish TermoDeck system, introduced to me by Andy Ford, president of Fulcrum First in London and shown in Figure 6.8.[17] Based on the principle of using thermal mass to moderate temperature swings in a building, this system essentially places the ductwork inside the precast concrete slab of an office building and provides passive cooling via a ventilated hollow-core slab. The interconnection of the hollow core slabs establishes the air paths, through which cooled or heated air is discharged via ceiling diffusers to the indoor spaces.

TermoDeck uses a fan-assisted ventilation system to push treated fresh air through a series of ducts formed within the individual concrete ceiling and floor slabs. As the air passes along the ducts, the concrete warms or cools the fresh air before supplying it to the occupied space.

The effects of using the heat storage capacity of hollow core slabs vary between summer and winter conditions. Surplus heat, generated from body heat, lighting, computers, and solar radiation, can be stored in the slabs, increasing their temperature by 2–3°C (35–37°F) during the day without affecting the comfort of the occupants.

In the summer this excess heat is dissipated from the slabs by cool night air in temperate climates or conventional chillers in hot climates, but up to 50 percent less capacity is needed than for conventional technologies. The fans keep running up to 24 hours a day, so more fan energy is needed for this technology.

In cold climates during winter heat is stored in the slabs overnight to maintain comfortable internal conditions for the occupants the next day. In some hot climates during winter, the cool night air alone can cool the structure, without the need for chillers, to provide comfortable conditions by the next morning.[18]

For example, for a new campus for the University of East London, adjacent to the London City Airport, engineer Edward Cullinan provided ventilation and air conditioning for a building sealed all along its south side, a planning stipulation because of aircraft noise. He encouraged the designers to use the TermoDeck heating and cooling system for 40 percent of the cost of conventional air conditioning.[19]

As another example of the utility of this system, the 33,000–square-foot (3,000–square-meter) Elizabeth Fry Building at the University of East Anglia in the United Kingdom, designed by Fulcrum, uses the TermoDeck system in a precast concrete slab, resulting in a total heating energy demand of 25 kilowatt-hours per square meter per year (about one sixth the demand of a

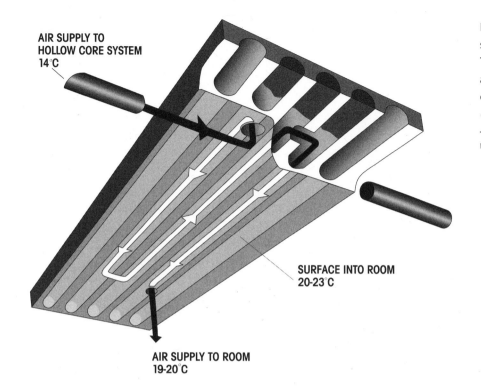

AIR SUPPLY TO HOLLOW CORE SYSTEM 14°C

SURFACE INTO ROOM 20-23°C

AIR SUPPLY TO ROOM 19-20°C

FIGURE 6.8 A unique solution to natural ventilation, TermoDeck tempers outside air with the thermal mass of the concrete slab. *(Courtesy of TermoDeck International, Ltd., redrawn with permission)*

typical "good" U.S. building).[20] Ford's firm also designed the Brighton Library, using a three-story TermoDeck system. Ford's basic philosophy is "simplicity, not systems." He says that if one pays attention to building physics, one doesn't really need systems.

In 2007, a commercial building in Leeds, U.K., the $11-million, 50,000–square-foot (4,500–square-meter) "Innovate Green Office" at Thorpe Park, designed by Rio Architects and King Shaw Associates, was awarded the highest-ever Building Research Establishment Environmental Assessment Method rating of 87.5 percent, using a TermoDeck system.[21] Energy savings for the building are estimated at $2.60 per square foot per year, close to 10 percent of the projected rent.

The building system technologies presented in this chapter are great approaches to green design but not universally applicable. Radiant heating and cooling systems and active façades are more popular in Europe, where the engineering and design community presents a more progressive approach to building system technologies. However, interest in such systems in North America is growing. Around the world, building system integration and operator–user interface continues to be an area of interest and growth, especially for high-end projects and multiple-building environments. In all cases, any building design team must consider many factors when evaluating the use of building system technologies, including the following:

- In overall building design, the purpose and intent of the building must be considered as well as the architectural design approach.
- Climate is a major determinant in what types of systems are viable and will best serve a building and its occupants. For example, heating and cooling systems that work well in the

moderate climates of Western Europe may not work as well in the more extreme climates in many parts of the United States.

- The economics of a given building project are a key element in the design process and must be factored into key system decisions.

In the United States, the preference is still for buildings with the lowest initial cost, even those with higher operating costs. This approach prevents engineers and architects from making sensible decisions that will result in far more energy-efficient, sustainable buildings.

WHAT CAN WE USE TODAY?

We put that question to Tim McGinn, an engineer and principal at Calgary-based Cohos Evamy architects and engineers. Tim is one of the leading practitioners of sustainable design in Canada and also a national speaker for ASHRAE, the mechanical engineers' professional society. Here's his list of ten technologies and approaches that might have good transferability from Europe to North America:[22]

- Design briefs concentrating on low-carbon design rather than solely a low-energy design, where the low-carbon design would include embodied energy
- Use of earth tubes to preheat outdoor air
- Decoupling of ventilation and cooling, predominantly using displacement ventilation with radiant cooling (chilled ceilings, low-temperature heating, and higher-temperature cooling systems)
- Increased use of high thermal mass in thermally active building systems, including slabs
- Mixed-mode (fan-assisted) natural ventilation through a central stack atrium also used for daylighting
- Chilled beams (to a limited extent in the right applications)
- On-site use of renewable energy, from wind and solar, to geothermal, and moving toward co-generation or tri-generation systems with biomass fuel
- District cooling and heating to allow more effective application of renewable energy toward a low-carbon approach
- A well-developed market that can support equipment manufacturers providing space-effective, modular packaged systems that provide high efficiency and reliability (for such applications as graywater reuse, rainwater reuse, heat recovery ventilation, solar domestic water packages, and integrated boiler heating systems)
- Exterior active solar control systems, such as movable shades and shutters

I think this is a pretty good list. Every one of these systems can be engineered and built in the North American climatic and cultural conditions. None of them requires new technology. Many of these approaches are already being used by more determined green architects and engineers, such as underfloor air distribution systems, light shelves, and displacement ventilation systems. However, one cannot say that they are mainstream yet in any way.

Economic feasibility will always be an issue, as will the availability of well-made products and systems. One experienced European architect now teaching at a major U.S. university told me that he had not seen the quality of manufacturing in American façades, for example, that would allow some of the European systems and approaches to be deployed effectively in the United States. This might be a current gap in the marketplace, but it's nothing that time and clear demand won't resolve.

McGinn also thinks that some very new influences are destined to have a major influence on sustainable design in the United States in the very near future. These include a focus on low-carbon design, the PassivHaus technology for residential and small commercial applications, thermoactive slabs in buildings that more carefully integrate thermal mass into climate control, fenestration systems using ethylene-tetrafluoroethylene membranes, and ground-source heat pump systems integrated with foundations and piles supporting buildings. Many of these systems are discussed in Chapter 1.

None of the European technologies profiled in this book would have particular difficulty in meeting U.S. and Canadian building codes, but many will not be familiar to North American architects and engineers, let alone the contractors and subcontractors, building operators, and managers who will have to install and operate them. They won't know how to specify them, estimate costs, and procure the systems or components, biasing design and construction decisions back toward tried-and-true approaches. After all, the current built environment is the result of an ongoing dialog between suppliers, designers, specifiers, builders, and users.

CHAPTER 7

Eco-Towns

From Austria to Estonia, England to Sweden, Germany to Denmark, eco-towns are all the rage. Everyone is trying to recreate Eden in the midst of densely settled urban environments. For purposes of definition, an eco-town is a new settlement that tries to dramatically reduce its carbon footprint through a combination of low-energy building, on-site or local renewable energy, renewable transport options, and other means. Such a settlement often emphasizes local agriculture, community gardens, waste recycling, water recycling, and other features of sustainable development.

There is much to be learned from some of these long-standing (15 years or more) projects. In a way, this movement mirrors what's been happening quietly in the United States for the past 15 years, with developments ranging from Civano, in the city limits of Tucson, Arizona, to new suburban and exurban environments such as Terramor at Ladera Ranch in Orange County, California, to a wide variety of new urban districts, typically with some aspect of brownfield redevelopment, such as the South Waterfront in Portland, Oregon and the Dockside Green project in Victoria, British Columbia, Canada.[1] The continental European eco-towns have been a mixture of brownfield redevelopment, urban infill, and waterfront recovery projects. In the case of the United Kingdom, there has been a mix of urban infill and proposed suburban development. European eco-towns typically are supported or even initiated by the national government and attempt to be sustainable in terms of renewable energy supplies while making use of damaged or marginal lands. In a few cases they have grown up organically, through local citizen action, but for the majority, government funding has kick-started the process.

FREIBURG, GERMANY

Freiburg im Breisgau, a city located at the southwestern tip of Germany, where the Danube and Rhine rivers converge, began its ecological experiment in an area known as Vauban in 1993, with a particular focus on solar technology (Figure 7.1).[2] (Until very recently, Freiburg had the largest solar photovoltaic power plant in Germany.)[3]

The southern suburb of Vauban in Freiburg is especially well known for its ecological initiatives, the redevelopment of about 100 acres of former French military barracks into homes for

FIGURE 7.1 Vauban is a classic car-free, low-carbon, self-organized urban revitalization and sustainable urban solution.

(Thomas Schroepfer and Limin Hee, "Emerging Forms of Sustainable Urbanism: Case Studies of Vauban Freiburg and SolarCity Linz," in Journal of Green Building, Volume 3, Issue 2, Spring 2008)

5,000 residents. In Vauban, the energy use is 70 to 100 percent below German standards, with 65 percent of power from renewable sources, primarily wood chips.[4]

Vauban was planned with a clear set of ideals or guiding principles that are modeled throughout Europe in designing new towns or new urban districts:[5]

- Diversity of residents, with a mix of private and public housing
- Design by choice, with individual architects working with small client groups
- Self-organizing communities, formed before the first buildings are erected
- Open-ended development, with flexible planning and design
- Good public spaces at different scales
- Environmental urbanism, with car-reduced neighborhoods, backed by good public transit, put in place before construction begins

The specific tools put in place include the following:[6]

- Sustainable building regulations, especially promoting greater density, green roofs, and rainwater harvesting.
- A nonprofit corporation to facilitate everything, now called Stadtteilverein Vauban, or "Forum Vauban," founded in 1994. (This is very different from the U.S. model of relying almost exclusively on private developers, with community input only at the plan approval stage.)
- Community building activities from the inception of the project.
- Use of existing buildings for student housing and community programs (the French military barracks).
- Mobility enhancement, with light rail and bus stops within 500 meters of all buildings.

- Redesign of the streetscape to serve pedestrians as well as cars, with traffic calming devices including very low speed limits (30 kilometers per hour [less than 20 miles per hour]).
- Green spaces, including preservation of existing trees, with bioswales for rainwater recovery and recharge.
- Environmental measures, with annual heating energy consumption below 65 kilowatt-hours per square meter per year (note that this is well above the PassivHaus and Minergie standards and is likely to be reduced dramatically in coming years).

LINZ, AUSTRIA

SolarCity is a public housing initiative in a new city quarter of Linz, Austria. Linz is Austria's third largest city, with a population of about 190,000 people.[7] The original SolarCity plan calls for a model residential community with a population of up to 6,000 people. The first phase began in 1994, with an initial 630 low-energy homes. By 1996, twelve nonprofit corporations were committed to building homes in SolarCity. Germany's Herzog and Partners built some of the original homes, along with Richard Rogers and Norman Foster from the United Kingdom. Germany's Atelier Dreiseitl provided the landscape planning and architecture.[8]

SolarCity is linked to the central city of Linz by streetcar. The overall aim is to have a car-free environment, as far as possible, with a density of about twenty people per acre, not unlike a typical "zero lot line" suburban development in the United States, factoring in household size. Building heights are kept low, to three stories. Overall, this is a model suburban rather than urban community, with strong open space preservation, making future growth rather difficult. Unlike in Vauban, there is little public engagement in planning, as the entire project stems from the city government.

MALMÖ, SWEDEN

Malmö is a city well known for its sustainability initiatives. Located very close to Copenhagen, Denmark, this Swedish city of 270,000 is frequently cited as the model for sustainable development. A new project for the city is the redevelopment of its Western Harbour. Called Bo01, City of Tomorrow, this development is an entirely new district in the Western Harbour with room for 600 dwellings as well as offices, shops, and other services on more than 300 acres (Figure 7.2).

The aim is for the district to be a leading example of environmental adaptation in a dense urban environment. It will also be a driving force in Malmö's development toward environmental sustainability. Bo01 is the first development stage of Västra Hamnen (The Western Harbor), one of Malmö's growth areas of the future. The area is typical of redundant industrial land, with contamination from past use as a shipyard. But the area has many positive aspects, especially its location by the Baltic Sea, adjacent to a beach and close to the city center. The city has adopted a fundamental ecological approach to planning, building, and construction as a key tool in the creation of the district.

The city also created a program to make the Augustenborg district into a more socially, economically, and environmentally sustainable neighborhood, called Ekostaden Augustenborg, one of Sweden's largest urban sustainability projects. One of the key aims of the project is to enable

FIGURE 7.2 A new project for Malmöis the redevelopment of its Western Harbor. Called Bo01, City of Tomorrow, this development is an entirely new district with room for 600 dwellings as well as offices, shops, and other services on more than 300 acres. *(City of Malmö, www.malmo.se/sustainablecity)*

FIGURE 7.3 Called Ekostaden (Eco-City) Augustenborg, this is one of Sweden's largest urban sustainability projects. Residents take a leading role in planning, design, and implementation of the eco-friendly program. *(City of Malmö, www.malmo.se/sustainablecity)*

residents to take a leading role in the planning, design, and implementation of the project. The project was launched in 1998, and the results so far indicate that Augustenborg has become an attractive, multicultural neighborhood in which residential turnover has decreased by almost 20 percent.[9]

A number of initiatives have been undertaken throughout Augustenborg to increase resource efficiency by up to 20 percent compared with 1995 levels. Measures to increase energy efficiency have been undertaken throughout the neighborhood, optimizing heating and hot water systems and cutting electricity use.

The residents of Augustenborg questioned why there was no renewable energy production in the area. That became the start of a new project between the city, Malmö University, E.ON Sverige and MKB Fastighets that includes a 450–square-meter (4,800–square-foot) solar thermal plant and 100–square-meter (1,076–square-foot) photovoltaic array, producing hot water for the district heating system and electricity for the homes (Figure 7.3).[10]

VAXJÖ, SWEDEN

Vaxjö is another Swedish city that is committed to sustainability initiatives. Located in southern Sweden, this town of 85,000 people is committed to being the greenest city in Europe. The city's goal is to reduce carbon emissions over time, as a model for the entire country. In 2006, more than half of the town total energy and 90 percent of heating energy came from renewable sources, primarily biomass from Sweden's northern forests, their "green gold." The Swedish government's announced goal is to end dependency on oil entirely by 2020. This transition is aided certainly by a significant carbon tax, in place since 1991.[11]

Since 1993, carbon dioxide emissions per capita have decreased 30 percent, compared with a 10 percent decrease in Sweden as a whole, and gross regional product per capita has increased by nearly 50 percent.[12] Vaxjö's example is engaging the country, and the entire Baltic region, but it wouldn't be nearly as dramatic without the commitment of the national government to an oil-free future, backed up by stiff carbon taxes.

GREENWICH MILLENNIUM VILLAGE, U.K.

In 1997, English Partnerships committed to transforming Greenwich Peninsula—previously the site of the largest gas works in Europe—into a thriving modern community. The Greenwich peninsula is one of the largest development sites in London and one of Europe's biggest regeneration projects. On this site, the Greenwich Millennium Village (GMV) was launched in 1999 and consists of about 1,500 homes, with an ultimate buildout of about 3,000 homes (Figure 7.4). Located in East London in the borough of Greenwich along the Thames River, GMV was built for the government's English Partnerships Millennium community scheme, which raised the bar in terms of new environmental sustainability standards.[13] At the time, GMV was widely considered to be setting new standards for environmental and sustainable development. More recently, the United Kingdom's Department of Communities and Local Government created the Eco-Towns program to build up to sixteen new settlements across the country.

The GMV spreads over 64 acres, with a mix of one- and two-story condos, townhouses, and live–work units, with each group of buildings having a landscaped courtyard. Total public and private investment for development on this former brownfield site was about $1.5 billion.[14] A study by the Building Research Establishment showed that the first 286 units reduced primary energy consumption by 65 percent and construction costs by 12 percent, with a reduction of 70 percent in defects at first occupancy. Construction waste was reduced by nearly 60 percent.

THE CARBON CHALLENGE PROJECT[15]

The Carbon Challenge Project has the principal aim of accelerating the home building industry's response to climate change. Delivered by English Partnerships on behalf of the national Department of Communities and Local Government, this 2008 competition aims to build more than 1,000 homes to Code Level 6, essentially a zero-carbon standard, in four different locations, with about 35 percent apartments and the rest single-family units. Development will be completed in 2011. There will be seven different housing types, and all developments will be built with combined heat and power (CHP) plants, using gas-fired turbines. Waste heat is used to provide hot water for domestic use and for some space heating. The basic idea is to make the community self-sufficient in terms of hot water and heating needs (neglecting the natural gas used to start the process). Although this is focused purely on the individual home level and not on the community level, it is still larger than most home developments.

U.K. ECO-TOWNS PROJECT[16]

Perhaps the most ambitious eco-town program is that announced by the British government in the spring of 2007 to build ten to thirteen new eco-towns on brownfield sites around the country. Inviting proposals from private developers and local town councils, the government proposed these to be models of ecological design, with 5,000 to 10,000 homes each. Each development is to be zero carbon and will be exempted from certain property taxes.[17]

There are many challenges in implementing sustainable urban design for some new towns.[18] First of all, building new towns from scratch outside existing cities takes a lot more energy for transport, first in building the town and then in supporting commutes to existing jobs. So is this really what is meant by *sustainable development*? Second, these developments aren't large enough to afford the infrastructure investment needed to create zero-carbon communities using, for example, district heating systems. Third, there is a question of economic viability. It's easy to build homes but a lot harder to integrate the commercial component. For example, although homes began to be sold and occupied at GMV in 2000, the commercial sector didn't begin leasing until 2006. That's a long wait for a close-at-hand loaf of bread. Therefore, it is unclear whether these experiments are replicable. Finally, forced technology choices are made that may not be the best in the long run. For the Eco-Towns the government wants at least 20 percent on-site renewable energy production, which gets harder as the community gets denser. By forcing investment in expensive on-site solar or wind technology, the directive might preclude better alternatives, such as contracting for off-site wind or wave power energy or integrating the development with existing district heating or CHP systems.

Right now, the estimated additional cost per unit for a Code Level 6 home is £19,000 (about $38,000) on a base cost of £200,000, about 9.5 percent more. This is harder to swallow than it seems, because the goal is to have 30 percent of the units affordable. If the "market rate" homes have to swallow the entire cost increase, that would add about 25 percent to the cost of these homes.

The fate of the government's Eco-Towns program is in doubt for two reasons. First and foremost, in 2008 the United Kingdom experienced the same housing and economic recession difficulties as in the United States. Second, there is growing local resistance to the Eco-Towns concept from established communities. Couple that with the possibility that the current Labour government might not survive an electoral challenge in 2009, and it's possible that the entire program will be put on hold in the near future[19] or deliver far fewer new eco-towns.

As of October 2008, the government was still moving ahead, planning to build up to ten Eco-Towns, with between 5,000 and 20,000 homes built to at least Code Level 4 of the Code for Sustainable Homes. According to one source, "These towns would include at least 30 percent affordable housing, 'high-quality public transport links' and enough community facilities and jobs to avoid them becoming commuter suburbs. Each would be an exemplar in eco-design, with all buildings achieving zero-carbon status."[20]

However, there is strong resistance from the communities where the new towns would be located. This is a classic "not in my back yard" (NIMBY) stance that one sees all over the world; resistance to change is universal, it seems. One source reported that the government has delayed the timetable for announcing the Eco-Towns shortlist, which was set to be published in October 2008 but will not come out until 2009. In one location, Rossington, which is in South Yorkshire, the development has been cut down from 15,000 to 5,000 homes.[21]

Regardless of the fate of the project, there are some interesting aspects to the Eco-Town experiment that bear mention. The first is the very existence of the project itself. It's extremely difficult to create change on a large scale in established cities. Most of the Swedish examples involved smaller districts, brownfield sites, or a massive commitment to change that requires a very stable political order, as is found in Scandinavia. The second is the government's intention to partner with private developers and local governments and to make the entire affair a competition.[22] The third is the government's willingness to subsidize the results, if necessary, with a strong commitment to affordable housing. The fourth is the insistence on strong environmental results such as zero-carbon homes and low-impact transportation.

As originally announced, the program intended to explore the potential to create a complete new settlement to achieve zero-carbon development and more sustainable living using the best new design and architecture. The key features the British government wants to achieve are as follows:[23]

- Places should have a separate and distinct identity but good links to surrounding towns and cities in terms of jobs, transport, and services.
- The development as a whole should achieve zero carbon and be a strong example in at least one area of environmental technology.
- There should be good range of facilities in the town, including a secondary school, shopping, business space, and leisure.
- Between 30 and 50 percent of the units will be affordable housing with a good mix of home sizes in mixed communities.
- There should be a strong organization to manage the town and its development and provide support for people, businesses, and community services.

Whether or not the U.K. Eco-Towns program survives the current economic turmoil, it has already changed the discussion in the entire country about how to proceed with sustainable development and the feasibility of reducing the country's carbon footprint by simultaneously tackling the energy use in housing, transport, and urban settlements.[24] For example, the Swindon town council is working on plans to create the first carbon-negative town in Britain.[25]

TALLINN, ESTONIA

Ecobay is a new master-planned community in Estonia, near the capital of Tallinn, on the Baltic Sea. Sustainability is the driving force behind the plan from Danish architecture firm Schmidt Hammer Lassen.[26]

The design intends to create a modern mixed-use development that will accommodate up to 6,000 people over the next 15 to 20 years. The master plan covers some 481,000 square meters (5,175,000 square feet, or about 120 acres). The aim is to provide housing that cuts conventional energy use by up to 70 percent.

Ecobay is a sustainable urban area located in a natural beauty spot in Tallinn. Adjacent to the Natura 2000 nature reserve on the Paljassaare Peninsula on the Baltic Sea, the site is part raised seabed and part landfill. The master plan provides a range of different building types, creating a new district with housing, shops, primary and secondary schools, commercial development, and green recreation areas. The project also includes extensive redevelopment of the existing harbor front, creating a promenade, marina, restaurants, and cafés. The community design has to take into account strong winds blowing off the Baltic, so it will use a system of artificial dunes spread across the site to afford some separation and wind shielding.

The green agenda supplements and supports the town plan's traditional guidelines with a number of new green prerequisites. Both orientation and massing will respond to prevailing wind conditions and the seasonal trajectory of the sun. The project aims to use sources of alternative energy, energy-efficient building methods, and an appropriate green strategy for infrastructure development. Expansion of public transport with electric-powered buses and trams or light railways is being negotiated with the city authorities in Tallinn. Ecobay will be a benchmark project for sustainable urban development of the future and will exceed the current stringent European Union energy conservation requirements.[27]

The mix of buildings, including residential, commercial, and retail uses, will be designed to minimize the need for auto use. The energy supply for the project will come from geothermal heat, wind energy, and surplus methane gas produced by a nearby wastewater treatment facility.

Ecobay is typical of the many smaller eco-towns growing up around Europe, in and adjacent to existing cities. Most of them are the result of competitions hosted by local authorities, a program of promoting excellence that most North American municipalities should adopt. In fact, it would make sense to have an entire program of international competitions for eco-settlements that would invite the European experience into our communities.

ECOTOWNS SPREAD BEYOND EUROPE

Planners, architects, and engineers from Western Europe, especially the United Kingdom, are beginning to spread the gospel of eco-towns all over the world. Some of the more striking examples include Masdar (designed by Foster + Partners) in the United Arab Emirates (UAE), a carbon-neutral town for 50,000 people in the Arabian desert, and Dongtan Ecocity (designed by Arup), near Shanghai, also aiming at 50,000 inhabitants.

Masdar, Abu Dhabi, UAE

Masdar is a great planning challenge. The UAE has lots of sand, the Persian Gulf nearby, and plenty of sun, so there's land, water, and energy, all available at a cost. Some will argue that there can't really be a sustainable city in the Arabian desert, but I'm willing to let the experiment play out and see how far they get. Others argue that the UAE government is quite serious about sustainability, knowing full well that the day will come when revenues from oil and gas extraction will disappear.[28]

Located near the emirate and city of Abu Dhabi, this 6.5–square-kilometer city expects to house 50,000 people eventually, in accordance with the WWF's "One Planet Living" sustainability standards, which include zero carbon emissions, zero waste generation, sustainable transport, sustainable materials, sustainable food and water, habitats and wildlife, culture and heritage, equity and fair trade, and social health and happiness.[29] The primary decision for this (and every) carbon-neutral city is to ban cars with combustion engines from the central city, to reduce the demand for ventilation in this hot, humid climate.

In terms of design, the first step will be to reduce demand by 80 percent through passive design strategies, such as thermal mass, narrow streets, solar shading, and proper home and building orientation. The basic design principle of the Masdar development is a dense walled city to be constructed in a two-stage phasing that relies on the creation of a large photovoltaic power plant, which later becomes the site for the city's second phase, allowing for urban growth yet avoiding low-density sprawl. Strategically located to be served by Abu Dhabi's principal transportation links, Masdar will be connected to surrounding communities and to the center of Abu Dhabi and the international airport by a network of existing roads and new rail and public transport routes.

The city plans to be car free. With a maximum distance of 200 meters to the nearest transport link and amenities, the compact network of streets encourages walking and is complemented by a personalized rapid transit system. The shaded walkways and narrow streets are designed to create a pedestrian-friendly environment in the context of Abu Dhabi's extreme climate. It also emulates the tightly planned, compact nature of traditional walled cities. With expansion carefully planned, the surrounding land will contain wind and photovoltaic farms, research fields, and plantations, so that the city will be entirely self-sustaining.[30]

In early 2009, the developer of Masdar announced that it planned to press ahead with the $22-billion project by taking advantage of the fallout of the global crisis. The world's first carbon-neutral, zero-waste Masdar City, due to be completed by 2016, seeks to benefit from cost reductions, a lack of business opportunities elsewhere, and strong government support. One executive said, "We will not scale back on our spending because our project cost is going down," adding that raw material and other development costs are falling steadily because of the global economic recession. The project is expected to create 50,000 jobs in Masdar City and add 2 percent to Abu Dhabi's gross domestic product.[31]

Dongtan Eco-City, China

Led by the head of Arup's "Integrated Urbanism" consulting practice, Peter Head, this team has been working since 2005 to plan, design, fund, and build a new town for 50,000 people adjacent to Shanghai. Partnering with its client, Shanghai Industrial Investment Corporation, Arup has plans for renewable energy and water supplies for what it hopes will be the world's first sustainable city.[32]

Dongtan is unique in its island location, wetland environment, and habitat quality. Yet it is close to one of China's fastest-growing cities and sits in the center of a region that is one of the most significant drivers of the global economy.

The Yangtze delta leads China's progress toward economic self-reliance and the growth of its consumer markets. As economic progress continues, the pressure for development in the Yangtze delta increases. As demographic and economic pressures grow, the threat to the Dongtan natural environment has also increased.

As a means of ensuring the continuing protection of the internationally recognized Nature Conservation Area to the east of Dongtan and to capitalize on the unique quality of the local environment, SIIC plans to set the country's highest standards for new development.

Dongtan is located on Chongming, the third largest island in China, at the mouth of the Yangtze River. The 8,600-hectare (20,640-acre) site is adjacent to a wetland of global importance.

The urban area will occupy just one third of the site, with the remaining land retained for agriculture and used to create a buffer zone of managed wetland between the city and the natural wetland.[33]

Dongtan will produce its own energy from wind, solar, biofuel, and recycled city waste. Clean technologies such as hydrogen fuel cells will power public transport. A network of cycle paths and footpaths will help the city achieve close to zero vehicle emissions. Farmland within the Dongtan site will use organic farming methods to grow food.

Dongtan will be a city of three villages, originally planned with a demonstration phase for up to 10,000 people, to be completed by 2010. Arup and its Chinese client hope that the development at Dongtan will represent a turning point in China's frenetic urban growth, incorporating all the economic, social, and environmental principles that combine to reduce the impact on the natural environment and provide a model for future development across China. Because of the global economic crisis and local political issues, this ambitious timetable now seems in doubt.[34]

What can we make of the proliferation of eco-towns? There is a strong movement for recreating urban environments for long-term sustainability, all around the world. These small experiments are no substitute for rehabilitating existing urban and suburban environments with green buildings, energy-efficient retrofits, large-scale renewable energy installations, sustainable transport, and urban agriculture. But they do provide a useful clean slate to try out new land use, planning, and settlement concepts that can gradually be introduced into larger urban environments. Let's hope they succeed beyond everyone's wildest imaginations.

CHAPTER 8

Green Building in the Retail Sector

Throughout this book I've highlighted commercial and institutional green buildings, for offices, schools and universities, public buildings, and large corporations. But environmental sustainability and green building are firmly on the global agenda in every building sector, including in the shopping center industry. There are many paths that shopping center developers and owners can take to create and execute a sustainability program. In the United States, retail construction is the second largest commercial construction sector, so retail buildings are important generators of carbon dioxide emissions that must be controlled.

In June 2008, in London I keynoted the first European green shopping center conference, Centrebuild, hosted by the International Council of Shopping Centers. At the conference it was obvious that the European retail development community is doing a lot to incorporate low-energy design and sustainability concerns into their new projects. At this time, few developers are tackling the refurbishment of existing centers for energy savings, except at normal (8- to 15-year) intervals when the retail environment itself needs major alternations.

Jerry Percy, head of sustainability for the United Kingdom's Gleeds management and construction consulting firm, says,[1]

> We've seen an acceptance of low-energy and sustainable design in the retail sector from some of the key leaders. The owners of most of the retail projects, particularly for new mixed-use developments, are looking to secure anchor stores and subsequent tenants. Because the vast majority of them are public companies, those large organizations have corporate responsibility targets that involve sustainability in their developments. They're setting building performance standards of BREEAM Excellent or Very Good, the LEED Gold equivalent.
>
> What we're finding is that some of the larger retailers are now demanding certain levels of building performance to be incorporated into the core and shell. In the U.K., Marks & Spencer is a good example; they're setting requirements, specifications, and design standards and making them a condition of signing up as the anchor store.

This chapter presents three different approaches taken by European retail developers. Their varied approaches should give guidance to other retailers launching a green agenda.

MULTI DEVELOPMENT, THE NETHERLANDS

Multi Corporation B.V. is headquartered in Gouda, the Netherlands, and is active in twenty-three countries throughout Europe, extending from the United Kingdom to Turkey. In 2007, Multi was named European Retail Developer of the Year at the International Market for Retail Real Estate conference in Cannes.[2]

CEO Glenn Aaronson is a firm believer in changing the world via the "2 percent solution," making things 2 percent better every year, instead of trying to make huge leaps all at once. He believes that any corporation can handle 2 percent change, such as 2 percent higher costs for green buildings and 2 percent per year improvement in results. In the space of 10 years, he notes, "you're then 20 percent better, and it's virtually painless." In his view, the solution to the challenge of achieving sustainability is "getting better" all the time, the well-known approach of continuous improvement. The question is how to audit the changes to make sure that the 2 percent change is happening each year, without backsliding.[3]

Multi's Sustainability Principles

Originally an American investment banker, Aaronson has led the charge at Multi toward incorporating sustainability into every aspect of the company's operations. The first shopping center to use the company's sustainability principles was built in Duisburg, Germany and occupied in the fall of 2008.

Multi has formalized its sustainability commitment into five key principles, known as the 5Es for a Sustainable Future program:

1. Everlasting design: Design should aim at creating flexible and timeless urban spaces that will hold their value far into the future.
2. Ecological footprint: Each project should optimize the use of land and reduce the consumption of resources, by both constructing new buildings more effectively and managing existing buildings more efficiently.
3. Equal benefits: Multi's projects should provide benefits to the local community, through a variety of "give back" programs.
4. Economic vitality: Multi's projects aim to create healthy business environments to ensure financial sustainability.
5. Education for all: Each project should raise public awareness of the changes required to preserve our planet.

Multi's five principles contain operational criteria that reflect Aaronson's belief that if a company holds strong beliefs internally—in this case about sustainability—it is also important to express these values externally.

Turning Principles into Development Activity

With the right focus on customer, shopper, employee, and community benefits, appropriate to time and place, it is straightforward for a company to develop operating guidelines for future development and to begin implementing specific green features.

A statement of core values such as the 5Es begins to suggest synergies to design teams. For example, a focus on light and daylighting immediately integrates with energy efficiency considerations. Studies of daylighting in retail show gains in sales of about 5 percent but also energy savings of about 10 percent of the initial investment per year.[4] Appropriate transport connections begin to reduce the carbon footprint of the development by encouraging more public transit and pedestrian access.

Aaronson strongly supports the use of BREEAM, the U.K. green building assessment and certification standard for shopping centers in the European Union. Aaronson believes that BREEAM is more flexible than other systems such as LEED, that it can be customized to fit many different development situations, and that it is focused appropriately on the social dimension of development, in addition to obvious considerations such as water and energy use.

Forum Duisburg received a BREEAM Very Good rating, about equivalent to LEED Silver or Gold in the United States. Consisting of 59,000 square meters of gross leasable area, the project cost about €170 million ($240 million).[5] The Duisburg project contains a combined heat and power district heating plant. In the main mall, there is an interesting ventilation scheme, achieved by overpressurizing shops by 10 percent (so that air moves out of the shops and rises through the atrium), green roofs, and a direct connection to the local transit line (S-Bahn) below the center.[6]

One interesting approach adopted by Multi is to use each shopping center as a forum for education about sustainability. In the case of the Forum Duisburg project, there is also a social program that trains disadvantaged local people in construction and center operations, in cooperation with the local municipality.

Getting the Entire Company on Board

Multi has gone through a fairly typical progression to reach its current level of commitment to sustainable development activities. Under Arco Rehorst's leadership, a sustainability committee was created in 2006, followed in 2007 by Aaronson's strong commitment to move forward with the committee's recommendations. Rehorst and the committee started with a long list of possible topics, some sixty-three in all, narrowing them down to the top twelve to create a focus for future work.

Each new investment proposal submitted to management now becomes an "investment plus sustainability" proposal in that it details the sustainability achievements that it targets. Each new development will carry tenant guidelines, for example, to set green cleaning standards. The purpose of this approach is to transform investment decisions over time by encouraging development executives to change what they consider to be appropriate considerations away from merely financial issues. In this case, sustainability has to be considered when money is being allocated, or the project is likely to fall by the wayside.

Getting the Customers on Board

Every developer has two sets of customers: directly, the retail tenants, and indirectly, the customers it hopes to attract to the shops. Because sustainability measures typically involve higher costs at the beginning, the developer's dilemma is to persuade the retail tenants to pay higher rents or to persuade the project's investors to accept slightly lower returns. This is an important business problem, but it is likely to disappear in the next 3 to 5 years. As the developed world moves toward sustainable development and tenants want to secure the reputational benefits of locating in green centers, getting green into shopping centers should become easier. Whether tenants will be willing to pay higher rents for these benefits is still an open question.

The problem of potentially lower returns to developers is also likely to be temporary for two reasons. First, the centers with lower energy, water, and waste management costs will be able to demonstrate those reductions in shared operating costs as time goes forward (and therefore have the potential for rent growth and higher real estate valuation); second, developers with green experience are likely to obtain other benefits such as attracting investment capital and recruiting and keeping key employees (a major emerging issue in most advanced economies).[7]

SONAE SIERRA, PORTUGAL

An innovator in the shopping center business, Sonae Sierra offers an integrated approach to owning, developing, and managing shopping centers. Sonae Sierra shopping centers integrate leisure with retail and other services, with a focus on green issues. Based in Portugal, the company currently operates 50 centers, with twenty-eight under development in Portugal, Spain, Italy, Germany, Romania, Greece, and Brazil. For fiscal year 2007, the company reported net operating revenue of €639 million.[8]

Sustainability Commitment

Sonae Sierra's CEO, Álvaro Portela, created a corporate responsibility policy a decade ago,[9] based on the firm "belief that no economic activity can take place in a vacuum."[10] The company was a founding member in 1995 of the World Business Council for Sustainable Development, one of the leading organizations in the field. The ultimate goal is for the business to be "sustainable, in the very long-term meaning of the word."

Sonae Sierra uses an environmental management system (EMS) certified under the ISO 14001 standard; the system is certified by Lloyds. The company's environment manager oversees the application of the EMS to company operations. The key to ISO 14001 is its focus on continuous improvement. Sonae Sierra ensures sustainable buildings by focusing on environmental responsibility in the design, construction, and operation phases. Portela believes that the corporate responsibility policy is essential to their brand, but "like all brand attributes, you have to deliver what you promise to your stakeholders to be taken seriously," hence the importance of each year's corporate responsibility action plan and the EMS system for monitoring performance.

Environmental Management Systems

Sonae Sierra's environmental focus covers four major areas: climate change, water, waste management, and land use. A centralized, online database gathers data for Sonae Sierra's water use, waste, and climate issues. This information generates reports that, for example, call for tighter water use, set annual targets for waste recycling, and provide directions for improving building management systems (BMSs).

Climate Change

The company's stated short-term goal is to reduce greenhouse gas emissions by 10 percent. Sonae Sierra uses the Environmental Standards for Retail Development (ESRD), an internal Internet specification tool, to come up with the best environmental practices in the planning and design of new shopping centers. The tool considers 190 standards that cover issues such as energy, water, waste, transport, health and well-being, site sustainability, and materials. The standards are based on Sonae Sierra's experience, best practices, and certification schemes such as LEED and BREEAM. The standards determine the use of technologies such as solar, ventilation, efficient boilers, air-conditioning units, advanced lighting, and combined heat and power in design. The company is committed to achieving a high rating under the EU's Energy Performance of Buildings Directive, which issues grades of A to G.[11] Furthermore, the company is part of a 3-year project (ending in 2009) called the World Business Council for Sustainable Development's Energy Efficiency in Buildings Project, which delineates the changes necessary to have all buildings become zero-net-energy consumers.

ESRD standards have led to transport impact studies at the design stage. These result in green travel plans, local transport partnerships, and greater use of public transport, walking, and cycling. Furthermore, the company encourages efficient vehicle use through priority lanes, and dedicated parking bays for carpoolers, refueling stations, and alternative-fueled vehicles.[12] Figure 8.1 shows Avenida 8, a Sonae Sierra shopping center in Portugal.

Water

The company's goal is to maintain water consumption at or below 4 liters (1 gallon) per visit per year, a target it claims to have achieved in 2007. ESRD standards require water-efficient designs, such as equipment specifications and water recycling, and wastewater treatment, such as oil and hydrocarbon separators in stormwater. Some of the water-efficient features are rain-

FIGURE 8.1 Avenida 8 in Portugal saves more than 14 million gallons of fresh water annually through rainwater harvesting and water reuse and recycling. The project's on-site energy production also saves 12 tons of greenhouse gas emissions per year. (*Sérgio Guerra, Sonae Sierra*)

water harvesting and graywater recycling, water-efficient sanitary fixtures (such as spray taps and low-flush toilets), efficient irrigation systems, and the use of non–water-intensive native or adapted plant species. Furthermore, to prevent pollution from rainwater runoff, filter drains and porous pavements are used.

Waste

The company's stated goal is to achieve a minimum 50 percent recycling rate and a maximum 30 percent landfill disposal rate. Sonae Sierra conducts site-specific waste management strategy studies to determine the necessary space for waste separation and recycling. The company calls for construction companies to provide reports of their waste management. Furthermore, it encourages tenants to manage waste responsibly, even though it has little control over tenant activities.

Land Use

Sonae Sierra's goal is to use previously developed land for new shopping centers and to protect biodiversity where possible in developing new sites. Where sites have been previously contaminated, the company takes remedial action according to the Canadian Environmental Quality Guidelines or the Dutch Standards for Soil Quality. ESRD standards specify planting indigenous plant species in landscaped areas and favor the use of hedgerows and green barriers.

Implementation Issues

Introducing a major change toward sustainability at the corporate level is not without its challenges. According to Portela, "The main challenge was the company's cultural evolution that we had to create in order to place the corporate responsibility management issues at the core of our strategy and mission. All the company, from board level to the rest of the staff, has to understand and believe that this [policy] is crucial for the growth of the company and it should impact the way we all do business." This challenge implies the need for a continuing "sales job" inside the company, as people are continually brought into the organization and as those inside the company need constant reminders about the mission.

Portela also points out one of the major areas of concern for all developers, saying that "another big issue is how to balance short-term [additional] costs against long-term externalities, since both the environmental and economic benefits are only visible during the operation phase. Only a company [like ours] that holds onto assets, and actively manages them, is able to recoup additional capital costs through reduced running costs."

SHOPPING CENTER TECHNOLOGIES

El Rosal, Ponferrada, Spain. Built to reflect local character, this shopping center achieved ISO 14001 certification for the construction phase. One of the center's environmental features is a solar roof with 600 photovoltaic panels on a 1,500–square-meter area that cost €620,300 (about $840,000). This results in energy production of 132,447 kilowatts per year, with annual savings of €58,300 (about $81,000). At current electricity prices, the company expects to recover the initial system cost after just 9 years for equipment with a 25-year life. On average, emissions are reduced by 48 metric tons of carbon dioxide per year, or 1,200 metric tons over 25 years.

Centro Colombo, Portugal. In this development, Sierra introduced the Green Travel Plan project. It analyzes the transport infrastructure and implements measures to encourage and improve the accessibility of the shopping center by public transport, bicycles, and pedestrians. Furthermore, in customer surveys Sierra asks what form of transport its customers use in visiting the centers so that it can monitor indirect greenhouse emissions.

Centro Vasco da Gama, Portugal. This project uses groundwater from a nonpotable water supply. The investment for the system consists of a pumping station and treatment equipment. Monthly water consumption has been reduced by 530 cubic meters (142,000 U.S. gallons), a saving of approximately €100 ($145) per month, corresponding to 11 percent of total water consumption. According to the company, the initial system investment was recovered in 2007, with an annual cost saving equivalent to €11,900 ($17,255) per year in the following years.

SES DEVELOPMENT, AUSTRIA

Filipa Fernandes is head of sustainability for a large Austrian-based developer, SES Spar European Shopping Centers. She led their sustainable development of the Europark center in Salzburg, Austria (Figure 8.2), which won several awards for the sustainability strategies at this project, including the International Design and Development Award in 2007 from the International Council of Shopping Centers. In Europark Salzburg, the nearly 51,000–square-

FIGURE 8.2 Europark in Salzburg received the industry's international award in 2007 for the most sustainable shopping center. *(SES Spar European Shopping Centers)*

meter (550,000–square-foot) shopping center contains 130 shops. It opened originally in 1996 and was later expanded by 20,000 square meters and reopened in late 2005. Europark sets a benchmark with its use of sustainable materials, its climate control system, and its reuse of the energy in exhaust airflow for heating incoming air.

Another important project for SES, and one that also garnered its share of awards, is the Atrio center, at the intersection of Italy, Austria, and Slovenia, in the Austrian province of Carinthia, town of Villach. Completed in 2007, the project's sales area is 38,000 square meters (400,000 square feet), with eighty-two shops, and it cost about $140 million. Unique to this project is the use of ground-coupled energy for heating and cooling, with 652 geothermal energy piles containing piping driven into the ground, supplying about 7,000 kilowatts of heating and cooling energy. The project uses trans-seasonal storage, with waste heat from summer cooling stored in the ground to facilitate winter heating. This has the major advantage of removing cooling towers from the roof and reducing exterior noise levels dramatically. The project saves an estimated 500 metric tons of greenhouse gas emissions per year.[13]

LESSONS LEARNED

Shopping center developers can create a meaningful sustainability program in many ways, yet there are common themes in the approaches that Multi, Sonae Sierra, and SES have taken, which provides a framework for corporate sustainability efforts not only in the retail sector but more broadly. The five common themes among the programs highlighted in this chapter are CEO leadership, internal and external communication, knowledge management, education and training, and corporate operations.

These common themes have contributed to the achievements of their sustainability programs and also underpin the successful programs of other companies.

First, CEO leadership is essential to any sustainability program. Without top-level leadership, nothing much happens beyond the operational adjustments that many firms are making to respond to higher energy prices and greater focus of local governments on green issues. Particularly in this time of retrenchment in the development industry, it is important for key employees to know that the CEO regards sustainability as essential to the organization's future and that they should spend time on this initiative. For Sonae Sierra, Portela made environmental responsibility a cornerstone of the company's development program many years ago.

Second, from the outset there must be an active communication program, both inside and outside the organization. Each of these companies has been active at getting its employees committed to the program and in getting external recognition for its sustainable achievements, especially through award programs.

Third, the organization needs to commit to education and training of its employees. In the case of the three developers, each company has a point person responsible for the success of its sustainability initiatives. For Multi, technical director Rehorst led the way by engaging the country managers to become advocates for the program through a training and monthly learning program. For Sonae Sierra, training its people in the ISO 14001 system was a critical element in gaining acceptance for the system. For SES, Fernandes has been the sparkplug for directing their achievements.

Fourth, the organization must be determined from the beginning to capture the lessons learned through its attempts to build certified centers and to create green operations programs for existing centers. The organization needs to capture cost data and determine which of its design consultants, contractors, and vendors are most cooperative and knowledgeable about sustainability issues.

Finally, the company needs to green its own operations. This means engaging employees with "personal sustainability" projects, reducing overall fuel use, perhaps buying carbon offsets for travel, implementing environmentally preferable purchasing programs, supporting employee car sharing and public transit use, and a host of other programs that show a strong corporate commitment to sustainability.

The retail industry in Europe is just beginning to wake up to the sustainability theme, but one can already see good examples of leadership in this arena. I fully expect that there will be a widespread movement to green building in European shopping centers, with the consensus that BREEAM will be the rating standard and with the growing number of European retailers who are embracing green and who would be the tenants in these centers. With its stronger environmental ethos, the European public is also more likely to reward green shopping centers with its patronage, although there are scant data at this time to support this thesis.

CHAPTER 9

Looking to the Future

W hat does the future hold for European green design? I think it's obvious that low-energy designs will dominate the future but also that BREEAM and LEED rating systems, or their variants, will spread, forcing European architects and engineers to open up their thinking to the broader concerns of sustainable design, including land use, water recycling, renewable energy, sustainable materials, and indoor environmental quality.

Here's a look ahead at a few trends that are likely to be more prominent in the future. The key to a low-energy outcome is to set stretch goals for the entire society, as we saw in Chapter 7 with the Swedish examples. Swiss researchers have done that with their goal of a 2,000-watt society. Building design and construction, along with existing building renovations, will be increasingly dependent on and driven by the availability of good software to guide results in the right direction, as we show with the Environmentally Viable Architecture (EVA) tool and Calcon's Energy Performance, Indoor Environmental Quality Refurbishment (EPIQR) software. Building designers will become increasingly interested in and guided by post-occupancy evaluations and more interested in the "soft landing" approach to finishing projects and improving the first year of occupancy. The implementation of the European Energy Performance of Buildings Directive (EPBD) will radically change building design and renovations because the penalty for not achieving high-performance results will be that the building's value will be degraded in the marketplace.

Zero-net-carbon buildings will replace zero-net-energy buildings as the goal for sustainable design as people become increasingly concerned about the life-cycle impact and embodied energy of buildings. Product manufacturers are likely to pick up on the Dutch approach to "slim and smart buildings" as they look for ways to integrate new building systems into the construction process, to save time and money in implementing sustainable buildings. Finally, we are already beginning to see the export of European design techniques and sustainable planning practices to Russia, the United Arab Emirates, and China. It won't be long before the same approaches start winning more design competitions in the United States and Canada.

THE 2,000-WATT SOCIETY

Most of the current North American green building rating systems such as LEED and Energy Star look at the percentage of improvement in energy systems, compared with today's existing codes. But the carbon challenge of this generation is to reduce energy use by absolute numbers, to much lower levels than today. Even stretch goals such as those found in the Architecture 2030 Challenge[1] are presented in terms of a 90 percent reduction by 2030 from today's high levels of energy use.

In 1998, the Swiss Federal Institute of Technology presented an alternative approach, not just for buildings but for an entire society.[2] The 2,000-watt society challenges the developed world to cut energy use to 2,000 watts (or 17,520 kilowatt-hours per year) by the year 2050, the current world average. This is a real stretch. Western Europe currently uses about 6,000 watts per capita, and the United States uses about 10,000 to 12,000 watts. This goal implies cutting U.S. energy use by 80 to 83 percent and Western Europe's by 67 percent. Table 9.1 shows what the average Swiss person uses today.[3]

The implications for buildings are clear. Only dramatic cuts in building energy consumption such as those found in the PassivHaus standard and the Architecture 2030 year 2025 goals will be sufficient. Cutting energy use by this much also involves radically reducing the energy use of the existing building stock, changing patterns of urban settlement toward much higher density, aiming at 100–mile-per-gallon autos powered by renewable sources, and so on. Of course achieving this average would mean that Chinese energy use would also have to fall by one third, whereas that of Bangladesh could climb 300 percent (Figure 9.1).

There's one other kicker to this concept. Within 50 to 100 years, 1,500 of the 2,000 watts would have to come from carbon-free sources such as solar, wind, biomass, hydro, and even nuclear, so that the net carbon drain would be only 500 watts, about 4,000 kilowatt-hours per person per year. Multiply that number by 7 billion people, and you still have a lot of carbon emissions, about 28 trillion pounds, or 14 billion tons.[4] (Carbon dioxide emissions in 2004 were about 30 billion tons.)[5]

TABLE 9.1 ENERGY USE PER CAPITA, SWITZERLAND, 2007.

CATEGORY	ENERGY USE PER CAPITA (W)
Living and office (heat and hot water)	1,500
Food and consumer items, including transport	1,100
Electricity	600
Auto	500
Air travel[a]	250
Public transportation	150
Public infrastructure	900
Country total	5,000

[a]One round trip between Zürich and Shanghai would be equivalent to 800 watts, so the 250-watt allowance covers only a few, much shorter air trips.

Source: Elizabeth Kolbert, "The Island in the Wind," The New Yorker, July 7, 2008, www.newyorker.com/reporting/2008/07/07/080707fa_fact_kolbert?currentPage=all, accessed August 7, 2008.

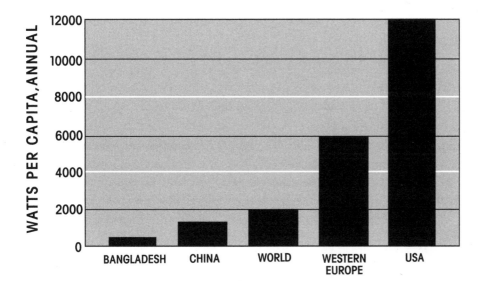

FIGURE 9.1 Average energy use in selected countries according to the Swiss research institute ETH, which is credited with pioneering the concept of a 2,000-watt society that reduces human impact to sustainable levels without giving up the amenities of modern life.

You can see the challenge to U.S. architects, engineers, and building owners and developers: Stop thinking that a 15 to 20 percent improvement over current codes is sufficient and begin designing zero-net-energy buildings with enough on-site and off-site renewables produced or purchased to offset the energy use in the building (Table 9.2). For a 100,000–square-foot building using 15 kilowatt-hours per square foot per year, that would mean buying or producing 1.5 million kilowatt-hours per year. With a $0.02 cost premium per kilowatt-hour, that's only $0.30 per square foot per year. With average urban rents at $30 per square foot per year, that's only a 1 percent premium. Why is that so hard to swallow? Even assuming that a project spent $3 per square foot extra to reduce energy use dramatically (i.e., about 2 percent on $150 per square foot

TABLE 9.2 THE COST OF A 100,000–SQUARE-FOOT ZERO-NET-ENERGY BUILDING.

Building net energy use after conservation measures	15 kWh/sq. ft./year	1,500,000 kWh/year
Additional cost to achieve this goal based on a $150/sq. ft. cost	$3/sq. ft. (2%)	$300,000
Annual additional cost of energy investments at 10% annual capital recovery	$0.30/sq. ft.	$30,000
Annual cost of purchased renewable energy at $0.02/kWh	$0.30/sq. ft.	$30,000
Average urban rent	$30/sq. ft.	$3,000,000
Percentage rent increase to cover zero net energy	2% ($0.60/$30)	—

construction cost) that would amortize at an additional $0.30 per square foot, the cost would only double to about 2 percent of rent (Table 9.2).

So why can't we accept the Swiss challenge and live on 2,000 watts per day? This was the average energy use in Switzerland, a very cold country by the way, in 1950. As a child in 1950, I knew no one who thought that we were suffering a great hardship, at least in energy terms. Since 1950, U.S. energy use per capita has grown 50 percent.[6] If we're a 12,000-watt society today, what would be the harm in going back to an 8,000-watt society (the 1950 level), especially when we know we could do it without giving up much because our buildings, cars, factories, and homes are much more energy efficient today?

Here's the saving grace: About two thirds of primary fossil fuel energy used today is just wasted, lost as heat in our engines, motors, power plants, and so on, primarily because energy has been so cheap that there hasn't been much incentive to save energy and make our physical plants more efficient.[7] So, if we can double the efficiency of primary energy conversion, we'll get down to 6,000 watts in the United States rather quickly. Then the remaining two-thirds drop to 2,000 watts can be made much less painfully.

Back to the Swiss 2,000-watt society: The metro area of Basel began a pilot project in 2001 to develop and commercialize some of the technologies involved. The city of Zurich joined the project in 2005. Recall that the 2009 Swiss Minergie standard is only 38 kilowatt-hours per square meter (about 3.5 kilowatt-hours per square foot, or about 6,000 kilowatt-hours annually for a 1,700–square-foot home or apartment, less than 1,000 watts) at the present time, and you'll see that the Swiss are well on their way toward 2,000 watts.[8]

TACKLING THE PROBLEM OF EXISTING BUILDINGS

Although it is technically not a green building issue, the problem of upgrading the energy efficiency and indoor air quality of existing buildings is critical to reaching the 2,000-watt society goal (or even remotely approaching that level of building energy use). My friend Christian Wetzel in Munich is a former researcher at the Fraunhofer Institute for Building Physics, Germany's leading energy research lab (comparable to the U.S. national laboratories such as Lawrence Berkeley National Lab) and now runs a small software company called Calcon.[9] His software tool is called Energy Performance, Indoor Environmental Quality Refurbishment, or EPIQR, after the Greek philosopher Epicurus (from whom we derive the word *epicurean*).

The goal of EPIQR is to evaluate a building as user-friendly, as holistically and independently as possible, with a maximum effort of a few hours to determine the most cost-effective (energy) retrofits. Imagine taking only a handful of easily gotten measurements of an existing building (preferably a group of buildings) and coming up with an estimate of energy demand within 10 percent, then generating a series of energy upgrades that yield whatever return on investment the building owner specifies. Wetzel and his colleagues have done this for more than 1.5 million flats and, including the commercial areas, altogether more than 100 million square meters (more than 1 billion square feet) gross area in just 5 years.

And it's all based on Fraunhofer's exhaustive research (along with other European energy researchers) into the key variables determining building energy use, which are easily observable, such as the roof condition, window type and condition, number of stories, number of apartments and stairwells, and age of a building. Wetzel has licensed this information database and created the software to make it into a practical analytical and investment tool. By reducing the front-end cost of energy audits, the EPIQR tool allows building owners to quickly and painlessly specify a series of economically beneficial retrofits to reduce energy consumption. The software evaluates the degradation state, estimates refurbishment and retrofit costs, and then generates actions and budgets over a 1-year, 5-year, and 10-year horizon. It also analyzes heating energy demand according to the European Union EPBD, allowing an Energieausweis (Energy Certificate) to be issued for the building.

LIFE-CYCLE DESIGN TOOLS

Everyone is looking for the ultimate tool that will assess how well a home, building, or urban development will affect the environment on a life-cycle basis. One Englishman, David Kirkland, has come up with a piece of software called EVA Tool that promises to do just that (Figure 9.2).[10] Kirkland says, "When just 1 percent of a project's up-front costs are spent, up to 70 percent of its life-cycle costs may already be committed. If you integrate green design directly into the processes and even the software that people use to design buildings, then thousands of designers will automatically do it right."

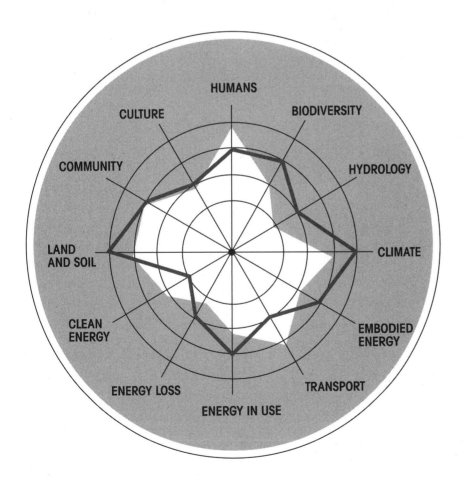

FIGURE 9.2 David Kirkland's EVA Tool's graphic interface allows teams to monitor a project's progress across 12 environmental impacts associated with the built environment.
(© *Enviarch, Ltd.* www.evatool.com, www.evacology.org)

Kirkland describes the purpose of EVA Tool in the following way:

One of the core things that we're concerned about is the current design paradigm for buildings. What we're finding on a lot of these projects is, although their design performance metrics are pretty good, the actual operations—the real-world operation once they've been running for a few years—fall short. Our feeling is that you can't separate sustainable design aspects from the core design process. Therefore, we've designed a tool that helps the designer to make the right decisions at the right time, without making life a burden with long checklists and those sorts of things.

The EVA Tool graphic itself summarizes twelve impacts that are within the control of the project's architect and design team. Kirkland says,

For each of those impacts, before you start your project, you must set yourself a benchmark of what your design goals are, and that's what the bold line is. That is something you establish beforehand. One of the key aspects of EVA Tool is that we're trying move away from generic benchmarking. We're finding that to make a building really work performance-wise, it boils down to very particular, local issues for that particular building. So, we push for setting a unique benchmark for each project, given the project parameters, which means it's much more finely tuned. The white space represents the self-scoring and self-measuring of how you're doing so far in terms of the goals that you set yourself.

Kirkland says that the lessons learned and recorded on each project provide a template of knowledge for the next one and provide a dynamic and ever-evolving "knowledge ecology" within an architectural practice. Armed with the right knowledge and process, design teams should do a much better job of developing the best green buildings.

SOFT LANDINGS FOR GREEN BUILDINGS

Bill Bordass works at the Usable Buildings Trust (UBT), a nonprofit based in the United Kingdom that promotes better buildings through improved understanding of how they actually work.[11] He and his colleagues have concluded that post-occupancy evaluation (POE) must become a routine activity for design and building teams.

In collaboration with the Building Services Research and Information Association,[12] UBT has converted a brilliant idea known as "soft landings" into a formal process that everyone can use. Soft Landings was initiated by architect Mark Way. He researched and tested it with the support of the Estates (Facilities) Department at Cambridge University and a team of designers and constructors with input from UBT. Soft Landings is designed to run alongside any procurement process, enhancing three critical stages: briefing and programming; before and after handover, known as the "finish" stage; and into the first 3 years of use.

Soft Landings includes the following key elements:

- A means of engaging the design and construction team beyond handover to help guide a new or refurbished building through the first crucial months of building operation and beyond. This helps to reduce the tensions and frustrations that can occur when people move into a new building.

- An opportunity for the design and building team to examine the operation of the building and its control systems and to undertake debugging and fine-tuning. This allows clients and users to get more out of their buildings and designers to improve their specifications for future work.
- Associated independent post-occupancy surveys to help inform the team, the building users, and the client about functionality, usability, manageability, energy efficiency, environmental performance, and occupant satisfaction.
- A way of managing client expectations and design intent by routine performance benchmarking throughout the design and construction process and into monitored performance use. The energy benchmarking provides additional technical and operation detail to augment the requirements of the energy certification, which is now mandatory in Europe.
- Aftercare is included as an additional paid service from the design and building team. It allows the designers to help the occupiers get the best out of their building and, if necessary, tackle the problems that can occur with complex systems. (Bordass believes that the present warranty arrangements often only treat symptoms.)
- Clients can respond to the basic framework by setting specific roles, responsibilities, and sign-off duties.

If one understands the difficulty of moving to truly sustainable buildings over the long run, then one will see the brilliance in the Soft Landings approach. It makes into a formal and accepted process the handover, troubleshooting, and fine-tuning activities that go with any complex modern building. POE and feedback also become routine activities that will benefit the industry, its clients, and the planet.

EPCs AND DECs

The most exciting thing I found in Europe was the EPBD (introduced in Chapter 3) and the associated Energy Performance Certificates (EPCs) and Display Energy Certificates (DECs) for existing buildings, based on annual kilograms of carbon dioxide emissions, considering primary energy sources. Figure 9.3 shows what the full EPC looks like, rating buildings on a seven-letter

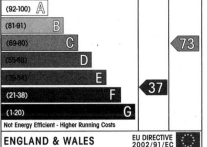

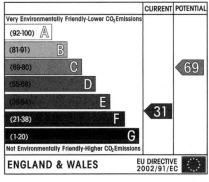

FIGURE 9.3 The energy performance chart shows relative energy use and carbon emissions from designs and gives an easily remembered grade and suggestions for improvement.

scale, from A to G, with A being a zero net energy use per unit area, and showing the carbon production equivalents. Most office buildings would rate between a D and an E on this scale.

The EPC certificates contain information about the building type, the asset rating, reference values and benchmarks, and a series of recommendations for investments to reduce energy use that have less than a 3-year payback ("no or low cost"), less than a 7-year payback ("medium cost"), and greater than 7 years ("strategic investments").[13] The asset rating is defined by using about 200 data inputs and then calculating energy use and determining a numerical ranking with the following formula:

Asset rating = Building emissions rating (kg CO_2/sqm)/National building rating (kg CO_2/sqm).

So if a building generates less CO_2 from its energy use than the national average for its type by 30 percent, for example, then its EPC score would be 70, giving it a respectable "C" energy performance asset rating. The certificate and rating are good for 10 years.

The DEC's asset rating is determined in a similar fashion, except that actual energy use data are used. The purpose is to determine actual energy use and to see whether the building is being operated as efficiently as it could be.

$$\text{Asset rating} = \text{Annual building emissions rating (kg } CO_2\text{/sqm)/}$$
$$\text{Typical building rating (kg } CO_2\text{/sqm).}$$

In the case of the DECs, the certificate is valid for only 1 year, the recommendations for 7 years. Every prospective renter or lessee must be given a copy of the certificate, and a poster with the certificate must be displayed publicly. The display must include ratings from a prior 3-year period, so that building occupants can see whether improvements have been made.

The British government expected that about 1.5 million commercial buildings could be affected by EPCs and DECs and that more than 200,000 certificates would be issued in 2008 alone.[14]

What I really like about this approach is that it substitutes information for regulation. All that's required is to rate the building's energy use against an objective scale and to tie energy use to carbon emissions. We do that in the United States already with the Energy Star program, but it's only a relative ranking (the top 25 percent) as opposed to an absolute scale. If we want to get serious about reducing energy use in buildings and inducing energy-saving remodels, refurbishments, and renovations, we have to start broadcasting energy use per unit area.

ZERO-CARBON HOMES AND BUILDINGS

To get to a zero-carbon home or zero-carbon building, first let's consider what a zero-net-energy use home might be. Once you start to look at it more closely, you find a series of ever more stringent definitions.

1. A sort-of zero-net home might just buy carbon offsets sufficient to provide for its total energy use, using the better economics of off-site renewables. A variant of this approach is to have specific renewable sources, such as a nearby wind turbine installation or solar photovoltaic (PV) farm tied directly to a specific development.

2. A zero-net-electricity home might consist of a grid-tied solar PV system that on an annual basis generates as much electrical energy as it consumes. (This assumes an efficient building envelope and efficient appliances, but total use still might amount to 50 kilowatt-hours per square meter per year, or about 10,000 kilowatt-hours per year for a 2,200–square-foot home.)

3. An all-renewable home might have solar PVs plus a small biomass boiler fed with purchased wood pellets and generating all the heating, hot water, and electrical power for the home.

4. An all-grid zero-net-energy home might buy renewable energy from the grid and indirectly power everything with solar, wind, biomass, and other renewables.

5. A zero-net-energy development might be in local balance with renewables, similar to Beaufort Court, or a British eco-town with 20 percent on-site renewables, the rest from a district energy plant or local combined heat and power (CHP) system running on biomass. This can be called on-site carbon neutral.

6. What about source energy, or all the wasted energy needed to get electricity from the initial fossil fuel to your home? If that were also considered (in Germany it's called "primary energy"), then you might need to generate four times your electrical use on site to produce the energy needed to run the home.

7. A true net-zero home might be totally disconnected from the grid and use its own harvested biomass to run a boiler. (There are thousands of such homes in the backwoods of the United States and Canada already.) This is called site autonomy.

8. But what about the gray energy, the embodied energy of all the building materials, transportation system, and so on? The Europeans are quite serious about measuring this also, and it appears to be about 20 percent of the total direct primary energy use of society. If you count that in the equation, you have to generate even more renewable power.

9. Finally, what about transportation energy use? One recent U.S. study put the energy use of the average 12-mile, one-way American commute at 130 percent to 237 percent of the energy use in a typical office building.[15] So it's clear that the location of a home and distance to work, along with options for getting to work, are also vital components of the low-carbon lifestyle equation.

Other sources of greenhouse gas emissions must be counted, such as refrigerant leaks from air-conditioning systems, methane emissions from waste treatment plants and herd animals, and other chemicals that have significant global warming potential. Yes, bovine flatulence is a problem at the global scale. Buildings are only part of the solution.

Obviously, if you care about the problem of global warming and CO_2 production, you know that nature doesn't care for any of these accounting niceties. She cares only whether CO_2 concentrations in the atmosphere are increasing. That's where we have our work cut out for us.

In the United Kingdom, the Beddington Zero Energy Development (BedZED) was an early attempt to find out how to create a zero-net-energy development. BedZED is located in Wallington, Surrey, and represents an eighty-two–unit, multifamily residential mixed-use development with about 27,000 square feet of commercial space. Built on a brownfield site and completed in 2002, BedZED had a goal of no net carbon dioxide generation from energy production.

After 1 year of monitoring, the development had reduced energy use for space heating by 73 percent and for hot water by 44 percent, along with a 25 percent reduction in electricity use, compared with average new homes built in the United Kingdom in 2000.[16]

The chief advocate for this approach is architect Bill Dunster, who continues to evolve his thinking about what to do to get British lifestyles back down to a "one planet" level. Figure 9.4 shows the estimated energy use of a well-designed BedZED town, contrasted with the British average, showing 70 percent lower carbon emissions, from an average of 12 tons per capita to about 3.5 tons. The authors of this most recent study state, "The only way of living in a low-carbon future is to reduce our current demand by 80 percent and then micro-generate the remaining 20 percent with building-integrated renewable technologies."[17]

The aim of the entire U.K. program is to show people how "Code 6" (zero-net-carbon) homes can be built. Figures 9.5 and 9.6 show production housing that represents Code 6 homes. In Figure 9.5 we see a building called "The Lighthouse" at Kingspan, located at the Innovation Park of the Building Research Establishment (BRE) in Watford, just outside London. According to the BRE, the timber-clad Kingspan Lighthouse has an elegant barnlike design derived from a 40° roof pitch that accommodates a PV array. The Kingspan Lighthouse has achieved Level 6 of the Code for Sustainable Homes. This means it is a zero-net-carbon home. It has a zero-carbon energy supply for space and water heating and all electrical power demand for the home, including electrical cooking and appliances.[18]

This superinsulated, airtight building fabric was designed to provide generous daylight levels and includes effective solar control. Integrated building services are based around a platform of renewable and sustainable technologies. These include water efficiency techniques, such as low-volume sanitary ware and appliances and wide-ranging renewable energy technologies.

The Code 6 home was built by Barratt, the United Kingdom's largest homebuilder, and

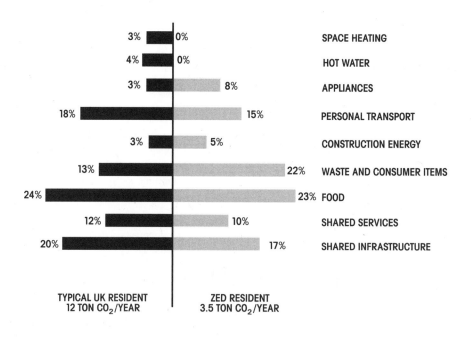

FIGURE 9.4 Bill Dunster Architects continues to push the envelope on zero-energy development; this chart compares the estimated energy use of a well-designed BedZED town with the British average, broken down by major life activities.

FIGURE 9.5 With a strong commitment to zero-carbon housing, the United Kingdom is pioneering stylish sustainable buildings such as this home, designed by Sheppard Robson.
(Sheppard Robson)

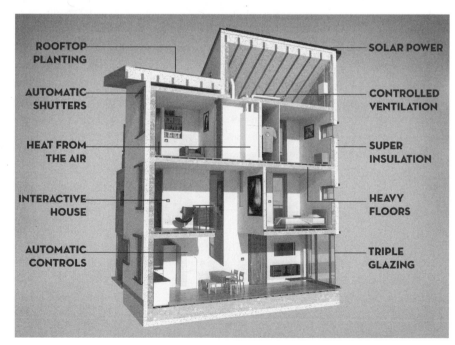

ROOFTOP PLANTING

AUTOMATIC SHUTTERS

HEAT FROM THE AIR

INTERACTIVE HOUSE

AUTOMATIC CONTROLS

SOLAR POWER

CONTROLLED VENTILATION

SUPER INSULATION

HEAVY FLOORS

TRIPLE GLAZING

FIGURE 9.6 The Barratt Green House includes well-insulated walls and windows, along with efficient heat recovery ventilation.
(Barratt Developments)

Figure 9.6 shows the sustainable features incorporated into the design of the Barratt Green House. A big difference between the Lighthouse and the Barratt Green House is the heating solution. The Lighthouse has a wood pellet–fired biomass boiler, but Barratt shied away from this. Andrew Sutton, project architect, said, "We don't believe biomass is a mass market solution. It's unrealistic to expect householders to run wood pellet boilers, and there are issues of supply, which might work on a district scale but not for individual homes."[19]

Instead, the team took a development-wide approach by assuming the Barratt Green House would be part of a bigger development and supplied by a district heating system. The home's heating needs are supplied by an air source heat pump located on the outside of the home; the hot water pipes run into the house, just like those from a district heating scheme. The power for the heat pump comes from PV panels located remotely. A second array of PV panels is mounted on the roof of the home to power appliances within.

The home uses six sustainable strategies that will be familiar to anyone who followed the PassivHaus story in Chapter 1:

- Mechanical ventilation with heat recovery
- Triple glazing to keep heat in during the winter
- Exposed concrete floors to increase thermal mass for summer cooling
- Super insulation, with 7 inches of insulation over 8 inches of aircrete planks
- External shutters to block solar gain
- Thermal storage for water and space heating, supplied by an external air source heat pump.[20]

A recent U.K. government report put the current extra cost of a Code 6 home between £19,000 ($38,000) and £47,000 ($94,000) per unit. The report commented that the lower costs would come from developments "where there is potential to use site-wide carbon-saving technologies (e.g., CHP systems)," typically sites with high numbers of housing units and greater densities.[21] The report concluded that "the costs of achieving the specific energy standards required at Code level 6 are typically higher than those associated with achieving zero carbon status" because of the "cost associated with the additional thermal efficiency measures and the impact of the reduced heat demand on the carbon savings from CHP systems." The bottom line is that the cost of trying to meet zero-net-energy standards with just on-site systems is unacceptably high. The report expected that by 2016, these costs would be reduced by 16 to 25 percent as builders acquired more experience with new systems.

SMART, SLIM BUILDINGS

Professor Jos Lichtenberg at Holland's Technische Universiteit Eindhoven has proposed a system he calls Slimbouwen, or smart buildings, as the way to bring sustainable design into the affordable realm by using standardized or industrially manufactured components.[22] Lichtenberg's idea is that Slimbouwen is based on a skeleton structure and the separation of services (such as heating, ventilation, air conditioning, and plumbing) from the building structure. A crucial development for this approach is a floor system that enables the installers to mount their prepared and prefabricated services practically as a whole. He believes that our current system of building has reached the end of its useful product life cycle.

In his view, one of the main ideas is to rearrange the building process from a parallel process into a serial process consisting of only a few main steps. He says, "The traditional building process, and especially the finishing process, can be characterized as a complicated process in which the participants carry out activities with a high rate of interdependency to other participants. The result is a lot of overlap, inefficiency, failure costs, complex coordination, lack of mutual respect, etc. Participants have to return on site several times since the proceeding is dependent of other participants. In fact this process is a kind of parallel process. By contrast, a sequential process containing only a few major sub-activities can only be obtained by a separation of services from the rest of the process."

I find this idea intriguing and a useful antidote to all the wonderful but highly customized architecture featured in this book because a basic tenet of good sustainable design is to "build it in, don't bolt it on," meaning that building systems should be completely integrated with the building. This is supported by the idea of getting rid of most finishes and most services, integrating them with the building structure, or making sure they can come in via a factory-built system. I also think that design process has to be attacked to secure better results, a topic I explored at length in a recent book.[23]

EUROPEAN GREEN DESIGN GOES EAST

In this book, we've been looking mainly at opportunities for European green design to go west, to North America. But it's also going east (to Eastern Europe, Russia, the Arabian Peninsula, and China). I met in April 2008 with Guy Battle, head of the Battle McCarthy firm at his office in London.[24] Battle has been at green design for at least 15 years. Designed in cooperation with U.K.-based international architects RMJM, the Okhta Tower in St. Petersburg, Russia is one of their largest projects to be based on sustainable design principles. The seventy-nine–story Okhta Tower (Figure 9.7), the new headquarters for Russian energy giant Gazprom, would be the tallest building in Europe when completed, about one third taller than the Commerzbank in Frankfurt.

RMJM won the competition to design this building in late 2006, amid a lot of controversy over the size of the tower. RMJM claims the tower will be the world's most sustainable building, consuming half the energy of an ordinary skyscraper, thanks to a "fur coat" of two double-glazed layers around the outside, with atrium spaces in between.[25]

The 396-meter (1,307-foot), $2.4-billion structure will have to battle winter temperatures of −30°C (−22°F), but in summer the outside air will only be about 25°C (77°F). To accomplish a low-energy design, the building will be encased in two giant glass-and-steel, sensor-lined envelopes, with plants and shrubs filling the buffer zones between them.[26] The plants are expected to provide natural thermal insulation in winter and a source of fresh air in summer to keep offices cool. Heavily sensored, the building will decide how to regulate its own climate, keeping offices at 21°C (70°F) in winter, with the buffer zone at 10°C (50°F) even when it's −30°C outside.

With the double-skin building, energy use is reduced about 65 percent, according to engineer Guy Battle. The building also has rainwater recovery systems and building-integrated PVs.

FIGURE 9.7 Slated to be Europe's tallest building, RMJM's Okhta Tower in St. Petersburg, Russia deals with a very cold climate in imaginative ways. *(RMJM)*

Battle calls his approach "decarbon-8" and has created a service mark called "Planet Positive" for his firm's approach to design.

The pentagram design of the tower maximizes access to daylight and allows spectacular views for the internal offices without heat loss through exposed surfaces.

In the earlier stages of the design process, results showed that 1,200 different-sized glass panels were needed, meaning a greater construction cost and a heavy environmental burden. After much analysis, RMJM found a more environmentally friendly solution by creating seven standard panels, allowing repetition and a much smaller environmental impact.

The design allows a generous number of social spaces and green breakout zones spread out along the floors. These enable office workers to access leisure areas without wasting valuable time and energy commuting to ground level.

Construction begins in 2008, with completion expected in 2012. Tony Kettle, RMJM's group design director, said of this project,

> Most buildings take a limited approach to sustainability, picking a handful of issues to concentrate on which are often considered at the latter stages of the design or building process. With the Okhta Tower, we thought about sustainability issues right from the start and as such it has been totally integrated into the design, frame and structure. The Okhta Tower is a complex, innovative building but we feel we have got the design right—integrating social, economic and environmental aspects in harmony.[27]

We began this exploration of European green building trends by noting some of the reasons why Europeans might be greener than we are, including culture, politics, economics, and climate. We then took a long look at the PassivHaus movement, the EPBD, and other trends that are driving European green building forward. Looking to the future, I think we will see the PassivHaus movement push into all the countries of northern and Western Europe within 5 years because it makes so much sense, both economically and environmentally. As the EPBD enters its second decade with real teeth, I think there will be a strong improvement in energy performance in new buildings and a growing importance of retrofitting or refurbishing older buildings to meet green building standards such as BREEAM, the French Haute Qualité Environnementale, and the German Gütesiegel. The likelihood that European green building improvements, designs, and installations will outpace those in the United States is still quite strong, and I think 5 years from now we will still have a lot to learn about green building and green development from our friendly colleagues and competitors across the pond.

CHAPTER 10

The Challenge and Promise of Green Buildings: Lessons from Europe

G reen buildings are growing rapidly in the United States, with cumulative new project registrations under the LEED rating system growing 50 percent in 2006, 75 percent in 2007, and more than 80 percent in 2008.[1] Yet more than half of LEED project certifications are still at the lower levels of Certified and Silver, indicating that the ability of design and construction teams to deliver high-level green buildings is still at an early stage of development. By contrast, the BREEAM system has certified about 9 percent of its buildings at the Excellent level, equivalent to LEED Platinum, the highest level, against about 5 percent in the LEED system.[2]

Green buildings in the United States are certified at only one-fifth the number (per capita) as in the United Kingdom. What might appear to be a stretch for U.S. design teams is considered normal design practice in the United Kingdom, Germany, and other countries. U.S. green building practice is still inhibited by the notion that the costs are significantly higher than conventional buildings; for example, one survey of more than 800 construction industry executives in 2007 showed that more than 40 percent of them thought that green buildings added 10 percent or more to cost, and almost 75 percent thought that the cost premium was at least 5 percent.[3] Fighting a heavy bias toward lowest-first-cost solutions, green building in the United States needs a stronger business case to succeed. In Europe, by contrast, cultural and political factors are stronger drivers for low-energy, green building solutions.

LESSONS LEARNED

We've taken a brief excursion through what for many American and Canadian building team professionals might be a strange and exotic world, intriguing and a bit familiar, perhaps, but still largely outside the realm of their daily practice. What lessons can we learn and apply from the European experience? What will need to change in North America before we can bring some of these ideas, systems, and technologies into more widespread use? What might be some of the competitive implications for North American design professionals, contractors and subcontractors, and manufacturers?

We started this exploration of European green building and sustainable design practices by recalling Nicolai Ouroussoff's challenging article from 2007. In that article he concluded that obstacles still remain but that progress might be made from a surprising quarter:

> Will America ever catch up with Europe's impressive green record? Mark Wigley, the dean of Columbia's graduate school of architecture, has noticed a sea change in how students here approach sustainability. Increasingly, he said, they see it as a central aspect of their work. . . . At the same time, Wigley admits that architects cannot accomplish anything without willing clients. "My prediction is that if we have a change in America, it won't be driven by politicians or architects but by the developers," he said. "We're at the moment where developers can gain a significant advantage if you reduce energy [costs]. For the first time you have clients who are willing to pay for this. So I think the one group we associate most with greed and inefficiency will lead the way in the future."[4]

I've seen this happening throughout the United States, where the most avid adopters of green building technology have been speculative office and mixed-use developers, ranging from the Durst Organization in New York City, to Hines in Houston, to Gerding Edlen Development in Portland, Oregon.[5]

We began this book with a Foreword from Behnisch Architekten's David Cook. The Behnisch firm is probably the foremost German architect involved with U.S. projects (there are many from the United Kingdom, of course). The systems used in the Norddeutsche Landesbank in Hannover (Figure 10.1) are good examples of what we might see in the United States. Considering both user well-being and low-energy systems, this 75,000–square-meter (807,000–square-foot) building for 1,500 people was built with no air conditioning. Daylighting was optimized, while avoiding unwanted solar gain and glare on computer screens. A double façade was installed, protecting against noise, vehicle emissions, and wind while serving as a supply air duct to adjoining offices. (To be sure, this is a benign climate, exceeding 72°F only 5 percent of the year, but most large American office buildings in a similar climate would be sealed and provided with massive heating, ventilation, and air conditioning systems.) Supplement cooling was supplied by inducing chilled water into the slab, with cold water provided by a ground-source heat exchanger connected to the foundation piles. And the story goes on.[6]

So what are the lessons learned?

- So much more is possible: European green building design and construction practice shows that it's possible to design a much better built environment, one that creates more livable buildings using far less energy than we do today. The prevalence of advanced design solutions also spurs industry toward product innovation. As Transsolar's Helmut Meyer remarked, it's easy in Europe to find six to eight good façade suppliers for advanced design ideas, whereas in North America it's hard to find more than two.

- A change in North American design culture is clearly needed; what's considered a good result today in the United States and Canada would not be considered very good in much of Western Europe. Although nearly 60,000 American architects, engineers, and other building industry participants have become LEED accredited professionals, the fact that fewer than 2,000 buildings have been LEED certified by October 2008 indicates that most of them have yet to put this knowledge into practice. Europeans are quite comfortable liv-

FIGURE 10.1 Designed by Behnisch Architekten, this bank headquarters incorporates natural ventilation and daylighting into a unique twisted geometry that still maintains human scale at the street level. *(Roland Halbe fotografie)*

ing with order, predictability, and clear limits, things that are anathema to the American spirit. We use twice as much energy as Europe (Figure 9.1) yet are no wealthier or happier. There must be a happier medium between tying ourselves in political and regulatory knots and continuing to trust in the laissez-faire approach of unbridled free enterprise to achieve the response we need to the perils of climate change. Among other things, the sense of entitlement to cheap energy has to go if we are to provide an economic rationale and set of signals that will encourage zero-net-energy solutions in the built environment.

- Culture and regulation should fit together more closely, as they do in Europe. For example, German law provides that every office worker has a right to fresh air, natural ventilation, and daylight. As a result, in Germany no one can be more than 5 meters from a window (unless ceiling heights are raised), making building floorplates much narrower than in North America. In other words, by law and custom, the health and comfort of office workers are valued much more than the concept of real estate "efficiency," defined as net leasable area as a percentage of gross floor area.

- The role of engineers in the building design process must be elevated. A European project wouldn't start without having the mechanical and electrical engineers at the table; most American architects design a building, at least preliminarily, before they engage the engineers. We need a revolution in design, toward a more integrated design process, one that puts the issue of zero carbon at the forefront of the design process.[7]

- Building design and construction practice will change only when there is a strong feedback from actual results, measured through post-occupancy evaluations, with the results communicated to the designers and builders. Bill Bordass of the Useable Buildings Trust indicated that this is still an issue in the United Kingdom, especially getting funding for this purpose. The obvious solution is to include funding for both advanced building commissioning and formal post-occupancy evaluations in the original building budget, as a quality assurance and performance verification measure. Most architects and engineers I've encountered are concerned that post-occupancy evaluations will only lead to lawsuits rather than constitute a critical element of the industry's learning curve.

- Educational practice for both architects and engineers must reemphasize building physics as a core element of the curriculum, not only in terms of building energy use but also with respect to all the elements that make buildings habitable and healthy places: fresh air, natural ventilation, moisture management, heat recovery, and use of radiant surfaces to promote comfort. The fact that more U.S. universities are inviting European architects and engineers to teach this subject indicates a wider recognition of the issue.

- A strong government role must be liberating, not oppressive. Right now, the U.K. building industry is having a very difficult time with the British government's eco-towns scheme and the requirement for zero-net-energy homes throughout the country by 2018. It's one thing to mandate zero-carbon results, then demand that 20 percent be provided by on-site renewables, and another to get builders to produce homes that don't cost 20 to 40 percent more to get that result.

- In the United States and Canada, the national government can play a much stronger role. Although the LEED rating system has grown up without much government oversight, mandating it has fallen primarily to state and local governments. What's needed is a quick update to the national building codes to incorporate LEED performance objectives into all codes; moreover, we will need a national energy code for new buildings and major renovations if we are to have a fighting chance to reduce energy use and carbon emissions to 1990 levels. States such as California could adopt stricter codes, but every state and municipality should be required to adopt a stringent building energy code that raises the standards every few years toward a zero-carbon goal. If we can have national energy efficiency standards for automobiles, why not for buildings?

- The European Union's Energy Performance of Buildings Directive, requiring all buildings to be labeled with their energy consumption, provides strong feedback from the marketplace to individual building owners and occupants. A similar system in the United States, going beyond making LEED a mandatory measures in public buildings, would require the Energy Star rating to be posted prominently on all buildings and would assign letter grades (probably A through F in our case) to all properties, would allow the marketplace to put a value on that information, and would pressure building owners and managers to perform the necessary upgrades.

- Formal commitments mean a lot. The fact that Sweden is committed to eliminating oil imports by 2020 or that Germany plans to reduce greenhouse gas emissions 36 percent below 1990 levels by 2020 wonderfully drives decision making at all levels of government, business, and society. Specific goals, such as 20 percent on-site renewables in U.K. housing, help to focus attention and bring forward capital, people, and innovations to make them happen. As the saying goes, "If you don't know where you're going, any road will take you there." Conversely, a strong social and political goal pushes and pulls the innovative energy of society in a specific direction.

- The North American housing sector has a lot to learn. My own research into U.S. and Canadian green homes convinced me that it's possible to design a home that reduces energy consumption by 50 percent without sacrificing comfort or adding significant cost.[8] The German PassivHaus standard shows that we can push the envelope even further, aiming at a 90 percent reduction in heating and hot water use, through a more comprehensive and systematic approach based on building physics.
- European cities offer clear models for U.S. cities. The example of Vaxjö, Sweden, reducing greenhouse gas emissions by 30 percent since 1993 while increasing gross regional and domestic product per capita by 20 percent, shows that we can decouple economic well-being from carbon dioxide production. Cities such as Freiburg, Germany show the power of citizen involvement in creating low-carbon futures. Many American city planners and developers have begun taking the grand tour of these European examples to gather ideas for urban redevelopment and mixed-use projects in the United States. What we need are changes in development incentives, zoning laws, and green building ordinances to turn these examples into reality.
- The German government has demonstrated that even a northerly country can promote solar power in cities with dedicated incentives ("feed-in tariffs" in the case of Germany and Austria, paying much more for solar electricity generated than just the current residential price of electricity). In North America, we are just beginning to encourage solar power in a serious way; in fact, in 2008 the U.S. Congress finally extended the federal solar power tax incentives through 2016, indicating that we're beginning to consider renewable energy not as an expensive luxury but rather as a vital national need.

WHAT WILL WE NEED TO CHANGE TO USE THE EUROPEAN EXPERIENCE?

In the Introduction we argued that the four key issues were climate, culture, politics, and economics. As I've pointed out, the climate regions of the United States and Canada are far more diverse than those of Western Europe, but I think that many of the "design with climate" approaches can be extended beyond their current narrow range of 45° to 60° latitude, in climates with little humidity to worry about.

European culture has grown up since the 1950s with a sense of place, resource scarcity, and land scarcity. There's no "back 40," no "outback" to dump waste or to site new cities. The idea of a closed loop is more real there, especially in an island nation such as the United Kingdom but also in small countries with more stable populations such as Norway, Denmark, and Sweden. There is also a stronger sense of social justice, primarily because of the greater strength of labor-dominated left parties, but also a greater coherence of community, with far more homogeneous populations.

There is also a sense that cities must become more like nature, more biomimetic, to become truly sustainable. An example might be the green wall placed on the side of a two-story conference center at Bennetts Associates' New Street Square to provide carbon dioxide production in the midst of a busy urban area (Figure 10.2).

Politics and economics are the bigger issues. Most Americans tend to view current resource

FIGURE 10.2 One of the
many examples of a green
wall, this two-story
conference center in central
London's New Street Square
attempts to bring nature
back into the city.
(Jerry Yudelson)

scarcities or rising costs as temporary market imbalances or inconveniences rather than a look at
the most likely future. As a result, our politics has yet to come to terms with higher energy prices
and greater demands on coherent policy formulation for a sustainable future. What I see coming
is a growing consensus that will play out over the next presidential term toward a national building code for green buildings and a national energy code for homes and structures, which will result
from a firm commitment to a low-carbon future.

The economic arguments for green buildings are strong, but not as strong as in Europe. Until
we see gasoline prices at $7 or $8 per gallon, we're likely to make few structural adjustments in
urban design and settlement patterns. Until we see average electricity prices above $0.15 or $0.20
per kilowatt-hour, we're likely to see only incremental improvements to new and existing buildings.

Over the long haul, this trend toward more sustainable buildings is irreversible. But it will
take a change in thinking to move us more quickly along this path. Understanding the European
experience can help with that change in outlook, understanding, and intention. I encourage all of
you to continue to follow European green building developments as closely as you follow those in
the United States and Canada. There's much to learn, digest, and implement.

WHERE SHOULD WE BE HEADING?

One of the clear lessons from this book is that there are major competitive implications to lag-
ging behind in adopting new approaches to sustainable design and development. The first

competitive implication is for North American firms wanting to stay in the running for major U.S. and Canadian projects as their clients become more demanding of low-carbon solutions and more aware of what's available from European architects and engineers. The second is for manufacturers of building products and systems having to compete with companies that have learned the art of sustainable design, products, and systems in the much larger European Union marketplace. The third is for the contractors and subcontractors as this market starts to become increasingly global, especially for major projects. How will they stay competitive if they don't know how to price and install the systems that leading architects and engineers will be specifying?

These are all meaty questions, far beyond the scope of this book. Nonetheless, the clear intention of this book is to force answers, to issue a wake-up call to North American building teams to learn how to design, build, and operate for an increasingly low-carbon future, to combine elegance with economy in design, creature comfort with cradle-to-cradle considerations. In a way, it's a revolution to return to the roots of North American design, learning how to design with climate.

Bob Berkebile is principal of BNIM Architects in Kansas City, Missouri. He's not sure that we should focus so much on learning from Europe if that means adopting only high-tech solutions to low-carbon demands. After all, these solutions are driven largely by conditions that might be very different there and also by the demands of the global economy. Here's what he thinks should happen instead:[9]

> I find that high-tech double-skin buildings are often too complicated and sophisticated. That means they're too expensive and/or too difficult to operate and maintain. Ultimately, they're fairly resource-intensive even though they may ultimately consume a little less energy. Typically the most published European projects are the most copied by Americans; they are often clever but complex and not integrated or elegant.
>
> In other words, they're not using nature as a model; they're using ever more sophisticated but outdated Western scientific thought. If you were to talk with Janine Benyus, author of *Biomimicry*,[10] she would suggest using nature as our source of innovation. This approach requires a deeper understanding of how nature works to achieve efficiency, diversity, and resilience. I believe that if we are creating design solutions for a more crowded, polluted, resource-constrained planet we must look for more elegant solutions.

Berkebile is a strong advocate for shifting our thinking and developing "a more holistic regenerative approach" that seeks "to understand the principles of nature well enough to divorce ourselves from the 'heat, beat, treat' strategy that much of the award-winning European architecture currently is using."

A British architect, Robert Adam, provided a similar sentiment in railing against purely technical fixes for glass boxes that perhaps shouldn't be built in the first place:

> What makes a building last a long time is really quite simple. It needs to be robust and adaptable. Robust buildings are made of solid, low-maintenance and preferably local materials. Adaptable buildings are daylit, easy to subdivide and service, and don't depend on machinery such as lifts and air-conditioning. In other words, they'll be solid, low and narrow. We're surrounded by buildings like this that have lasted for centuries.[11]

You'll have to make your own choice about whether to adopt more contemporary (and more technologically advanced) European green building approaches or to take the road less traveled and follow Berkebile's and Adam's recommendations. Should we be adopting high-tech but low-carbon solutions from Europe or taking a different approach entirely, one based on biomimicry?

This might be a good place to pause in our journey and take stock. As we look to accommodate over the next 40 years a projected 50 percent increase in the U.S. population and perhaps even a 30 percent increase in world population, with the pressures of resource depletion and climate change growing yearly, should we still be committing so many resources to the building sector?

Can we figure out how to build more timeless contemporary buildings that imitate nature in the way that indigenous buildings throughout the world always have, by using local materials, human ingenuity, passive systems, and natural water, wind, and sunlight? Can we understand and communicate human comfort and health considerations to building designers who are increasingly removed from the people they are serving with their work?

Ultimately, resolving these questions is more about culture than technology, ecology than economics, behavior than biofuels. It's about using the collective human intelligence, applied to design of products, systems, technologies, and buildings, to allow our urban civilization to be sustainable over the long haul. In that respect, we might take another, more humble look at the European experience, because they've operated cities, governments, cultural institutions, and places of learning for at least 500 years longer than we have in North America and done a pretty good job of it. It's time for more voyages and conversations of discoveries between two great civilizations.

Bon voyage!

DESIGN AND DEVELOPMENT FIRMS AND PROJECTS

NOTES

Preface

1. www.breeam.org, accessed August 28, 2008.

2. Nicolai Ouroussoff, 2007, "Why Are They Greener Than We Are?" *New York Times Magazine*, May 20. www.nytimes.com/2007/05/20/magazine/20europe-t.html.

Foreword

1. This text is based on extracts from the catalog titled "Ecology. Design. Synergy," which accompanies the exhibition currently touring North America and Asia and documents the collaborative efforts of Behnisch Architekten and Transsolar.

2. Herbert Girardet, 2007, *Surviving the Century: Facing Climate Chaos and Other Challenges* (London: Earthscan).

Introduction

1. The three-story building is V shaped in plan, with the extreme ends of the V splayed away from each other. A central core is located at the apex of the V. The building incorporates a 66-meter-long, south-facing, inclined solar façade, at the center of which is the main entrance. Behind it is located a three-story atrium and an internal "street" between it and the splayed wings. Quite cleverly, the building also exploits prevailing winds from the nearby sea to create an updraft from the sloping south wall that helps naturally ventilate the building.

In normal operation, the building should function in its low-energy passive solar mode, but a tenant with high heat loads (e.g., from a data center) can augment this strategy with a displacement ventilation and cooling system. The building is designed to be robust and versatile. If necessary, it can be divided into up to six individual tenant occupancies.

2. Interview with John Echlin, August 2008.

3. Interview with Larry Malcic, August 2008.

4. Obviously, latitude alone doesn't explain climate. For example, proximity to the ocean and altitude are also important. In the British Isles and northwestern Europe, the warm Gulf Stream also plays a strong role in moderating annual temperature.

5. These are called Workplace Directives, or "Die Arbeitsstaattenrichtlinie," www.vdi.de, VDI6000, accessed January 20, 2009. Behnisch Architekten and Transsolar Climate Engineering, *Ecology. Design. Synergy*, p. 60. Personal communication, Dr. Thomas Spiegelhalter, University of Southern California, September 4, 2008. "Die Arbeitsstaattenrichtlinie, VDI 6000, Blatt 2," www.vdi.de/401.0.html?&no_cache=1&tx_vdirili_pi2[showUID]=92588&L=0, accessed January 21, 2009.

6. In a May 2008 survey, only 20 percent of people polled said they would take no action to improve their EPC rating on a retrofit project. As many as 43 percent would try to increase their rating by two or more grades. *Building* (U.K.), 2008, May 2, p. 59.

7. "EPC Costs Balloon to Ten Times More Than Planned," 2008, *Building* (U.K.), May 2, p. 13.

8. European Lifestyles of Health and Sustainability study, available at www.environmentalleader.com/2007/10/29/europeans-greener-than-americans/, accessed October 30, 2007.

9. Vincent James, Jennifer Yoos, and Nathan Knutson, 2008, "Bridge from the Past," *High Performing Buildings*, Fall, pp. 28–42. www.hpbmagazine.org.

10. California's new energy standards apply to all new buildings beginning in July 2009. See www.greenerbuildings.com/news/2008/07/18/california-adopts-green-building-code-all-new-construction, accessed August 28, 2008.

11. McKinsey Global Institute studies include "The Case for Investing in Energy Productivity," 2008, www.mckinsey.com/mgi/publications/Investing_Energy_Productivity/index.asp, accessed August 28, 2008.

12. U.S. Green Building Council, www.usgbc.org/DisplayPage.aspx?CMSPageID=1496, accessed August 28, 2008.

13. U.S. Conference of Mayors, www.usmayors.org/climateprotection/, accessed August 28, 2008.

14. Throughout this book, you'll notice various comparisons between the green buildings and "standard" or "conventional" buildings. It's always better if the actual energy use of a building is measured. But in many cases I have had to rely on claims based on energy modeling, comparing a given building with a "standard" building based on local codes or measured average energy consumption in a specific country. In most cases, no one is actually publishing energy use on a per-square-foot basis so that one can compare actual use from one building to another. This is a widespread problem in architectural and engineering building reports, not just with green buildings, one that is being slowly remedied as the realization sinks in that even "green" buildings do not always perform as well as advertised. So I advise the reader to take all claims of energy performance with a grain of salt, to understand the specific reference standards used in the comparison, and to adopt a skeptical attitude about such assertions until a building has several years of measured and evaluated data, compared with generally agreed-upon reference standards.

15. Anja Caldwell, 2008, "Green Schools in the United States and Germany," *Educational Facility Planner*, 42(4), pp. 10–11.

16. See "Engineering a Sustainable World," the story of the Oregon Health & Science University's Center for Health and Healing, the world's largest LEED Platinum-certified building as of mid-2008, downloadable from Interface Engineering, Inc. at www.interfaceengineering.com.

17. See Jerry Yudelson, *Green Building through Integrated Design*.

18. See the information on the CCI at www.clintonfoundation.org.

19. See the work of Professor Norman Miller at the University of San Diego, with colleagues Jay Spivey and Andy Florance of CoStar, "Does Green Pay Off?," working paper of the Burnham Moores Center for Real Estate, San Diego, CA. www.sandiego.edu/business/documents/July142008DoesGreenPayOff-Ed.pdf.

20. Brian Edwards, 2006, "Benefits of Green Offices in the UK: Analysis from Examples Built in the 1990s," *Sustainable Development*, 14, 190–204, at p. 192, available at Wiley Interscience, www.interscience.wiley.com, accessed September 7, 2008.

21. Interview by Friedrich H. Dassler, 2007, *Intelligente Architektur*, 01–03, pp. 17–25.

22. Interview with John Echlin, July 2008.

23. Interview with Bruce Fowle, July 2008.

24. Interview with Robert Shemwell and James Andrews, August 2008.

25. A German-trained architect practicing in the United States for 10 years, Anja Caldwell emphatically disagrees with this conclusion. She and Bill Caldwell, also a U.S. architect who practiced in Germany, say, "The worst firm in Germany is still better educated about integrated design and sustainability than any middle-ground firm in the U.S." Personal communication, January 2009.

26. Interview with Dr. Katy Janda, August 2008.

27. See www.thisislondon.co.uk/standard/article-23574021-details /Miliband+toughens+UK+emission+targets/article.do, accessed December 31, 2008.

28. Interview with Kevin Burke, August 2008.

29. See www.c2ccertified.com, accessed January 20, 2009, and www.mcdonough.com/cradle_to_cradle.htm.

Chapter 1

1. Joan Sabaté, Christoph Peters, and Jordina Vidal, 2008, "Factor 10: Toward a 90 Percent CO_2 Reduction in Mediterranean Building, New and Retrofit," *Conference Proceedings, 12th International Conference on Passive Houses 2008*, PassivHaus Institut, Darmstadt, Germany, pp. 453–460.

2. 2001 U.S. Household Energy Consumption data for single-family homes, available at www.eia.doe.gov/emeu/recs/recs2001/detailcetbls.html#total, accessed August 27, 2008.

3. Information in this section is taken from an interview with Dr. Wolfgang Feist in the journal *Energy Design Update*, January 2008, pp. 1–6, used by permission of Aspen Publishers, New York, www.aspenpublishers.com.

4. www.roofhelp.com/Rvalue.htm, accessed August 27, 2008.

5. For a list of such subsidies, see www.dsireusa.org, accessed August 27, 2008.

6. "An Interview with Dr. Wolfgang Feist," *Energy Design Update*, January 2008, used with permission of Aspen Publishers, www.aspenpublishers.com, accessed September 11, 2008.

7. The same insulated Thermos bottle that protects against winter cold also helps keep the home cool during the summer.

8. Jerry Yudelson, *Choosing Green*.

9. www.solardecathlon.org/faqs.html, accessed August 27, 2008.

10. www.solardecathlon.org/contests_scoring.html, accessed August 27, 2008.

11. www.dgnb.de, accessed August 27, 2008.

12. Werner Sobek, *R 128*, pp. 18, 20, and 22.

13. Ibid., p. 84.

14. www.minergie.com/download/Faltblatt_Minergie_Standard_e.pdf, accessed August 27, 2008.

15. www.postfinance.ch/pf/content/en/seg/priv/prod/eserv /dossier/realestate/realestate3.html, accessed August 7, 2008.

16. Georg W. Reinburg, 2008, "History, Present and Future of Passive Houses: A Case Study," in *Proceedings, 12th International Conference on Passive Houses 2008*, pp. 257–264. www.reinberg.net.

17. Interview with Georg Reinberg, August 2008.

18. Ronald Rovers, *Sustainable Housing Projects*, p. 28.

19. Ibid., pp. 80, 103.

20. This conclusion was verified in a conversation with Katrin Klingenberg, a German architect leading the PassivHaus movement in the United States and in her paper at the PassivHaus conference, "A Passive House on Martha's Vineyard," pp. 113–118 of the conference proceedings. The Passive House Institute US can be found at www.passivehouse.us, accessed August 27, 2008.

Chapter 2

1. It also helped that I can speak and read German reasonably well, so I was able to delve more deeply into the projects and design culture of architects

and engineers in that country during four visits there.

2. David Lloyd Jones, *Architecture and the Environment*, p. 9.

3. Peter Buchanan, essay in Ingeborg Flagge, Verena Herzog-Loibl, and Anna Meseure, *Thomas Herzog*.

4. Personal communication, White Design, July 18, 2008.

5. Interview with Rab Bennetts, May 2008.

6. www.permasteelisa.com, accessed January 12, 2009.

7. www.hopkins.co.uk, November 19, 2008, information release.

8. Donati, *Michael Hopkins*, p. 275.

9. www.arup.com/sustainability/feature.cfm?pageid=4927, accessed August 30, 2008.

10. Interview with David Richards, director, Arup Associates, London, June 2008.

11. www.shortandassociates.co.uk/page.asp?pi=28, accessed August 17, 2008.

12. www.holcimfoundation.org/T177/Gold-Germany.htm, accessed September 7, 2008.

13. Herbert Dreiseitl and Dieter Grau, *New Waterscapes*, p. 16.

14. Ibid., p. 42.

15. Ibid., p. 64.

Chapter 3

1. www.spaingbc.org, accessed August 29, 2008.

2. www.worldgbc.org/council-development/where-worldgbc-is-active, accessed August 29, 2008.

3. www.usgbc.org/LEED/Project/CertifiedProjectList.aspx ?CMSPageID=244, accessed August 29, 2008.

4. www.buildingsplatform.org/cms/, accessed August 28, 2008.

5. europa.eu/abc/european_countries/others/index_en.htm, accessed August 28, 2008.

6. Interview with Bill Bordass, July 2008.

7. In Europe there are two sorts of energy certificate. Energy Performance Certificates are designed to inform property transactions; they use "Asset Ratings" (based on theoretical calculations) and provide a standardized basis for comparing buildings on the market, be they old, new, or refurbished. Display Energy Certificates (DECs) are for display in public buildings. Countries can choose whether to base their DECs on calculated Asset Ratings (as in Scotland) or on measured annual energy use Operational Ratings (as in England, Wales, and Northern Ireland).

8. *Building* (U.K.) magazine, www.building.co.uk/sustain_story.asp ?storycode=3116537&origin=bldgsustainnewsletter, accessed August 27, 2008.

9. Ibid.

10. www.breeam.org, accessed August 29, 2008.

11. Presentation at Ecobuild conference, February 2008, by Thomas Saunders and Anna Surgenor of BRE Global, at www.breeam.org/page _1col.jsp?id=54, accessed August 29, 2008.

12. Personal communication, Simon Guy, BRE, December 23, 2008.

13. www.propertyweek.com/story.asp?sectioncode =274&storycode=3119943&c=1, accessed August 29, 2008.

14. Brannon Boswell, "Europe Seeks Common Green Code: European Leaders Push for Union-Wide Environmental Standards," *SCT: Shopping Centers Today*. www.icsc.org/sct/sct_article.php?i=sct0608&s=1&d=6.

15. www.building.co.uk/sustain_story.asp?storycode=3126140&origin =bldgsustainnewsletter, accessed January 2, 2009.

16. www.usablebuildings.co.uk/rp/index.html, accessed August 29, 2008.

17. Interview with Bill Bordass, July 2008.

18. To understand the U.S. Energy Star benchmarking system for buildings,

go to www.energystar.gov, accessed August 29, 2008.

19. However, the current population growth rate is slightly negative, reflecting a rapidly aging population and a severe dropoff in births, typical of many European countries. www.cia.gov/library/publications/the-world-factbook/print/gm.html, accessed August 29, 2008.

20. These two sources supplied 92 percent of electricity in 2001 versus 71 percent in the United States. www.cia.gov/library/publications/the-world-factbook/print/gm.html, accessed January 20, 2009, and www.eia.doe.gov/cneaf/electricity/epa/epat1p1.html, accessed January 20, 2009.

21. europa.eu/abc/european_countries/eu_members/germany/index_en.htm, accessed January 12, 2009.

22. www.bellona.org/articles/articles_2007/Germany_save_money_gas_emission, accessed August 17, 2008.

23. www.germanwatch.org/klima/ccpi.htm, accessed August 17, 2008.

24. www.ipsnews.net/news.asp?idnews=36470, accessed August 17, 2008.

25. www.dgnb.de, accessed August 29, 2008.

26. Interview with Anna Braune, August 2008.

27. www.nytimes.com/2008/08/07/world/europe/07solar.html?ref=world, accessed August 17, 2008.

28. Courtney Tenz, 2007, "Germany Goes Green," *German Life*, April/May, 13(6), p. 40. germanlife.com/Archives/2007/0704-01.html, accessed August 17, 2008.

29. www.hic-net.org/document.asp?PID=187, accessed August 17, 2008.

30. www.rolfdisch.de/project.asp?id=48&sid=-1755599670, accessed August 23, 2008.

31. www.rolfdisch.de/project.asp?id=70&sid=-1755599670, accessed August 23, 2008.

32. Personal communication, Prof. Thomas Spiegelhalter, September 5, 2008.

33. www.buildingsplatform.eu/cms/index.php?id=118&publication_id=3143, accessed August 29, 2008.

34. Ibid.

35. europa.eu/abc/european_countries/eu_members/france/index_en.htm, accessed January 12, 2009.

36. Rose-Marie Faria, April 2008, "France: Green Building Market," U.S. Commercial Service, Washington, DC, p. 1.

37. www.assohqe.org, accessed August 23, 2008.

38. www.areneidf.org/english/hqe.html, accessed August 23, 2008.

39. "HQE Challenges for 2010 in the Ile-de-France Region," www.areneidf.org/english/hqe.html, accessed August 23, 2008.

40. Faria, "France: Green Building Market," p. 5. U.S. estimates for LEED certification are based on the author's experience.

41. Ibid., p. 2.

42. Southface Energy Institute, 2006, *Southface Journal*, Summer. www.southface.org/web/resources&services/publications/journal/sfjv206/sfjv206_green-n-france.htm, accessed January 12, 2009.

43. Frank Hovorka, 2008, "Coloring Paris Lights," *High Performance Buildings*, Summer, 48–55, www.HPBmagazine.org; www.brenac-gonzalez-architectes.com/index-en.html, accessed August 23, 2008.

44. Hovorka, "Coloring Paris Lights," p. 52.

45. Ibid., p. 55.

46. Herbert Guttinger, Bob Gysin, and Stefan van Velsen, 2008, "Eawag Forum Chriesbach: A Step towards the 2000-Watt Society," in *Proceedings of the World Conference SB08*, Tokyo. www.sb08.org, accessed January 21, 2009.

47. "Resultate und Erfahrungen der ersten beiden Betriebsjahre des 'nachhaltigen' Neubaus Forum Chriesbach, Eawag/Empa Dübendorf" ("Results and Experiences of the First 2 Years of Operation of the Sustainable New Building Forum Chriesbach"), n.d., available from Herbert Güttinger of Eawag, www.eawag.ch, p. 4.

48. Mark Zimmerman, 2008, in *Proceedings of the 12th International Conference on Passive Houses*, pp. 381–386.

49. www.buildingsplatform.org/cms/index.php?id=118&publication_id=3184, pp. 5–6, accessed August 29, 2008.

50. www.anab.it, accessed August 31, 2008.

51. Federico Bevini, *Green Building in Italy*, U.S. Commercial Service, ID#137287, September 2006.

52. Ibid.

53. Ibid.

54. www.mcarchitectsgate.it/index.php?id-198-projid-100, accessed August 17, 2008.

55. Rose Owen, 2001, "Sounded Breath, Cast Shadow: Sustainability, Connectedness, and the Workplace," M. Arch. thesis, McGill University. Montreal, Canada. Data from www.ecosensual.net/drm/thesis/ziguzzini2.html, accessed July 9, 2008.

56. Greencalc is a government system in the Netherlands for rating buildings.

57. Marlon Huysmans, OVG, personal communication, October 2008.

58. Behnisch Architekten and Transsolar Climate Engineering, *Ecology. Design. Synergy*, p. 54.

59. Project description provided by BEAR Architects, www.bear.nl, accessed August 27, 2008.

Chapter 4

1. *Miscanthus* is a fast-growing nonfood crop that can be harvested annually.

2. www.beaufortcourt.com/about-beaufort-court/design—performance.aspx, January 12, 2009.

3. Sandra Mendler, William O'Dell, and Mary Ann Lazarus, *The HOK Guidebook*, pp. 218–227.

4. Ibid., p. 223.

5. A brise soleil ("sun breaker" in French) is a permanent sun-shading technique, typically in the form of horizontal or vertical louvers, projected out from a building's façade.

6. Sandra Mendler, William O'Dell, and Mary Ann Lazarus, *The HOK Guidebook*, p. 227.

7. www.24hourmuseum.org.uk/nwh_gfx_en/ART31044.html, accessed September 1, 2008.

8. www.fulcrumfirst.com/pages/portfolio/brightonlibrary.htm, accessed September 1, 2008.

9. RIBA Award citation, personal communication from Bennetts Associates, May 2008.

10. www.building.co.uk/sustain_story.asp?storycode=3115327, accessed January 21, 2009.

11. Maria Cristina Donati, *Michael Hopkins*, p. 106.

12. Ibid., p. 120.

13. www.newlondonarchitecture.org/project.php?id=70, accessed August 30, 2008.

14. www.propertyweek.com/story.asp?storyCode=3037179, accessed August 30, 2008.

15. www.arup.com/europe/newsitem.cfm?pageid=1069, accessed August 30, 2008.

16. www.shortandassociates.co.uk, accessed August 17, 2008.

17. R. Watkins, J. Palmer, M. Koloktroni, and P. Littlefair, 2002, "The Balance of the Annual Heating and Cooling Demand within the London Urban Heat Island," *Building Services Engineering Research and Technology*, 23(4), pp. 207–213.

18. Quinton Pop, 2005, "Going Green: From UK to SA," *Journal of the SA Institute of Architects*, March–April.

19. www.shortandassociates.co.uk/pages.asp?pi=35&cp=4, accessed August 17, 2008.

20. UCL Estates & Facilities Division, www.ucl.ac.uk/efd/?bldg=ssees, accessed January 12, 2009; Short and Associates Architects, School of Slavonic and East European Studies, www.shortandassociates.co.uk/pages.asp?pi=35&cp=4, accessed August 17, 2008.

21. Pop, "Going Green."

22. Ibid.

23. www.shortandassociates.co.uk/page.asp?pi=35, accessed August 17, 2008.

24. Pop, "Going Green."

25. Ibid.

26. Ibid.

27. Michael Wiggington and Jude Harris, *Intelligent Skins*.

28. *Architecture Today*, AT23, November 1991.

29. Rockwool batts have about 10 percent greater R-value than fiberglass batts. www.sizes.com/units/rvalue.htm, accessed August 17, 2008.

30. B. Howe and J. W. Twidell, 1994, *Passive Ventilated, Daylight Optimized, Low Energy Engineering Building* (Leicester, UK: De Montfort University, AMSET Centre), pp. 243–250.

31. Not all green buildings use, or need to use, thermal mass in the building envelope or structure to achieve their energy-saving objectives.

32. www.architecture.uwaterloo.ca/faculty_projects/terri/125_W03/king_helicon.pdf, accessed August 17, 2008.

33. www.sheppardrobson.com/sr_master.html, accessed August 17, 2008.

34. www.permasteelisa.com, accessed August 17, 2008.

35. www.ecda.co.uk/, accessed October 14, 2008.

36. www.innovateoffice.co.uk/leeds-offices/green/, accessed August 29, 2008.

Chapter 5

1. Max Hollein and Nicolaus Schafhausen, *Kunst/Art at Lufthansa Aviation Center*, p. 165.

2. All project information in this section was provided by Foster + Partners; see www.fosterandpartners.com.

3. Presentation by Carlos Esteves, architect with Somfy, at Frankfurt architectural conference, September 2007. Somfy provided the product for the retrofitting of exterior solar control blinds onto the building in 2007; see www.somfy.com.

4. Sheila J. Bosch, 2000, "Green Architecture: Symbolic Sustainability or Deep Green Design?" maven.gtri.gatech.edu/sfi/resources/pdf/TR/Symbolic%20sustainability.pdf, accessed August 28, 2008.

5. www.nationsencyclopedia.com/Europe/Luxembourg-CLIMATE.html, accessed January 12, 2009.

6. "European Investment Bank Energy Audit," section 3.5, "Mechanical Ventilation," pp. 12–21, provided by Ingenhoven Architekten office.

7. Based on Marina Flamme-Jasper, *NORD/LB, Hannover*.

8. Behnisch Architekten and Transsolar Climate Engineering, *Ecology. Design. Synergy*, p. 34.

9. Flamme-Jasper, *NORD/LB, Hannover*, p. 105.

10. Taken from Till Briegleb, *High-Rise RWE AG Essen*.

11. Behnisch Architekten and Transsolar Climate Engineering, *Ecology. Design. Synergy*, p. 56.

12. Transsolar information sheet, www.transsolar.com, accessed September 7, 2008.

13. Kristin Feireiss, *Energies*.

14. Competition brief, www.holcimfoundation.org/T177/Gold-Germany.htm, accessed September 7, 2008.

15. Project description from a case study at www.behnisch.com, accessed September 7, 2008.

16. Rolf-Dieter Lieb, *Double-Skin Façades*, pp. 170–172.

17. Wiggington and Harris, *Intelligent Skins*.

18. Lieb, *Double-Skin Façades*, p. 170.

19. Peter Buchanan, 2000, *Renzo Piano Building Workshop*, Volume 4. Phaidon Press, pp. 169–181.

20. Project information provided by Atelier Dreiseitl.

21. Dreiseitl and Grau, *New Waterscapes*, p. 55.

22. gaia.lbl.gov/hpbf/casest_f.htm, accessed January 19, 2009.

23. www.architecturalreviewawards.com/dec2000/gsw/gswheadquarters.htm, accessed January 19, 2009.

24. www.berlin.de/tourismus/sehenswuerdigkeiten.en/00054.html, accessed January 19, 2009.

25. www.aia.org/SiteObjects/files/Trumpf_Administration_Building.pdf, accessed September 7, 2008.

Chapter 6

1. Paul Ehrlich is principal of Building Intelligence Group, LLC, www.buildingintelligencegroup.com, accessed September 7, 2008. See our report at www.mcaa.org.

2. Yudelson, *Green Building Through Integrated Design*.

3. Interview with Andy Ford, Fulcrum Consulting, London, May 2008.

4. Behnisch Architekten and Transsolar Climate Engineering, *Ecology. Design. Synergy*, p. 71.

5. See ohioline.osu.edu/aex-fact/0120.html, accessed August 9, 2008.

6. Anja Thierfelder, *Transsolar Climate Engineering*, book jacket quote.

7. On this subject, see my recent book, *Green Building through Integrated Design*, especially Chapters 3 and 4.

8. Interview with Helmut Meyer, July 2008.

9. Matthias Schuler interview with Friedrich Dassler, 2003, in *Intelligente Architektur 07–08*, p. 38.

10. www.schueco.com/web/us/architects/home#, accessed September 7, 2008.

11. www.schueco-profile.com/cda//mgz_AR/?GrOUP=1&STRUC=44&DATA=1903, accessed September 7, 2008.

12. Interview with Peter Mösle, August 2008.

13. This section is based on research by Paul Ehrlich and Jeff Seewald of Building Intelligence Group, conducted for Yudelson Associates on behalf of the Mechanical Contractors Education and Research Foundation.

14. Adapted from *Consulting-Specifying Engineer Magazine*, www.csemag.com/article/CA6492841.html, accessed June 30, 2008.

15. T. Moore, F. Baumann, and C. Huizenga, April 20, 2006, "Radiant Cooling Research Scoping Study," Center for the Built Environment, University of California, Berkeley, Internal Report.

16. Geoff McDonell, December 14, 2007, "Selecting Radiant Ceiling Cooling and Heating Systems," *Consulting Specifying Engineer*, www.csemag.com/article/CA6513022.html, accessed January 12, 2009; www.cbe.berkeley.edu/research/pdf_files/IR_RadCoolScoping_2006.pdf, accessed January 19, 2009.

17. Interview with Andy Ford, Fulcrum First, London, June 2008.

18. TermoDeck Web site, www.termodeck.com/termodeck.html, accessed July 28, 2008.

19. *The Independent*, London, December 6, 1999. findarticles.com/p/articles/mi_qn4158/is_19991206/ai_n14275674, accessed July 28, 2008.

20. CRed, the Community Carbon Reduction Project at University of North Carolina at Chapel Hill. www.ie.unc.edu/content/research/cred/cambridge_ac.html, accessed July 28, 2008.

21. Information from www.termodeck.com/newspage.html?news=853, accessed July 28, 2008. See also the story in the *UK Building Services Journal*, www.bsjonline.co.uk/story.asp?storyType=45%A7ioncode=93&storyCode=3094004. See also www.concretecentre.com/main.asp?page=1733, accessed January 20, 2009.

22. Interview with Tim McGinn, September 2008.

Chapter 7

1. See my book *Choosing Green* pp. 114–153.

2. www.solarregion.freiburg.de, accessed September 7, 2008.

3. Personal communication, Professor Thomas Spiegelhalter, University of Southern California, September 4, 2008.

4. Chris Turner, *The Geography of Hope*, p. 139.

5. Thomas Schroepfer and Limin Hee, "Emerging Forms of Sustainable Urbanism," p. 68, information used by permission of the publisher and authors.

6. Ibid., pp. 68–69.

7. www.linz.at/english, accessed October 12, 2008.

8. Thomas Schroepfer and Limin Hee, "Emerging Forms of Sustainable Urbanism," pp. 71–72, information used by permission of the publisher and authors.

9. www.malmo.se/servicemeny/malmostadinenglish/sustainablecitydevelopment/augustenborgecocity.4.1dacb2b108f69e3b8880002078.html, accessed September 7, 2008.

10. www.malmo.se/servicemeny/malmostadinenglish/sustainablecitydevelopment/augustenborgecocity/energyeffeciencyandproduction.4.1dacb2b108f69e3b8880002114.html, accessed September 7, 2008.

11. www.commondreams.org/archive/2007/06/23/2050/, accessed September 7, 2008.

12. "Vaxjö and Sweden have decoupled," www.vaxjo.se/vaxjo_templates/Page.aspx?id=1661, accessed September 7, 2008.

13. www.englishpartnerships.co.uk/gmv.htm, accessed October 16, 2008.

14. Jo Allen Gause, *Developing Sustainable Planned Communities*, pp. 152–161.

15. www.englishpartnerships.co.uk/carbonchallenge.htm, accessed October 16, 2008.

16. See the British government's prospectus at www.communities.gov.uk/publications/housing/ecotownsprospectus, accessed October 16, 2008.

17. www.timesonline.co.uk/tol/news/politics/article1782025.ece, accessed September 7, 2008.

18. Heather Topel, EDAW, personal communication, October 2, 2008. EDAW has acted as town planning consultants to Greenwich Millennium Village since 2004.

19. "Eco-Town Champion Admits Programme Is Likely to Fail," 2008, *Building* (U.K.), December 19, p. 19.

20. Tom Dyckhoff, "Eco-Towns: A Design for Life," *Times Online*. entertainment.timesonline.co.uk/tol/arts_and_entertainment/visual_arts/architecture_and_design/article4458938.ece, accessed August 9, 2008.

21. www.building.co.uk/sustain_story.asp?storycode=3120671&origin=bldgsustainnewsletter, accessed August 27, 2008.

22. www.communities.gov.uk/news/corporate/newecotownscould, accessed September 7, 2008.

23. "Eco-Towns Prospectus," 2007, p. 4, available for download at www.communities.gov.uk/publications/housing/ecotownsprospectus, accessed September 7, 2008.

24. See the report of the private Commission on Architecture and the Built Environment, "What Makes an Eco-Town?" www.cabe.org.uk/default.aspx?contentitemid=2762, accessed October 16, 2008.

25. "Swindon Could Become First Carbon-Negative Town in U.K.," 2008, *Building* (U.K.), December 19, p. 9.

26. www.shl.dk, accessed August 23, 2008.

27. Information provided by Schmidt Hammer Lassen, the project designers.

28. See Katie Puckett, 2008, "The Next Generation," *Building Gulf* October, pp. 4–8. www.building.co.uk/global.

29. www.panda.org/about_wwf/what_we_do/policy/one_planet_living/about_opl/principles/index.cfm, accessed September 7, 2008.

30. www.fosterandpartners.com/News/291/Default.aspx, accessed September 7, 2008.

31. www.gulfnews.com/business/Industry/10276674.html, accessed January 20, 2009.

32. www.arup.com/integratedurbanism/project.cfm?pageid=8020, accessed September 2, 2008.

33. www.arup.com/eastasia/project.cfm?pageid=7047, accessed September 2, 2008.

34. www.building.co.uk/story.asp?sectioncode=284&storycode=3117554, accessed January 20, 2008. "In China, Overambition Reins in Eco-City Plans," 2008, *Christian Science Monitor*, December 23. features.csmonitor.com/environment/2008/12/23/in-china-overambition-reins-in-eco-city-plans, accessed January 20, 2009.

Chapter 8

1. Interview with Jerry Percy, Gleeds, August 2008. Gleeds can be found at www.gleeds.co.uk, accessed September 7, 2008.

2. www.multi-development.com/web/europe.nsf/wwwVwContent/l2multipleawardsformultidevelopmentatmapicincannes.htm, accessed January 12, 2009.

3. Interview in April 2008 with three top executives at the company's headquarters: Glenn H. Aaronson, CEO, Multi Corporation B.V.; Arco Rehorst, technical director for Multi Asset Management; and Arno G. N. Ruigrok, adjunct director of Multi Vastgoed B.V.

4. See 2003 studies by the Heschong Mahone Group, sponsored by California's Pacific Gas & Electric Company, available at www.h-m-g.com/downloads/Daylighting/A-5_Daylgt_Retail_2.3.7.pdf, accessed June 13, 2008.

5. www.forumduisburg.de/Aktuelles.php, accessed June 3, 2008.

6. Interview with Glenn Aaronson, April 2008.

7. See Jerry Yudelson, *The Green Building Revolution*, for evidence that this is already happening in other commercial development sectors, especially Chapter 7.

8. Sonae Sierra company Web site, www.sonaesierra.com/Web/en-GB/home/default.aspx, accessed July 20, 2008.

9. General sources for this article are from presentations by Joana Barata Correia on You Tube, youtube.com/watch?v=pVRgKWmgYgU&feature=related (Part 1) youtube.com/watch?v=5C9VNoanVfg (Part 2).

10. All quotes from an e-mail interview with CEO Álvaro Portela, August 7, 2008.

11. See the European Union, ec.europa.eu/energy/demand/legislation/buildings_en.htm, accessed July 20, 2008.

12. Presentation by Elsa Monteiro, head of institutional relations, environment, and communication, Sonae Sierra, at ICSC Centrebuild Europe, London, June 20, 2008.

13. www.atp.ag/frameset/news.html, accessed September 6, 2008.

Chapter 9

1. www.architecture2030.org, accessed January 12, 2009.

2. See a 2002 summary of research to date at www.cepe.ch/research/projects /2000_watt_society/2000_watt_society.htm, accessed August 7, 2008. Also, see K. J. Morrow and J. A. Smith-Morrow, 2008, "Switzerland and the 2000-Watt Society," *Sustainability: The Journal of Record*, 1(1), p. 32.

3. Elizabeth Kolbert, 2008, "The Island in the Wind," *The New Yorker*, July 7. www.newyorker.com/reporting/2008/07/07/080707fa_fact_kolbert ?currentPage=all, accessed August 7, 2008.

4. Assumes an emission of 1 pound of carbon dioxide per kilowatt-hour of electricity.

5. www.eia.doe.gov/bookshelf/brochures/greenhouse/Chapter1.htm, accessed August 7, 2008.

6. From 1950 to 2000, total primary energy consumption per capita grew from 227 million Btu to about 350 million Btu; *Annual Energy Review 2007*, U.S. Energy Information Administration, Table 1.5, p. 13. www.eia.doe.gov/emeu/international/energyconsumption.html, accessed August 7, 2008.

7. At the 2007 Greenbuild conference of the U.S. Green Building Council, chairman George David of United Technologies asserted that worldwide efficiency of energy conversion is only about 9 percent. So, there's plenty of room for improvement, a task I'll happily leave to tomorrow's engineers and scientists.

8. "Minergie Buildings: A Model for the Future." www.postfinance.ch/pf /content/en/seg/priv/prod/eserv/dossier/realestate/realestate3.html, accessed August 7, 2008.

9. www.calcon.de, accessed September 6, 2008.

10. Interview with David Kirkland, July 2008. See also www.evatool.com, accessed September 2, 2008. There is also an open source wiki devoted to this topic at www.evacology.org.

11. www.usablebuildings.co.uk, accessed August 29, 2008.

12. www.bsria.co.uk, accessed August 29, 2008.

13. "Energy Certification of Non-Domestic Buildings," 2008, Fulcrum Consulting, p. 5. www.fulcrumfirst.com/pages/knowledgebase /knowledgebase.htm, accessed September 6, 2008.

14. Ibid., p. 9.

15. "Driving to Green Buildings: The Transportation Intensity of Buildings," 2007, *Environmental Building News*, 16(9). www.buildinggreen.com /articles/IssueTOC.cfm?Volume=16&Issue=9, accessed September 6, 2008; subscription required.

16. Alison G. Kwok and Walter T. Grondzik, *The Green Studio Handbook*, p. 281.

17. Bill Dunster, Craig Simmons, and Bobby Gilbert, *The ZEDbook*, pp. 49–50.

18. www.bre.co.uk/page.jsp?id=959, accessed January 12, 2009.

19. "The Barratt Code Level Six House: A Guide," *Building*, April 18, 2008. www.building.co.uk/regen_story.asp?sectioncode=331&storycode=3111357 &c=3, accessed September 6, 2008.

20. www.building.co.uk/story_attachment.asp?storycode=3111357&seq=3 &type=G&c=3, accessed September 6, 2008.

21. "Cost Analysis of the Code for Sustainable Homes," U.K. Department of Communities and Local Government," p. 40. www.communities.gov.uk, accessed September 6, 2008.

22. Jos Lichtenberg, "Slimbouwen."

23. Jerry Yudelson, *Green Building*.

24. Interview with Guy Battle, February 2008.

25. www.guardian.co.uk/artanddesign/2008/mar/03/architecture.russia, accessed September 6, 2008.

26. www.sourcewire.com/releases/rel_display.php?relid=39516&hilite=, June 10, 2008 press release, accessed September 6, 2008.

27. www.businessforum.net/general-chat/7969-europes-tallest-tower -among-most-sustainable-buildings.html, accessed September 6, 2008.

Chapter 10

1. U.S. Green Building Council data, monthly "LEED Matrix," author's analysis, current through August 2008.

2. See analysis in Chapter 4; author's analysis of LEED certification data found at www.usgbc.org/LEED/Project/CertifiedProjectList.aspx, accessed September 11, 2008.

3. Building Design & Construction, 2007 Building Industry White Paper, November 2007, p. xx. www.bdcnetwork.com, accessed September 11, 2008.

4. Nicolai Ouroussoff, "Why Are They Greener than We Are?" *New York Times*, May 20, 2007. www.nytimes.com/2007/05/20/magazine /20europe-t.html, accessed July 17, 2008.

5. See my 2007 book, *The Green Building Revolution*, Chapter 7. "The Revolution in Commercial Development."

6. Behnisch Architekten and Transsolar Climate Engineering, *Ecology. Design. Synergy*, pp. 32–34.

7. See my 2008 book, *Green Building through Integrated Design*, for more on this subject.

8. See my 2008 book *Choosing Green: The Home Buyer's Guide to Good Green Homes*.

9. Interview with Bob Berkebile, August 2008.

10. Janine Benyus, 2002, *Biomimicry: Innovation Inspired by Nature* (New York: Harper Perennial).

11. Robert Adam, 2008, "They're Having You On," *Building* magazine (U.K.), September 26, p. 37. www.building.co.uk/sustain_story.asp?storycode

BIBLIOGRAPHY

Bauer, Michael, Peter Mösle, and Michael Schwarz, 2007, *Green Building: Konzepte für Nachhaltige Architektur* (Munich: Callwey).

Beatley, Timothy, 2000, *Green Urbanism: Learning from European Cities* (Washington, DC: Island Press).

Behnisch Architekten and Transsolar Climate Engineering, 2006, *Ecology. Design. Synergy* (Berlin: Aedes International Architecture Forum), Exhibit Catalog.

Behnisch, Behnisch & Partner, 2002, *NORD/LB Hannover* (Ostfildern-Ruit, Germany: Hatje Kantz Verlag).

Behnisch, Behnisch & Partner, 2003, *Genzyme Center* (Stuttgart: FMO Publishers).

Briegleb, Till, 2000, *High-Rise RWE AG Essen, Ingenhoven Overdiek und Partner* (Basel: Birkhäuser).

Donati, Maria Cristina, 2006, *Michael Hopkins: 1976–2006* (Milan: Skira Editore).

Dreiseitl, Herbert and Dieter Grau, 2005, *New Waterscapes: Planning, Building and Designing with Water* (Basel: Birkhäuser).

Dunster, Bill, Craig Simmons, and Bobby Gilbert, 2008, *The ƵEDbook: Solutions for a Shrinking World* (London: Taylor & Francis).

Feireiss, Kristin, Ed., 2003, *Energies: Ingenhoven Overdiek und Partner* (Basel: Birkhäuser).

Feist, Wolfgang, Ed., 2008, *Conference Proceedings, 12th International Conference on Passive Houses 2008*, April 11–12, Nuremberg (Darmstadt, Germany: Passivhaus Institut).

Flagge, Ingeborg, Verena Herzog-Loibl, and Anna Meseure, 2001, *Thomas Herzog: Architecture + Technology* (Munich: Prestel).

Flamme-Jasper, Martina, 2002, *Nord/LB, Hannover* (Ostfildern-Ruit, Germany: Hatje Kantz Verlag).

Gause, Jo Allen, 2007, *Developing Sustainable Planned Communities* (Washington, DC: Urban Land Institute).

Girardet, Herbert, 2007, *Surviving the Century: Facing Climate Chaos and Other Challenges* (London: Earthscan).

Guy, Simon and Steven A. Moore, 2005, *Sustainable Architecture: Cultures and Natures in Europe and North America* (New York: Spon Press).

Herzog, Thomas, Ed., 2006, *SOKA-BAU: Utility, Sustainability, Efficiency* (Munich: Prestel).

Hindrichs, Dirk U. and Klaus Daniels, Eds., 2007, *Plus Minus 20°/40° Latitude: Sustainable Building Design in Tropical and Subtropical Regions* (Stuttgart: Edition Axel Menges).

Hindrichs, Dirk U. and Winfried Heusler, Eds., 2006, *Façades: Building Envelopes for the 21st Century*, 2nd ed. (Basel: Birkhäuser).

Hines Immobilien GmbH, 2006, *Uptown München* (unpublished brochure).

Hollein, Max and Nicolaus Schafhausen, 2007, *Kunst/Art at Lufthansa Aviation Center* (Ostfildern, Germany: Dr Cantz'sche Publishers).

Hyde, Richard, Ed., 2008, *Bioclimatic Housing: Innovative Designs for Warm Climates* (London: Earthscan).

Kwok, Alison G. and Walter T. Grondzik, 2007, *The Green Studio Handbook: Environmental Strategies for Schematic Design* (Amsterdam: Elsevier/Architectural Press).

Lichtenberg, Jos, 2004, "Slimbouwen, a Rethinking of Building, a Strategy for Product Development," 21st Conference on Passive and Low Energy Design, Eindhoven, the Netherlands, pp. 19–22.

Lieb, Rolf-Dieter, Ed., 2001, *Double-Skin Façades: Integrated Planning* (Munich: Prestel).

Lloyd Jones, David, 1998, *Architecture and the Environment: Bioclimatic Building Design* (London: Laurence King).

Mendler, Sandra, William O'Dell, and Mary Ann Lazarus, 2006, *The HOK Guidebook to Sustainable Design*, 2nd ed. (Hoboken, NJ: Wiley).

Reinberg, Georg W., Matthias Boeckl, and Pedro M. Lopez, 2008, *Ökologische Architektur: Entwurf, Planung, Ausführung / Ecological Architecture: Design, Planning, Realization* (Berlin: Springer).

Rovers, Ronald, Ed., 2008, *Sustainable Housing Projects: Implementing a Conceptual Approach* (Amsterdam: Techne Press).

Schroepfer, Thomas and Limin Hee, 2008, "Emerging Forms of Sustainable Urbanism: Case Studies of Vauban Freiburg and SolarCity Linz," *Journal of Green Building*, 3(2), Spring, pp. 67–76.

Sobek, Werner, 2002, *R 128: Architecture in the 21st Century* (Basel: Birkhäuser).

Thierfelder, Anja, Ed., 2003, *Transsolar Climate Engineering* (Basel: Birkhäuser).

Thomas, Randall, Ed., 2006, *Environmental Design: An Introduction for Architects and Engineers*, 3rd ed., written by Max Fordham LLP (London: Taylor & Francis).

Turner, Chris, 2007, *The Geography of Hope: A Tour of the World We Need* (Toronto: Random House Canada).

Webb, Michael, 2005, *Innovation in Sustainable Housing: Tango*, Moore Ruble Yudell Architects & Planners with SWECO FFNS Arkitekter AB (New York: Edizioni Press).

Wiggington, Michael and Jude Harris, 2002, *Intelligent Skins* (Oxford: Elsevier Architectural Press).

Yudelson, Jerry, 2007, *The Green Building Revolution* (Washington, DC: Island Press).

Yudelson, Jerry, 2008, *Choosing Green: The Home Buyer's Guide to Good Green Homes* (Gabriola Island, BC: New Society Publishers).

Yudelson, Jerry, 2008, *Green Building through Integrated Design* (New York: McGraw-Hill).

INDEX